Humanism in Business Series

Series Editors
Ernst von Kimakowitz, Humanistic Management
Network, Humanistic Management Center, Geneva,
Switzerland
Wolfgang Amann, HEC Paris in Qatar, Doha, Qatar
Pingping Fu, University of Nottingham Ningbo China,
Ningbo, China
Carlos Largacha-Martínez, Fundación Universitaria del
Área Andina, School of Management, Bogotá, Colombia
Kemi Ogunyemi, Lagos Business School, Pan-Atlantic
University, Lagos, Nigeria
Agata Stachowicz-Stanusch, Canadian University of
Dubai, Dubai, United Arab Emirates
Shiv S. Tripathi, IIHMR University Campus, Jaipur, India

Since its inception in the year 2011, the Humanism in Business book Series is brought to you by a dedicated editorial board representing the Humanistic Management Network (www.humanisticmanagement. network). The Humanistic Management Network is a global network registered as a Swiss association that lives, works and acts through chapters and collaborations in many countries around the globe. Its purpose is to encourage, promote and support economic activities and business conduct that demonstrate unconditional respect for the dignity of life.

Following the purpose of the Humanistic Management Network this book series serves to enhance and consolidate the body of knowledge on Humanistic Management and surrounding topics such as business ethics, leadership, CSR, corporate citizenship, sustainability, executive education, impact investing or purpose driven organizations to name but a few.

The books in this series all view Humanistic Management through their own lens, focusing on different aspects and highlighting different dimensions of humanism in business. What unites the books in this series is that they are all aligned to the three stepped approach which defines how we view Humanistic Management. It is based on the unconditional respect for the dignity of life, the integration of ethical reflection in managerial decision making and the active and ongoing engagement with stakeholders.

Furthermore the volumes in the series are an open invitation to join our efforts to make impact towards a more equitable and a more sustainable planet.

More information about this series at
https://link.springer.com/bookseries/14862

Kemi Ogunyemi · Ebele Okoye ·
Omowumi Ogunyemi
Editors

Humanistic Perspectives in Hospitality and Tourism, Volume II

CSR and Person-Centred Care

Editors
Kemi Ogunyemi
Lagos Business School
Pan-Atlantic University
Lagos, Nigeria

Ebele Okoye
Afara Leadership Centre
Lagos, Nigeria

Omowumi Ogunyemi
Institute of Humanities
Pan-Atlantic University
Lagos, Nigeria

ISSN 2662-124X   ISSN 2662-1258   (electronic)
Humanism in Business Series
ISBN 978-3-030-95584-7   ISBN 978-3-030-95585-4   (eBook)
https://doi.org/10.1007/978-3-030-95585-4

© The Editor(s) (if applicable) and The Author(s), under exclusive license to Springer Nature
Switzerland AG 2022
This work is subject to copyright. All rights are solely and exclusively licensed by the Publisher,
whether the whole or part of the material is concerned, specifically the rights of translation,
reprinting, reuse of illustrations, recitation, broadcasting, reproduction on microfilms or in any other
physical way, and transmission or information storage and retrieval, electronic adaptation, computer
software, or by similar or dissimilar methodology now known or hereafter developed.
The use of general descriptive names, registered names, trademarks, service marks, etc. in this
publication does not imply, even in the absence of a specific statement, that such names are exempt
from the relevant protective laws and regulations and therefore free for general use.
The publisher, the authors and the editors are safe to assume that the advice and information in this
book are believed to be true and accurate at the date of publication. Neither the publisher nor the
authors or the editors give a warranty, expressed or implied, with respect to the material contained
herein or for any errors or omissions that may have been made. The publisher remains neutral with
regard to jurisdictional claims in published maps and institutional affiliations.

This Palgrave Macmillan imprint is published by the registered company Springer Nature Switzerland
AG
The registered company address is: Gewerbestrasse 11, 6330 Cham, Switzerland

Foreword

Tourism and Hospitality are the industries that have been hardest hit by the restrictions on travel and distancing due to the Covid crisis of 2020 and 2021. Yet there is no better opportunity to transform an industry that has existed for millenia. These long and deep roots, some of which hark back to much more unequal times have persisted, that do not take into account the impact on the planet of human actions, nor the impact on humans of corporate decisions.

Humanizing an industry, especially one like hospitality requires re-thinking to a greater degree than one book can manage. So, I am glad to see volume 2 and look forward to the continuation of this series, kicking off an entire movement to transform the hospitality industry globally.

This book is an important precondition to that greater re-thinking, this book should become essential reading for all in the industry. I am glad to see it include working examples of how when these things are done, people are happier (both employees and customers and owners/lending institutions). We lack standards and globally applicable ways to measure in this industry, to force us to pay attention to what is important for the industry to survive, and the people who work in the industry to survive.

Finding ways to measure "resilience" for the hospitality industry to build into global economic crisis, and disasters—will drive to diversifying the portfolio of products and services that the hospitality industry offers—and open up avenues and trails for innovation that look currently like thick jungle or dry deserts, and people are choosing the paths that others have begun, spanning highways or footpaths… sometimes the footpaths of animals can also help us wander around to find new pathways to the destinations we seek.

Finding ways to measure social impact so that customers can make choices of where to go and where to stay based on social impact measures—will also inspire more virtual journey's so that people can taste, see, feel without having to take a plane. And when they eventually take a plane, they will be much more integrated into the way of living and being in that "distant" or "foreign" place because they will be prepared for how to make the most of that high carbon footprint decision. As chair of the IEEE working group, ICSIM—the Industry Connections Social Impact Measurement—we continue to find ways to compare and measure so communities and industries can share and learn.

Developing alliances and partnerships around the world to drive for this change—no one hotel, no one country, no one group can do it alone—so being able to operate in a networked world, where each player (hotel owners, tourist guide associations, tourist service industries—of which there are many) can see their place and how their individual actions and decisions lead towards a better world in general, and a more humanizing experience for customers and employees, this is a radical shift in perspective that will allow the industry to thrive and flourish in ways that support the thriving and flourishing of the people in the industry and at the same time being good stewards for the planet that makes our industry and our lives possible, that is the Spaceship Earth.

November 2021

Mei Lin Fung
People-Centered Internet
Northern California, USA

Acknowledgements

The idea of writing a book that would showcase the richness of the contributions of hospitality and tourism to human flourishing came to light during a seminar for lecturers in the humanities. The project seemed daunting, partly because the project required a deep knowledge of the practices within the industry and at the same time a rigorous exploration of philosophical and humanistic roots of the practices presented in a way that make it easy to appreciate the work of professionals in the field and their contributions to societal growth. The process of getting experienced authors from around the globe required the collaboration of many people and we thank everyone whose contributions and suggestions made it possible to arrive at this point in the project. It would be impossible to give a comprehensive list of everyone's contribution but we would like to highlight some.

We would like to thank all the lecturers who were present at the inception for the book for their ideas and for the support that they gave to all the contributors during the various phases of the writing project. We thank all those who reviewed the texts and gave suggestions to the authors thus enriching the work from many perspectives. Many of the

viii   Acknowledgements

authors reached out to professionals in the field who shared their experiences and helped to contact more people in the field and we thank them for their generosity in sharing their knowledge and time.

Gratitude is due to all the contributors for the in-depth research and their efforts to enrich the reader's knowledge with their work. Indeed, a lot of hard work and dedication goes into every good quality academic work and all the effort to work with the editors at attaining optimal result are highly appreciated. It is important to thank the families of all the contributors and all those who supported them during the process of working on the drafts.

The work of those who cared for the authors, editors, and everyone involved in the project, as they worked on the project is part of the hidden service contributing to human development which the book series highlights.

We would like to thank the publishers for their recognition of the importance of the contents of the book to human development and their interest in seeing that the project reaches all those who can benefit from the knowledge the books contain.

Special thanks go to the editors whose encouragement, tenacity, and belief in the project kept everyone going throughout the project, in the smooth and rough patches. The timely feedback and positive feedback given to contributors helped to guide the work and ensure that the work truly achieves its purpose and can be a tool for promoting excellence in practices within the hospitality and tourism industries.

As one will discover on reading the book, there are often many people whose hidden work within the production phase of many products goes unnoticed. Often, those people are not the first who come to mind when reflecting on the indispensable contribution to success but we would like to specially thank all those whose dedication and service to the production phase of this book made the final versions possible.

Contents

1   CSR and Person-Centred Care in Hospitality
and Tourism   1
Ebele Okoye and Omowumi Ogunyemi

Part I   Cultural Perspectives

2   The Essence of Hospitality Extracted
from the Odyssey of Homer: Its Relevance
for Hospitality Professionals Today   19
Fabiola Saul

3   Hospitality in Indigenous Nigerian Cultures   41
Ezinne Ukagwu

4   Celebrations and the Cultural Aspects of Hospitality   59
Adaora I. Onaga

5   Harnessing Technology for Hospitality and Tourism   79
Ngozi Nnamani

x   Contents

Part II   Customer Care Perspectives

6   Hospitality as Gift-Giving and Leadership   105
Ebele Okoye

7   Internal Customers: The Asset of the Humanistic
Workplace   125
Adaeze Eloka

8   Training for Effectiveness: Case Studies of Two
Hospitality Schools in Nigeria   147
Moyinoluwa Okunloye and Amaka Okpalla

9   Nursing Homes: The Person-Centred Care (PCC)
Model   167
Africa Bértiz Colomer

10   Exploring Guests Relations, Brand Loyalty,
and Repeat Visits in Luxury Hotels of China: A Case
of Tianjin   185
Dijin Wang, Asad Mohsin, and Jorge Lengler

Part III   Societal Impact Perspectives

11   Hospitality, Tourism and Vulnerability   211
Vivian Isichei

12   Sustainability Dimensions of Hospitality
and Tourism: Care for Our Common Home   229
Omowumi Ogunyemi and Andrew Onwudinjo

13   Corporate Social Responsibility in Hospitality
Industry: A Humanistic Perspective   247
Obinna Ikejimba

14   COVID-19, Its Effects on the Hospitality
and Tourism Sector in Kenya and Recommendations
Towards Recovery   269
Jane Wathuta, MaryJoy Karanja, and Clara Kariuki

Contents xi

15 Corporate Social Responsibility as Person-Centred Care 287
Kemi Ogunyemi

Index 307

Notes on Contributors

Vivian Isichei has a B.Sc. in Home Science and Management with a specialty in child development and family studies, an M.A. in International Tourism and Hospitality Management and an M.B.A. She has been a lecturer at Wavecrest College of Hospitality for nine years and has experience in teaching hospitality related courses, nutrition, research and philosophical anthropology. She has given hospitality trainings to employees of International and indigenous brands. She also coordinates a girls' youth club especially in the areas of mentoring on personal study, self-esteem/worth, self-identity, respect and other core values needed in the family and society at large.

Africa Bértiz Colomer has studied the degree of Assistant Manager and Humanities degree at the University of Navarra (Pamplona, Spain). In 2018 she completed the Master's Degree in Hotel Management at Francisco de Vitoria University (Madrid, Spain) and has just completed a Course of Directors of Centers for Dependency at the same University. For 30 years she has worked as a director of services in different residential, hospital and hotel institutions combining management work with

xiii

xiv   Notes on Contributors

a humanistic vision of orientation to the person and service. She collaborated in the implementation of the general services of several clinics (Chile, Argentina, Congo).

Adaeze Eloka is currently the facility manager at Pan-Atlantic University, Lagos, who believes that solving problems should be a facility manager's priority. Customer satisfaction is at the heart of what she does. Adaeze ensures that customers have a conducive environment to work and learn, by keeping the infrastructure and installations optimally maintained. She always seeks to align her decisions with the big picture of the organization.

Apart from her professional work, she volunteers time in the integral formation of schoolgirls. Playing the guitar in the company of family and friends is one of her favourite ways to spend leisure time.

Obinna Ikejimba is currently a lecturer at the Institute of Humanities, Pan-Atlantic University, Nigeria. He is a doctoral student of Philosophy at the Department of Philosophy, University of Ibadan. Prior to joining Pan-Atlantic University, he had worked for over five years in the management consulting sector as a human resource business partner. His experience spans organizational design and strategy, business process development, talent management and HRIT business solutions. He has very keen interest in business ethics. He has in the last three years taught undergraduate courses that encourage standards of good business practice, philosophy, logic and critical thinking.

MaryJoy Karanja is currently a 4th year student pursuing a B.A. in Development Studies and Philosophy (BDP) in at Strathmore University based in Nairobi, Kenya.

Clara Kariuki is currently a 4th year student pursuing a B.A. in International Studies (BIS) at in Strathmore University based in Nairobi, Kenya.

Jorge Lengler is an Associate Professor in International Marketing at Durham University Business School. He has published in top journals such as the *British Journal of Management, Tourism Management, International Marketing Review, International Journal of Hospitality Management,*

Journal of International Management, International Journal of Small Business, Journal of Small Business Management, International Journal of Contemporary Hospitality Management, Journal of Marketing Management, Advances in International Marketing, among many others.

Asad Mohsin is the Associate Professor and Convenor of the Tourism and Hospitality Management at the Waikato Management School. He is also Associate Director—New Zealand–India Research. He has accumulated several years of industry and academic experience working in different countries in the Middle East, Southeast Asia and Asia Pacific regions including Australia. He has published in several leading international journals. His main research interests and publications are in the area of—Tourism, Hospitality customer perceptions and contemporary trends, human resource issues and challenges, and product and service quality assessment.

Ngozi Nnamani is a technophile, currently in school management. She avidly follows technological trends, analyses, and advises on them. She believes that technology is most efficient when implemented by policymakers with a high level of emotional intelligence founded on positive work ethics. Before starting her career in Education, she worked for over five years in systems and application integration. After a successful career helping small businesses create payment solutions for their customers, she works full time in education, mentoring youths and in the formation and growth of school stakeholders. She holds two bachelor's degrees in Computer Science/Mathematics and Sacred Theology.

Kemi Ogunyemi Associate Professor, holds a degree in Law from the University of Ibadan, an LLM from University of Strathclyde, and M.B.A. and Ph.D. degrees from Pan-Atlantic University. She teaches business ethics, managerial anthropology, self-leadership and sustainability at Lagos Business School. She is also the director of Christopher Kolade Centre for Research in Leadership and Ethics. She has authored numerous publications, including Responsible Management—Understanding Human Nature, Ethics, and Sustainability, and is editor of the 3-volume resource for faculty in tertiary institutions—Teaching

Ethics across the Management Curriculum and of African Virtue Ethics Traditions for Business and Management.

Omowumi Ogunyemi obtained her first degree in medicine and surgery. She holds licentiate and doctorate degrees in philosophy (anthropology and ethics). She attended an international school of interdisciplinary research in Rome (Scuola Internazionale Superiore per la Ricerca Inter-disciplinare, SISRI) and won the 2014 DISF award (Documentazione Interdisciplinare di Scienza & Fede) for best interdisciplinary research paper. She was a finalist for the Expanded Reason Awards for 2018. Her research interests include interdisciplinary studies between philosophy and practical sciences and research on teaching the practice of virtues.

Ebele Okoye is a Nigerian pharmacist with a licentiate in philosophy. Her interests include women empowerment and education for the girl child bioethics and topical issues in character education for young adults. She applies both her knowledge from the practical science and human-ities in coordinating activities that promote development. She won the 2018 Harambee award for women development. She has many years of experience in mentoring and is currently the director of Afara Leadership Center in Lagos, Nigeria.

Amaka Okpalla is the Director of Lantana School of Hospitality, Lagos where she works with other trained professionals to guide students into a long-lasting career in the hospitality industry.

Moyinoluwa Okunloye is a research assistant at Lagos Business School, Pan-Atlantic University, Lagos. Her interests range from social respon-sibility and anthropology to communication ethics and other subdisci-plines that touch on humanity and social science.

Adaora I. Onaga is a lecturer at the Institute of Humanities, Pan-Atlantic University (PAU), Lagos, Nigeria. She holds an MBBS degree in medicine and surgery with specialization in Internal Medicine and Nephrology from the College of Medicine, University of Ibadan, Nigeria. She also holds licentiate and Ph.D. degrees in philosophical anthro-pology and ethics. She has worked in private and public hospitals where she taught medicine and nephrology to students and resident doctors.

She has also taught courses in philosophical anthropology and ethics both in Italy and Nigeria. Her current research interests include medical humanities and general ethics.

Andrew Onwudinjo teaches Ethics, Peace Studies, Conflict Resolution and Philosophical Anthropology at the Pan-Atlantic University Lagos, Nigeria. He had his Bachelor and Master of Arts degrees in Philosophy from the University of Lagos, Nigeria. His research interests include Ethics, Socio-Political Philosophy and Peace Studies. He is completing his doctoral studies in Philosophy at the University of Lagos focusing on the ethics of migration.

Fabiola Saul Ph.D. in History of Ideas at Universidad Panamericana (UP). Visiting Research Fellow at the Classics Department of Brown University (USA). Bachelor's and Master's Degree in Education at UP. Bachelor's Degree in Theology at Pontifical University of the Holy Cross (Rome). Certifications as English Teacher by diverse institutions.

She teaches the courses of Anthropological Theology I and II, Ethics, and Philosophy of Hospitality (ESDAI). She has recently published a book titled Hospitality in the Odyssey, and various articles related to Philosophy of Education and Language. She is a Teacher-Researcher of the Institute of Humanities of UP since 2011.

Ezinne Ukagwu has a B.Sc. in Accountancy from the University of Nigeria, Nsukka. She has many years of training experience in the hospitality industry. She was involved in starting schools of hospitality, Iroto School of Hotel and Catering in Ogun State, a project of Women's Board Educational Co-operation Society and Lagoon Institute of Hospitality Studies, a project of Nigerian Association for Women's Advancement, Lagos. She also regularly engages in rural promotion projects in Iloti, Ogun State. She won the *Harambee* award in 2012 for the promotion of equality for African women.

Dijin Wang originates from China. He completed his Master of Tourism at the Waikato Management School, majoring in the Hospitality Management. He has worked in Luxury Hotel, Hyatt Regency Tianjin East and Conrad Tianjin. He is very interested in customer relationship management in the luxury hotel industry in Tianjin and intends to promote the development of the Tianjin hotel industry through his effort.

Jane Wathuta is currently the Director of the Strathmore Institute for Family Studies and Ethics (IFS) and the Academic Director of Strathmore Law School (SLS). She is also a lecturer, researcher, co-trainer in research ethics and student mentor in Strathmore University based in Nairobi, Kenya. She is the author of several journal articles, book chapters and reports and has presented in various local and international conferences.

List of Figures

Chapter 5

Fig. 1 An overview of the history of technology in the hospitality industry 86

Fig. 2 A receptionist robot greets a hotel employee, demonstrating how to check-in at the new hotel, aptly called Weird Hotel, in Sasebo, south-western Japan (Photograph: Shizuo Kambayashi/AP) 89

Fig. 3 The same chatbot can give excellent or poor answers depending on the information the hotel made available (*Source* www.hotelhero.tech) 90

Chapter 6

Fig. 1 The RATER model (*Source* Carroll et al., 2017) 120

Chapter 7

Fig. 1 The internal customer 134

Chapter 10

Fig. 1   Final model   195

Chapter 13

Fig. 1   Carroll's social responsibility framework (1979)   252
Fig. 2   Humanistic CSR model   257

Chapter 14

Fig. 1   Employment   272

List of Tables

Chapter 2

Table 1 Some previous studies about Hospitality in Homer or Antiquity 35

Chapter 6

Table 1 California Critical Thinking Skills Test (CCTST) 117

Chapter 10

Table 1 Constructs measurements summary: confirmatory factor analysis and scales reliability 194

Table 2 Coefficients of structural relationships and goodness-of-fit indices of the structural model 196

1

CSR and Person-Centred Care in Hospitality and Tourism

Ebele Okoye and Omowumi Ogunyemi

E. Okoye (✉)
Afara Leadership Centre, Lagos, Nigeria
e-mail: ebele.okoye@afaraleadershipcentre.com

O. Ogunyemi
Institute of Humanities, Pan-Atlantic University, Lagos, Nigeria
e-mail: oogunyemi@pau.edu.ng

© The Author(s), under exclusive license to Springer Nature
Switzerland AG 2022
K. Ogunyemi et al. (eds.), *Humanistic Perspectives in Hospitality and Tourism,
Volume II*, Humanism in Business Series,
https://Doi.org/10.1007/978-3-030-95585-4_1

1 Introduction

Hospitality commonly refers to the friendly, generous, and warm welcoming of strangers, relatives, guests. The above description of hospitality implies that the guest is away from home, surrounded by strangers and yet feels very much at home. It also denotes the business of taking care of clients, customers, or other official visitors. Hospitality has its roots in ancient history and the meaning of hospitality has not changed since then, even though there are a variety of contexts within which it is practised. Indeed, even in ancient times when travelling was a lot more complicated, strangers would arrive in a foreign land and rely on the kindness of a local to seek shelter. Inns and taverns were developed in Europe during the age of pilgrimage and the development of trade routes throughout the continent. It was not until the eighteenth century that the idea of a hotel built solely for hosting guests appeared. With technological advancement that brought about faster and more reliable modes of travel, the need for accommodation has led to unprecedented growth in the hospitality sector. The prospects of space travel for tourism points to a possibility for more contexts for the practice of hospitality.

To understand hospitality more, it is useful to look at the word itself. The word "hospitality" comes from the Latin word "*hospes*", which means "host". It refers essentially to the relationship between a host and a guest. Considering the rate of influx of strangers to foreign lands, hospitality is an important aspect of human relationships. It is an indispensable tool for a successful and peaceful co-existence among humans. It simply means that we need to look at hospitality from a humanistic perspective since it is a human quality. A perspective that focuses on the human person as a free being endowed with intelligence and will, capable of making choices and self-actualisation. Most of the discussion in the current series is based on this affirmation. In fact, the interactions of humans with themselves and with the environment need to be guided by humanism in order to protect the interests of all stakeholders.

Hospitality is a human quality; nevertheless, it may have different expressions in different cultures. Over the years, due to its importance, hospitality has grown to be one of the most profitable industries globally. It has gradually become one of the largest and most diverse industries, employing hundreds of millions spread over different sectors. With the huge growth in the industry, together with its importance in the lives of humans, it needs a strong basis on which to anchor. One can sometimes feel a kind of tension between the drive to amass wealth, considering that hospitality is a lucrative industry and the initial compassion to care for another human be it a stranger, refugee, or guest. Indeed, hospitality transcends the financial negotiations as the industry offers a direct service to humanity. Based on the identity of humans as social beings, it is not surprising that there are calls for professionals in all fields, including the hospitality sector, to ensure that their work promotes fulfilment of other people around the places where they work and to work in such a way that their activities, safeguard resources that should be available for future generations.

2 Hospitality: A Person-Centred Approach

These days, there is a lot of conversation on corporations doing good and doing well. In other words, corporations are expected to be dedicated to serving the interest of stakeholders while simultaneously making profits. This work proposes that an optimal framework to achieve the necessary balance between profits and care of people and the environment should be person-centred, orientated towards fulfilment and human flourishing.

These book volumes contribute to the discussion in the hospitality and tourism industry from a person-centred perspective, since a humanistic perspective is a firm foundation for these industries. Such an approach will ensure the protection of the stakeholders while at the same time promoting the industry. Both the first and second volumes of the book, take on various topics in the discussion that helps one take a closer look at the humanistic themes in hospitality. Both synthesise core anthropological and historical aspects that lead to a better understanding of the industry, in scope and depth.

For anyone involved in the field of hospitality, the wealth of information provided in the book is a key to success. The richness of both volumes is also derived from the contributing authors who are drawn from among professionals in humanism and hospitality, some of them with over twenty years of industry experience.

The first volume explored in detail the anthropological foundations of hospitality and tourism while setting the foundational principles that will act as a background for the discussion in the entire series. The philosophical principles in the very first chapter of that volume have a lot of practical implications and these implications are explored throughout the volumes. An important topic under humanistic perspectives is the issue of self-fulfilment. The first volume was very concise in addressing the question of work as it pertains to the industry and how to find fulfilment through work done in the field of hospitality.

As mentioned earlier professionals in the industry need a deep understanding of the human person since the core business in hospitality involves people and interpersonal relations. Therefore, they must acquire an enriched view of the human person in the context of the industry. This understanding should be in such a way that they understand human needs and the benefits of the industry in fulfilling those needs. In the first volume, apart from the anthropological principles in hospitality, a good portion was dedicated to humanism and humanistic management in hospitality and tourism, from a personal dimension, exploring aspects of human dignity and how the industry, while respecting this dignity, contributes to human flourishing.

The second volume builds on the knowledge provided in the first. After exploring the personal dimension of hospitality, the second volume explores hospitality from a viewpoint, which goes beyond the individual. Topics like sustainability, CSR models, service, internal and external customers, COVID recovery strategies for the industry, etc., are now taken up in this current volume. Here, we find the practitioner in dialogue with people with whom they may not relate with directly.

In this volume, we have followed the same aim as the previous one, which is to bring together hospitality professionals and other professionals to have an enriching discussion on various topics that are covered under humanism as it pertains to hospitality. We have not only achieved this, but we have also been able to get authors from very different countries, thereby giving the conversations a more global perspective and a wider reach.

2.1 Hospitality in Culture

In the current volume, we have interesting aspects of history, which helps us discover the aged traditions of hospitality, that is as old as man. Truly hospitality is perennial, and it has universal manifestation as shown from the historical analysis. Historically, hospitality began in 15,000BC in the Lascaux cave in France which developed to accommodate members of other tribes who were away from home. In classical antiquity, the Greek and Roman spas were popular for those seeking rest and relaxation. The current volume explores the history of hospitality in various regions in Nigeria, which affirms that indigenous hospitality is also perennial and it is part of the social dimension of the human person. Through the lens of history, one readily appreciates the various ways the industry has evolved. Though it has continued to grow to the extent that it has become a major source of revenue to the world economy, the key elements are still the same. Man is a social being and so he must move around, and he will find himself in search of a home away from home, entertainment, etc. It is no wonder that, globally, hospitality is the fastest growing industry, and it ranks highest in job creation and employment of labour.

2.2 Hospitality as Service

Since the concept of hospitality implies service, this volume has a chapter dedicated to the theory of service. While hospitality may involve service, hospitality and service are two different concepts. Service is defined as the action of helping or doing work for someone, while hospitality refers more to the emotional connection one makes with the customers. The latter definition is the true meaning of service as shown in the third chapter of the second volume. It explains the theory of service and the philosophical basis of service. Serving others is an intrinsic human dimension and it enriches both the one serving and the one that receives the service. A service is a form of gift to the other. It is true self-giving, and it is comparable to giving the other person a gift, the only difference in the case of service is that what is given is intangible, whereas a gift many times refers to a tangible item.

For customer service delivery, the humanistic perspectives discussed in this volume are indispensable as a foundation for person-centred service delivery. Since service is not the same as hospitality, the volume shows that hospitality because it connects emotionally with the guest is that true self-giving, which in the final analysis is service par excellence. The volume also explores the aspect of "receiving as a gift". Customers, guests, and clients also have to receive this gift of self humanely. Feedback and recommendations should be given as a way of showing appreciation for a kind service received. Any negative feedback should be given in a way that respects the host and respects the dignity of a person.

True service involves leadership. The hospitality professionals through their desire to serve and care for the needs of their guests are true leaders. A good professional in this field must possess a good self-leadership which is an important part of effective servant leadership. It is an important prerequisite for consistently providing quality services to others. They constantly remind the rest of mankind of our humanity through their service carried out with an untiring, cheerful, and hospitable attitude. This can be very demanding, for this reason, the third chapter of the volume explores a few leadership qualities needed by hospitality professionals which enable them to carry out their duty effectively.

Customer service is key in hospitality and tourism since customer interactions are a core component of all the operations in most areas of the industry such as hotels, restaurants, bars, resorts, parks, and tourist destinations. Customer service affects sales and customer retention rates. The RATER method is discussed in the current volume as an effective tool to measure the quality of customer service delivery. Using this tool to measure the service quality is priceless as, nowadays, guests expect to be recognised and treated as individuals. Many establishments are going the extra mile to give personalised service delivery to their guests. Understanding the RATER model and how it works helps to modify the parameters to meet the needs of each client.

2.3 Hospitality Professionals and Professionalism

Guest experience is becoming more significant within the hospitality industry and research has shown that the involvement of front-line employees is important to the guest experience. Generally, people fail to realise that both service delivery and guest experience cannot be relegated to only the front-line personnel. Internal customer service, which includes both the front-line staff and those "behind the scenes", on which the front-line ones depend, must be included in the conversation when discussing customer service delivery. The humanistic management approach demands that employees are not seen merely as economic assets valued primarily according to the profit they make for the organisation. Since hospitality professionals are persons and persons must not be used as objects, managing human resources must be person-orientated. This idea is highlighted in the discussions on the internal customers.

A humanistic workplace actively creates an ambience for personal development and individual flourishing. All the employees in such an environment feel trusted, find it easier to innovate, and remain motivated. This is a more sustainable way of ensuring quality service delivery. Another way of ensuring quality customer service delivery and invariable high customer retention rate is when all the employees share the vision of the organisation. With an enabling environment for human flourishing, the internal customer relationships and service delivery yield the desired result in the external customer services.

In order to overcome the current challenge—which is not peculiar to only the hospitality industry—of hiring and retaining qualified staff, a good grasp on key humanistic management principles is necessary for overcoming this challenge. The "360 degrees" consideration of the internal customer relationship, which has to do with communication with bosses, colleagues, and subordinates, is part of the communication skills that are needed in any organisation for smooth operations. Suggestions on how to achieve excellent internal communication form part of the resources in this volume. Other aspects like respecting the dignity of the internal customer, handling power, soft skills, and the general work environment are also important aspects of the humanistic perspectives considered in the current volume. The external customers were also discussed. Who they are? What are their needs? What is the role of hospitality in enabling them to flourish? What is the role of hospitality in their lives and to society at large? What is the importance of the internal customers for the external customers? etc.

People each day are more sensitive to environmental issues. Nowadays, consumers know when an organisation is committed to a sustainable approach in manufacturing and service delivery. Consumer decision to patronise one product or the other could be influenced by how the organisation handles issues on sustainability. For instance, if the organisation avoids disposables, reduces, or even eliminates unnecessary paper consumption, conserves energy, reduces food wastage, etc. Hospitality management level policies and decisions are more and more shaped by these environmental and ethical considerations. Other issues on sustainability include simple questions like if the organisation uses eco-friendly appliances and switches, replaces toiletries with locally sourced ones, chooses ethically produced bedsheets made from organic materials and if it reduces energy consumption by using smart bulbs etc.

2.4 Hospitality: A Sustainable Approach

Sustainability is a topic of concern to many scholars, governments, and non-governmental organisations today. Tourism and the hospitality practices involved in it can influence the future of the planet in relation to the way we manage resources. It is therefore impossible to omit such an important subject in this work. Sustainability is important not just because it saves money by plugging wastage and reducing expenditure, but also because it saves our planet. There is no industry today that is not renovating towards a more sustainable and less wasteful culture. The hospitality industry cannot be left behind when it comes to sustainability. As part of this volume, there is a whole chapter dedicated to sustainability which recommends principles that will aid the industry to do good and do well at the same time. Indeed, there is an increasing need for businesses to see environmental sustainability and other aspects of sustainability as values that should influence business decisions. There are hotels that already have policies aimed at protecting the environment (Khatter et al., 2019).

Sustainability is key to caring for the earth to ensure that resources are sufficient not only for those who are currently living in the world but also for future generations. The activities and attitudes of professionals in this field go a long way to contribute to sustainability in our times. Sustainability is not only important because it leads to making more profit in the hospitality industry. It is important since it involves the care of others and so it requires a humanistic approach. Environmental sustainability in hospitality and tourism is very important, as our common home ought to be managed in such a way that even though we depend on it, we must care for it to sustain us and the generations after us. It simply means that both guests and their hosts must reflect on the various approach and methods in their relationship, to adopt a more environmentally friendly approach. This volume suggests some ways by which clients and their hosts can contribute to the goals of sustainability. Some of the solutions to issues with corporate social responsibility and sustainability in hospitality and tourism including green building, waste and pollution reduction, and employee development, as well as building community relations by providing help especially in times of need (Rhou & Singal, 2020).

2.5 Socially Responsible Hospitality

Corporate social responsibility (CSR) refers to the fact that businesses play a great role in the life of society and, for this reason, they must bear more responsibility. Corporate organisations' responsibility must go beyond only building wealth. They must care, not only for their investors and customers but also for their employees, the larger society and community, and the environment, thus, giving rise to the triple-bottom-line approach of enhancing profit, people, and the planet. The hospitality industry is a huge one, and its footprints in the environment cannot be overlooked. The industry consumes huge amounts of natural resources like water, food, and energy. It must also shoulder the responsibility of promoting practices that mitigate the negative impacts of its business on the environment. There are records of companies that have formally integrated CSR into their strategy to align the actual identity with the desired and conceived identity in view of the critics in its local community (Martínez et al., 2014).

There are various models of CSR proposed to meet the responsibility of corporate organisations. The question is which one of them is the best, which approach best creates a sustainable corporate responsibility practice that offers value, not only to the emerging market of socially and environmentally conscious consumers but also to all stakeholders in the business. In other words, how do corporations balance consumer emerging appetites with the demand to make their businesses more socially and environmentally responsible and at the time maximise profit? The best approach to CSR should follow a humanistic approach. It should be a model that takes into account the significant role of ethics in promoting the conditions for human flourishing through a humanistic approach to CSR.

In traditional marketing activities, hotels will usually focus on engaging new customers and neglect to maintain existing customers. Such actions lead the hotel management to concentrate on pre-arrival activities generally. The topic of customer retention is humanistic since it comprises human relations in form of guest and customer relations. Customer Relationship Management (CRM) can assist hotels to increase their customer satisfaction and loyalty, attract new customers and achieve long-run profitability with effective management strategies. CRM is defined as the strategic use of information, process, technology, and people to manage the customer's relationship with your company (Marketing, Sales, Services, and Support) across the whole customer life cycle. The role of CRM is to assist corporations to increase their customer satisfaction, loyalty, retention rate, build and manage long-term relationships with customers.

The chapter on feasts and the philosophy of celebrations highlights the importance of hospitality in aiding us humans achieve this intrinsic dimension of our everyday lives. Humans celebrate and without an adequate reflection on this important aspect of our existence, we may not realise the key role the industry plays in making our celebrations unique and unforgettable. In fact, as social beings (Lombo & Russo, 2014), we tend to wish to share our achievements and any significant life events with other people, and that wish is often expressed as celebrations.

2.6 Hospitality Technology and the Management of Crises

The twenty-first-century advancement in the area of technology is so important that it was not excluded in the conversation. Harnessing technology for hospitality and tourism, looking at developments in technology (e.g. artificial intelligence) and their potential to enhance the quality of human life, as well as possible harm to human flourishing, are discussed in detail. Innovative technologies and business models have transformed the service environment and integration of innovative ideas into hospitality can enhance its effectiveness (Bilgihan & Nejad, 2015). The chapter in the volume dedicated to technology in hospitality took a bold look at technological advancements and how to harmonise them with ethics and the question of possible loss of employment opportunities for humans. Topics such as AI, privacy and security concerns were not left out in the analysis. Technology increases efficiency: it has been known to reduce waiting times, improve customer experience when menial tasks are outsourced to robots, and use big data to optimise processes. For instance, using AI-powered chatbots both during the booking process and in responding to frequently asked questions on a particular service. It has also proven to be a customer service asset on the protective measures on COVID-19. There are many ways that management systems are deploying technology in hotel operations to monitor and optimise revenues, customer relationships, property, channels, and reputation. Many of them use mobile, cloud-based, and integrated solutions to achieve these needs. There is also the rising need for integrated messaging, predictive analytics, customer profiling, and middleware, which seeks to connect any disparate systems. The use of these tools has been made even more imperative with the challenging pandemic situation.

COVID-19 has affected practically every single sector of the world's economy, but there is no doubt that the hospitality industry is one of the worst-hit by the global pandemic. Even though tourism was booming a few years ago, the recent outbreak of the COVID-19 pandemic has been particularly catastrophic for it (Liew, 2020). The lockdown and other restrictions of movement and social gatherings greatly reduced the possibilities of tourism and the options for provisions of hospitality practices. Research suggests that full recovery to pre-COVID-19 era levels will take until 2023 or more. According to the US Travel Association, travel spending declined by 42% in 2020 (nearly $500 billion) from 2019, with international travel and business travel suffering the sharpest declines. International travel spending fell 76% (compared to 34% for domestic travel) while business travel spending reduced 70% (compared to 27% for leisure travel) (U.S. Travel Association, 2020). Since the World Health Organization declared COVID-19 a global pandemic in March 2020, hotels worldwide have seen precipitous declines in occupancy.

Nevertheless, the crisis was not all a negative experience for humanity. It has taught us to live better global fraternity. Moreover, the hospitality industry has grown more innovative during the crisis, learnt to adapt better, has become more resilient, and is more prepared to pursue new opportunities and better navigate the next crisis. It has also shown once more the richness and capacity of the human intellect to adapt and overcome challenges in different spheres. It has forced governments to re-assess their preparedness when it comes to emergency health situations like that of the pandemic. With the advent of the vaccine and as things return to normal, the volume makes various recommendations on how to speed up this recovery.

As the COVID situation evolves, other challenges may appear which will compel hotel owners and hospitality managers to think through various strategies for building the industry. We hope that, eventually, the crisis will be over, and the lessons learnt during this time will lead to a more robust industry, that is better prepared to face any future crisis. Different stakeholders of hospitality are already preparing operations as life gradually returns to normal. With the gradual increase in demand for travel, there is a slow recovery. For this recovery to be maintained all must learn to face some other challenges that came with the pandemic which has not fully disappeared. Challenges like recruiting employees, training, maintaining safety protocols, managing the guest experience etc.

3 Conclusion

The hospitality industry is exposed to various external factors that can weaken it. These factors and their prevention are discussed in this volume. It is important to deliberate on these vulnerabilities since the industry's weakness in a variety of events could more readily drive hospitality into a fragile business. Among the most dangerous threats to the sector are climate change, safety, and security issues, as well as unprecedented migration streams. These issues need to be discussed from a humanistic perspective and this is what the present volume seeks to achieve.

The current volume, together with the first volume remains a very valuable contribution to the field since both constitute one of the most comprehensive textbooks in hospitality from the point of view of humanities. It is written with students, lecturers, researchers, and professionals in mind. We hope that with this series, there is practically no major topic that you are looking for in the field of hospitality that you would not find some light within the lines here. The series doesn't claim to be exhaustive in any way, but we hope it has opened up a meaningful conversation that will help to trigger further discussion. Discussion on the ethics of hospitality and a rethinking of the basis of the industry, challenging and changing the existing paradigm. We hope that in the final analysis, we will have a hospitality and tourism sector that is people-oriented. A person-centred industry, where the people come first, and they are the centre of policies and frameworks that run the industry.

Chapter Summary

Common definitions of hospitality refer to the care of the persons who are often guests away from home, although such professional work can be carried out in homes. At the basis of the many definitions and descriptions of hospitality is the notion of the care for a person in need of it. It is therefore unsurprising that this volume focusses on the clients, customers, various stakeholders and indeed the future generations yet unborn, and explores possible contributions of hospitality and tourism to their growth and development. The dignity of the human person underlies the notions explored in the different chapters of the volume and unites it. The chapter gives an overview of the volume expressing its aim and the means through which it achieves those aims. The subjects covered in the volume include relationships between the hospitality professionals and their clients, corporate social responsibility, sustainability, technological advancement, and hospitality in special situations such as a pandemic.

It is possible to make profits while using methods that promote the dignity of the human person and that express care for other members of the human species and protect our future. It is also advisable for practitioners to engage in practices that contribute to their own personal flourishing by caring about the effect of their work on the environment. Hospitality and tourism professionals are called to reflect on the role their work plays in the care of humanity and to explore innovative ways to carry out the task of caring for others with a sense of responsibility for collaborating with others to achieve fulfilment. Human interactions and relationships within organisations are important for success, and a good understanding of the best ways to manage those relationships is even more important in a field that involves direct care for people. There is a need to explore the applications of ethics in hospitality and tourism industry.

References

Bilgihan, A., & Nejad, M. (2015). Innovation in hospitality and tourism industries. *Journal of Hospitality and Tourism Technology, 6*(3). https://doi.org/10.1108/JHTT-08-2015-0033

Khatter, A., McGrath, M., Pyke, J., White, L., & Lockstone-Binney, L. (2019). Analysis of hotels' environmentally sustainable policies and practices: Sustainability and corporate social responsibility in hospitality and tourism. *International Journal of Contemporary Hospitality Management, 8*(5). https://www.emerald.com/insight/content/doi/10.1108/EUM0000000001079/full/html

Liew, V. K.-S. (2020). The effect of novel coronavirus pandemic on tourism share prices. *Journal of Tourism Futures, ahead-of-print* (ahead-of-print). https://doi.org/10.1108/JTF-03-2020-0045

Lombo, J. Á., & Russo, F. (2014). *Philosophical anthropology: An introduction.* Midwest Theological Forum.

Martínez, P., Pérez, A., & del Bosque, I. R. (2014). Exploring the role of CSR in the organizational identity of hospitality companies: A case from the Spanish Tourism Industry. *Journal of Business Ethics, 124*(1), 47–66.

Rhou, Y., & Singal, M. (2020). A review of the business case for CSR in the hospitality industry. *International Journal of Hospitality Management, 84*, 102330. https://doi.org/10.1016/j.ijhm.2019.102330

U.S. Travel Association. (2020). *COVID-19 travel industry research.* Retrieved October 30, 2021, from https://www.ustravel.org/toolkit/covid-19-travel-industry-research

Part I

Cultural Perspectives

In this second volume, building on the foundation already laid down in the previous, the first part considers hospitality from cultural humanistic perspectives. In this part we see hospitality as it is practiced within indigenous cultures of Africa (Nigeria) and Europe (ancient Greece). There is also a discussion on the anthropology of feasts and celebrations. This part ends with a chapter on humanism in the applications of technology, which is continuously creating new cultural trends in the industry.

2

The Essence of Hospitality Extracted from the Odyssey of Homer: Its Relevance for Hospitality Professionals Today

Fabiola Saul

F. Saul (✉)
Universidad Panamericana, Mexico City, Mexico
e-mail: fsaul@up.edu.mx

© The Author(s), under exclusive license to Springer Nature
Switzerland AG 2022
K. Ogunyemi et al. (eds.), *Humanistic Perspectives in Hospitality and Tourism,
Volume II*, Humanism in Business Series,
https://doi.org/10.1007/978-3-030-95585-4_2

1 Introduction

A study of hospitality and tourism from a humanistic perspective should not lack a philosophical and a literary approach. This chapter, based in the works of two of the most famous Greek thinkers, Homer and Aristotle, will try to shed some light on how their works, so apart from the twenty-first century, contain valuable knowledge that may help understand this phenomenon. The main objective is to show how the predominant tendency to view hospitality strictly from the management or commercial perspectives can be enriched by elements gleaned from a humanistic approach, particularly regarding the practitioners in the industry.

The humanistic study of hospitality is not a novel approach. As Morrison and O'Gorman (2008, p. 216, Table 2) point out, areas such as Anthropology, Archaeology, Biblical studies, Philosophy, etc. have tried to analyse this phenomenon from their own perspective, and all of these analyses have proven to be valuable. This is possible because the action of receiving someone in the home—sometimes even a stranger—seems to be millenary. For an overall approach of the most relevant literature relating Homer and Hospitality, see Table 1.

Any philosophical study tries to answer the question of *what* something is, or *for what* it exists. Therefore, the present chapter will try to answer the question: what are the essential elements of hospitality within the Greek ancient tradition, and from there try to find implications for professionals in the hospitality and tourism industries today.

The present chapter is divided in three parts: the theoretical framework provided by Aristotle and Homer's Odyssey as a repository of examples of hospitality practices. The second part, where five essential elements of hospitality will be explained, and finally, the implications that can be derived from those essential elements for professionals today. The idea that unites the entire chapter is that of hospitality as a moral virtue because this perspective entails an enrichment of the personality of professionals who have chosen hospitality, tourism and many ways of service as their way of finding happiness and a life well-lived.

2 Theoretical Framework

The specific scope of Aristotelian thought that will be used in this chapter is Aristotle's theory of virtue.[1] First of all, it is necessary to recall that this Greek Philosopher defines man as a rational or a political animal (*Politics*, 1253a). The political aspect emphasises his need to create bonds, to have a circle of close relations, to belong to a public entity (in his case, the Greek City or *polis*), etc. But above all this, Aristotle is certain that man (as well as animals, plants, etc.) have a certain nature (*Physics*, 192b), and in the case of human beings, this nature is eminently rational, also sharing many characteristics with animals (growing up, nutrition, sensations, etc.).

The term rational, underlines man's ability to think, solve complex problems, communicate, create, etc. And according to what is usually called the 'function argument' (the Greek word for function is *ergon*), each being has a proper function according to its nature, and man is no exception: "the Good of man is the active exercise of his soul's faculties in conformity with excellence or virtue, or if there be several human excellences or virtues, in conformity with the best and most perfect among them" (*Nicomachean Ethics*, 1098a). So, the philosopher concludes, it is in the nature of man to acquire virtues, and thus, he becomes better man, or what man is supposed to be.

In other words, man achieves perfection through the acquisition of virtues, and these can be either intellectual or moral, depending on the faculty that is put in motion. Thus, intellectual virtues are such as wisdom, science, etc., and moral virtues perfect the appetites, the will, etc., and examples of these are fortitude, justice, temperance and many others. Prudence is the only virtue that is both intellectual and moral, since it not only helps a person to know what is the right thing to do at a certain moment, but also helps the person do it.

---

[1] For this section, the necessary works of Aristotle will be cited according to the academic usage, that is, with the Bekker numbering, and in the final reference list the links to these works in the public domain will be included.

It is important to note that in Aristotle's theory of virtue the matter of habituation (*ethismos* in Greek) in moral virtues is crucial, as a means to acquire virtue but also to build up character (*ethos*):

> Virtues are cultivated and not chosen in any simple sense, for it is not as a direct result of calculation, deliberation, resolution, or any other relatively simple mode of human activity that we become courageous, temperate or wise. We become these through a process of *ethismos*, or habituation, through the habitual acting out and embodying of those actualizations which the dispositions are dispositions toward. (Kosman, 1999, p. 270)

In the end, virtues become part of a person's moral character, creating like a second nature (*Eudemian Ethics*, 1220b), or more precisely, a state (*hexis*) of the soul. That is why in his view, once a person consolidates a certain virtue, the actions related to it become easier and easier every time.

In this sense, it is illuminating that Aristotle uses the Greek word *hexis* to explain virtues. It is a term from the Greek verb *echo*, which in a broad sense means 'to have' but can be translated as "a permanent condition as produced by practice" (Liddell et al., 1996, p. 595). He defines virtues as such in the *Rhetoric* (1367b), and in his *Nicomachean Ethics* (1117a, pp. 21–22), he states that a person who possesses a certain virtue acts accordingly to it when improvisation is needed and he lacks time to deliberate.

Finally, there is a central question to understand Aristotle's theory of virtue. And that question is: why should a person choose the path of virtue? Some authors find this view as narcissistic because they interpret it as if he proposed moral superiority for some persons (those who can achieve virtue), but that misinterpretation lacks focus. What Aristotle proposes in his ethical works is that human beings through the exercise of virtues achieve *eudaimonia*: or happiness.[2]

---

[2] Other ways of understanding this term could be human flourishing, a life well lived or prosperous (see LSJ, pp. 708–709).

As he states: "... our definition accords with the description of the happy man as one who 'lives well' or 'does well'; for it has virtually identified happiness with a form of good life or doing well" (Nicomachean Ethics, 1098b).

Some of the moral virtues Aristotle examines are: liberality, magnificence, greatness of soul, gentleness, etc. He only mentions hospitality in chapter VIII, that he dedicates to the topic of friendship, but as this study will prove, everything that Aristotle says about virtue in general can be applied to hospitality also.

On the other hand, the *Odyssey* of Homer will serve as the place from where to draw examples from. The decision to choose this Classic piece of literature is twofold: first, because understanding the origin of a word and the context in which it was born, the form it was used, etc., always leads to a better understanding of the nature of any cultural reality. And second, because it is the most remote testimony that can be found in Western culture of many cultural practices, and one of them is hospitality.

It is important to mention, though, that the method to be used is not the philological or hermeneutical examination, but rather an analysis that could be denominated humanistic. That is, a deep study of the hospitality scenes in the poem to deduce from them the essence of this phenomenon.

Also, it is very relevant to say that the Ancient Greeks contribute greatly to the understanding of the nature of hospitality because the word used for the stranger or foreigner was *xenos* (ξένος). Interestingly, this same word can also have the meaning of 'friend'. But not any kind of friend. It designates the friend that has come to be so through the specific deployment of hospitality.

From the moment that somebody was received as a stranger, becoming thus guest-friend, that relationship would never cease to exist, and would even be bequeathed to the following generations. This bond had its own name, *xenia*, which authors often translate as 'guest-friendship'.

So, as Moses Finley explains (2002, pp. 90–91):

Guest-friendship was a very serious institution. 'Guest-friend' and 'guest-friendship' were far more than sentimental terms of human affection. In the world of Odysseus they were technical names for very concrete relationships, as formal and as evocative of rights and duties as marriage....

Xenia was so important for the Greeks that their hospitality traditions connect with the religious realm, for all strangers were protected by Zeus, hence his epithet of the stranger's god (*Zeus Xenios*). As Herman (1987, p. 36) states: "like ritualised relationships in many cultures, *xenia* was surrounded by an aura of sacrosanctity".

In order to facilitate the readers' understanding of the analysis proposed by this chapter, the following paragraphs will offer a brief summary of the most relevant events in the *Odyssey* from the point of view of hospitality.

Ulysses[3] stops in twelve locations on his way home, but he is badly treated or even confronted in some places. Therefore, it is impossible to say that those scenes are a model of hospitality. But in four places the elegance and generosity displayed by the hosts towards him show ancient hospitality at its best. That is why these four scenes will be emphasised in the narration. This will be done following a chronological order, not the narrative one.

The War of Troy, that took Odysseus and many other Achaean leaders to that city, lasted ten years. Having beaten the Trojans, Agamemnon and all other leaders start the voyage home, but for Ulysses and his crew the journey will last ten more years.

After being attacked by the Lotus-eaters and the Cyclops called Polyphemus, the first hospitable encounter takes place on the island named Aeolia, home of Aeolus, king of the winds. He receives Odysseus and his companions, hosting them for a month and presenting as gifts of hospitality goods for the journey, including the wind to expedite their arrival. The lack of hospitality comes afterwards when Odysseus and his crew are sent back to Aeolia because Odysseus' friends open the bag containing the winds thinking it was full of gold and richness. Aeolus,

---

[3] It is important to keep in mind that Odysseus and Ulysses are the same person.

2 The Essence of Hospitality Extracted from the Odyssey of Homer ...

interprets their return as a sign that they were hated by the gods and decides to reject them this time.

They continue the journey, arriving at Aeaea, the island-home of the enchantress Kirke. She seems to be an excellent host, receiving some of Odysseus' men into her home and entertaining them with all kinds of abundant goods. But it turns out she only wanted to turn them into swine and keep them prisoners. She later tries to do the same to Odysseus, but when she realises she is not able to, she takes him as a lover and helps him with advice and supplies for his voyage home. It is like an ambivalent passage that shows hospitality on display, but for the wrong reasons.

Having survived wreckage, Odysseus manages to reach Ogygia, another island, this time home of the nymph Calypso. She entertains him, but trying to convince him to be her husband, she keeps him there for seven years. She finally decides to let him go, at the request of the goddess Athene. Once again, what seems to be magnificent hospitality loses its merit by depriving the guest of his freedom.

But in revenge for having wronged Poseidon's son, Polyphemus, this god's father, destroys his ship and the hero barely makes it alive to the beach of Scheria, the island of the Phaeacians and the kingdom of Alcinous. He is received in the palace, welcomed according to the traditions, and above all, he is treated as the most important person, varying the daily activities of the realm until his departure three days later.

A small but relevant gesture of the king is to be noted. On the first supper, the rhapsode sings by order of king Alcinous to entertain the attendees. But when he starts singing about the War of Troy, Odysseus, who has not been asked his name according to protocol, begins to weep. The only person in the room to notice is the king, and to avoid the embarrassment of the guest, he just asks the rhapsode to sing something else.

Reece (1993) has studied all hospitality scenes in the Odyssey, trying to establish a pattern of what ought to be done to receive a stranger. The only scene that fulfils all 25 steps identified by Reece is the one in Scheria. Therefore, it could be considered the prototype of Homeric Hospitality, with all the abundance, magnanimity and respect for the stranger. The matter of certain specific traditions to be followed in ancient Greece that this author studies underlines the ritual aspect that hospitality entailed in some ancient cultures.

Finally, after all the mishaps, Odysseus returns to Ithaka, but he is warned that 108 suitors are trying to marry his wife Penelope, and to obtain her acceptance they visit her every day. So, in order to enter the castle without exposing himself, the goddess Athene changes his appearance to that of a beggar. Penelope treats the beggar with respect and even sends the maids to offer him food and prepare a space for him to sleep.

Because of the particularities of this last scene, there has been much discussion about whether this could be considered or not a hospitality scene (for example, Harsh, 1950). This is so because according to the Greek ancient tradition, beggars were not subjects of *xenia*, since they cannot reciprocate the reception or the gifts, and did not have the possibility to travel. Therefore, they were never strangers and were not capable of withholding the bond of guest-friendship. But to the present analysis this scene contributes greatly to show how someone can receive generously even a man who cannot pay back in any way.

The other particularity of the scene is that it has been questioned whether it could be considered hospitality, since Odysseus is at *his* home, and what he is been offered is in fact *his*. But again, for the purpose of finding contributions for the twenty-first-century hospitality, this example is not only useful, but indispensable, since it talks about the reception of a human being regardless of his condition, and that connects significantly with moral virtue.

It can be observed how Homer builds his 12,000-verse poem upon the matter of hospitality, offering a certain kind of *in crescendo*. He presents examples of a stranger being mistreated (Lotus-eaters or Polyphemus), then some ambivalent passages of receiving but then rejecting the visitors (Aeolus), or receiving for the wrong reasons (Kirke or Calypso), up to the climax of exemplary reception in Scheria and Ithaka.

As a general conclusion concerning the Odyssey, it could be said that the persons who prove to be hospitable appear to possess like a sort of practical wisdom. In other words, it seems that they naturally know what needs to be done to make the guest feel welcome. They show a special sensitivity towards the guest's needs and the fact of putting this virtue of hospitality in practice seems to entail some other virtues, like liberality, generosity, prudence, etc. This is opposed, obviously, to those characters who do not have this virtue or have it but in an imperfect way.

The following section attempts to find the common traits in all of Homer's hospitality scenes in order to define the essential elements of this practice. As it answers a question about the essence, it could be considered as the specific part of this chapter where a philosophy of hospitality is intended.

3   Hospitality Essentials

As mentioned above, the following elements have been found present in those that can be considered 'successful' hospitality scenes in the *Odyssey*, and therefore are considered in this chapter as the five essential elements of this practice.[4]

3.1   Binarity

The most evident aspect of hospitality is that there are always two main agents, who usually receive the name of host and guest. Another way to express this same idea would be to use the word dichotomy, but sometimes this term entails a certain negative nuance, as implying opposites. It is interesting that in some ancient languages, like Latin and ancient Greek, there were not two words but only one to describe these two roles. Thus, the Greek word *xénos* can be translated into Latin as *hospes*, referring to both the host and the guest (Autenrieth, 1967, p. 222).

In the Odyssey, the distinction between hosts and guest is always clear. Ulysses is the guest *par excellence*, since he is received (or not) in the places he is forced to stop on his way home. The most remarkable hosts are Alcinous, his wife the queen Arete, and of course, Penelope. As hosts of Telemachus, who is in search of his father Odysseus, the notable hosts are Nestor, the king of Pylos, and Agamemnon, the king of Sparta.

---

[4] Brotherton (2019) mentions three: liminality, place, and exchange. In a broad sense those elements match with numbers 1, 2 and perhaps 4. The contribution of the present chapter lies in the other two, and the scope used to define them all.

Describing hospitality as a binary phenomenon may sound like a truism, but it is important to distinguish this phenomenon from others in which a person is welcomed and received, offered shelter, food, etc. For example, in the case of adoption, the distinction between the orphan and the adopting family ceases to exist after having received the child in his new home.

In this sense, there is a case in the Odyssey that is usually considered as hospitality, but according to this element, it is not. That is Penelope's reception of Odysseus who through the divine action of Athene has taken the form of a beggar. She defends him from the suitors, who are mocking and bullying him, and offers a bed, food, drink, etc. The issue is that in reality, it is Odysseus' home, therefore, according to this element, there is no hospitality in this case. Of course, from Penelope's perspective it would be hospitality and in its most sublime form, because beggars did not hold the 'right' to hospitality in the Homeric-ancient tradition.

If we consider the fact of hospitality creating an everlasting bond, then we could say that binarity turns into duality,[5] in which the two agents are still two different entities but have become united through the practice of hospitality. Thus, encircled by the term guest-friendship, they maintain their identity but have become united forever.

3.2 Space

Hospitality cannot occur without a physical site, which in the case of the Odyssey is always a home (from a palace to a simple hut). This is so because the stranger or traveller needs shelter, and if this necessity cannot be met it would be impossible to affirm that he or she has been offered hospitality.

In the Odyssey, the greatest hospitality performed happens in the kingdom of Scheria and Ithaka, as well as in Pylos and Sparta (palaces in all cases). The descriptions of these places vary, but the main feature of all is that they protect the guest from cold, wind, etc., and also have the necessary elements to provide certain comfort (water, tubs, places

---

[5] Duality is "the quality or state of having two different or opposite parts or elements". https://www.merriam-webster.com/dictionary/duality. Retrieved October 15, 2021.

2 The Essence of Hospitality Extracted from the Odyssey of Homer ... 29

to sit or lie down to rest). In this sense, what Brotherton (p. 30) highlights about hospitality spaces being usually non-mobile underlines the fact that something essential for hospitality is that it provides a safe space for somebody who is precisely on the move.

3.3 Limited Period of Time

For a stay to be considered hospitality, it is necessary that its duration is determined. If not, the person who is welcomed to a home becomes part of it (as in the aforementioned case of adoption) and therefore it is not hospitality anymore. This is crucial, because if the time lapse is not specified and the guest stays for too long, a pleasant relationship may turn into a stressful one, converting the guest into a pest for the host.

In the *Odyssey* this is clearly depicted by Homer and is also derived from the fact that Ulysses is striving to get to Ithaka. Therefore, he wishes to spend the least possible amount of time at every stop (even though Calypso manages to retain him for seven years).

3.4 Nourishment and Service

Alongside the element of space (home, roof, shelter), food and drink are usually identified with hospitality. This is a necessity for Odysseus, not a commodity, since he suffers from tiredness, thirst, hunger because his journey has become too long and because he keeps facing danger.

In general, we can say that someone in need of hospitality experiences certain vulnerability. And this is connected to the fact that human beings have a material principle, their body, which has certain needs to be satisfied. So, when Aristotle points out that man can be defined as a rational or a political animal (*Politics*, 1253a), he is using the term 'animal' to highlight the aspect human beings share with other living creatures: a body.

In the *Odyssey*, Ulysses is bathed, anointed, dressed, and served with abundance, not only by the amount of food or beverage, but also by the materials used to serve him (gold, silver, ancient trays, etc.). In addition, at the end of most of the hospitality scenes he is presented with gifts, a traditional practice in Ancient Greece. Hence, it is possible to say that all attentions towards the guest that look to fulfil any need take into consideration his bodily existence.

The gifts which were given to the guest, thus opening the possibility of further reciprocation, were also aimed at the material principle of human being but superseded it since certain immaterial aspects of them were stressed, such as their manufacture and their story. There are many moments in the *Odyssey* in which the host describes in detail how he acquired a specific object or the precious elements that it was made of. As Saúl (2019, p. 111) has indicated, this highlights not only the body of man but also his soul, for it promotes the depth of the bond and certain emotions around the gift-giving ceremony. It stresses the immaterial aspect of human beings, meeting his social need to create bonds (ibid., p. 111).

3.5 Human Moral Virtue

The deepest consideration that can be made about hospitality is that it implies a habit, and according to Aristotle's theory of virtues, being a good action that goes through the process of habituation, it would therefore be a virtue (in opposition to an evil repeated action that would then become a vice).

According to the description given above of some of the scenes in the *Odyssey*, it can be said that by receiving strangers and offering welcome, a space, food, etc., the host masters those actions, attitudes and sensibility that hospitality entails.

But the main point about virtues is not only the fact that they are acquired through repetition, but rather, that they create a sort of *forma mentis* in the person who develops them, a certain pattern in the way he acts. That is what Aristotle meant with the expression 'second nature' mentioned above.

So, in accordance with the entire theory of virtue Aristotle has proposed, hospitality may be considered a moral virtue, because it implies a practical knowledge, it is acquired through habituation, creates a certain sensitivity that facilitates the respectful reception of the guest,

2 The Essence of Hospitality Extracted from the Odyssey of Homer ...

and implies many other virtues, especially generosity. Telfer (1996, p. 83) seems to agree, but she uses the term hospitableness.

Of course, a moral virtue implies that a person chooses to behave in a certain way (depending on what virtue is the aspect that is emphasised) for the sake of the good that the virtue suggests, and not for a personal gain, or at least not only for this gain, as Aristotle explains concerning the necessary rectitude of intention (*Eudemian Ethics*, 1227b–1228a).

From the essential elements of hospitality explained above, the implications for professionals in this field will be deduced.

4 Implications for Professionals in the Field of Hospitality

By extracting these implications, the following point will be proven: that a historical approach through the reading of the Classics can yield interesting elements that have perennial human value and are therefore relevant to the human activity of hospitality. Therefore, this next section is the specific contribution of this chapter to understand Hospitality and Tourism from a deep humanistic perspective since it is the personal elaboration of the author.

For the implications, all institutions whose mission is to welcome people in any kind of situation will be considered: hotels, resorts, restaurants, cafeterias, persons who offer their homes through a web page or an App, etc. A special focus will be placed on those who chose hospitality as a profession and therefore look forward to excelling in the way they accomplish this virtue.

From the first element, that is, *binarity*, it could be said that all hospitality professionals ought to be aware that they hold responsibility for their own end of the relationship. If a guest arrives and they do not exercise the duties proper of the host, there will be no hospitality. This may sound obvious, but it boosts personal involvement in the process, since the hospitality professional cannot 'rely' on the institution, the facilities, the systems, etc. For example, if *only* one person from the staff of a hotel does not display on a personal basis all the attitudes and behaviours that hospitality entails, the guest will not feel welcomed. And it will not matter if the hotel where he stayed is one of the finest in the world.

Also, the hospitality professional must consider that the 'other', that is, the guest, is a human being, an individual in his own right. Therefore, homogeneity should not be the prevailing way of offering reception, assistance, or service. Of course, there are some limits to what each institution is capable of offering, but if the personal perspective of the hospitality professional is stressed, then hospitality professionals should try to be creative and innovative. Hospitality as a product to be mass-manufactured does not exist.

Finally, the host in this relationship must never forget the guest needs his own space to exercise his freedom, making his own choices, within the limits of respect required from him by the institution. This helps prevent the phenomenon of servility, which in the end provokes the opposite reaction of hospitality: wanting to leave instead of wanting to stay.

The element of *space* stresses the material element necessary to the proper reception of guests. The main implication for the hospitality professional is to keep spaces clean and cosy, aiming to resemble the *ambiance* of a home. For this purpose, the role of the maintenance and cleaning service personnel is crucial. Whereas for some views these jobs are second-rate, from the point of view of hospitality, they are of the utmost relevance, for without them the reception is either less possible or could even become a barrier. Think, for example, of the occasions when someone arrives at a friend's house that is so messy that they do not wish to stay.

Also, concerning domestic work, it should be noted along with Chirinos (2002) that this kind of work should never be considered less important, not only for the social utility they have (making Earth a habitable place), but precisely because they do not imply less rationality as it is commonly thought. They require practical reason (not the theoretical one), and therefore can only be done by rational beings.

Concerning the *limitation of time* that the hospitality relationship requires, it seems that this is solved in a hotel or a restaurant. But the modern types of hospitality that are by their own nature more flexible (for example an Airbnb), may need to consider this aspect. For it is necessary that the duration of the reception is clear for both guest and host. Of course, delimiting the duration of the hospitality relationship implies neither lack of flexibility in the dates or contracts, nor throwing somebody out on the streets if he continues wanting to stay. This is rather a matter of transparency in the relationship that fosters reciprocal trust, indispensable in hospitality.

Nourishment in hospitality highlights many elements, but especially the marvellous realm of gastronomy. All animals need food, but the only one who does something more than digesting or feeding is the human being. Not only because of recipes but, most of all, because everything around each recipe (the setting of the table, the cutlery, the conversation, the atmosphere) humanises a biological action.

Of course, the diverse institutions dedicated to offer hospitality may delimit the type of service they offer (formal, informal, take out, etc.), but from the point of view of those who either prepare the dishes or serve the table, the attitude is different if they see beyond a purely technical activity. Elegance in service is not a matter of money but of dignity in both host and guest.

Finally, the implications of hospitality being a *moral virtue* could become matter for a whole study. For the modest purpose of this chapter, only some will be mentioned.

The obvious consequence is that hospitality requires repetition and effort. This is where the term *openness*[6] becomes indispensable to understand hospitality as a virtue. Openness as a philosophical concept refers to the ability to perceive the 'other' and his circumstances, needs, desires, etc. Of course, to create this habit it is necessary to overcome selfishness and narcissism. In this mood, the host not only learns to 'read' the guest, or to anticipate his guest's needs, but above all, learns to make space within his soul to let others 'enter' (for a more detailed analysis of these concepts, see Torralba, 2003).

---

[6] It is interesting to note the lack of two words in the English language. First, the verb *acoger* in Spanish is usually identified as the *action* of hospitality and may be more expressive than the verb 'receive' or 'entertain'. The same happens with the term *apertura*, which is used to express the idea explained here with the word *openness*.

This radical openness towards the other shapes in the moral personality of the possessor of hospitality a proficient sensitivity towards the vulnerability of others, along with the capacity to overcome prejudice. Becoming thus an open person in the most radical sense of the term.

Definitively, seeing hospitality as a moral virtue stresses the necessity of being hospitable for the sake of being so, not in pursuit of a personal benefit. Of course, in the industry of accommodation or food, there needs to be an economical transaction. But the truly hospitable person does not behave only looking forward to a good tip or a raise in his salary. He behaves with hospitality because he understands the inalienable dignity of all human beings and enjoys making others happy.

5 Conclusions

One first conclusion may be that the humanities always contribute to deepening our study of reality. In this case philosophy as well as one piece of Classic Literature were used to find some implications for leadership and for managing people in hospitality and tourism.

It should also be noted that Homer's poems are Classic in both possible senses: because they are ascribed to the field of study referred to as Classics, but also in the sense that they are texts that will never be *démodé*. Their relevance stands the test of time because what they do is describe human nature, the depths of the human soul.

Of course, our industrial, systematised and informatic world does not look like ancient Greece at all. But the aim of the paper was to take some of the concepts depicted in the Odyssey and in Greek ancient tradition in general and use them to both understand the phenomenon of hospitality and to enhance it through these reflections.

Finally, it is logical to consider that hospitality has been present since man is man. There is something in human nature that made the first dwellers of planet Earth receive their neighbours in their hut (cave, or the like) after their (the neighbours') home was destroyed by an earthquake. There might be no archaeological ways to prove it, but if hospitality is a moral virtue, then it could be declared that it is inseparable from humanity. The task will always remain how to make people, spaces or even countries more hospitable.

2 The Essence of Hospitality Extracted from the Odyssey of Homer ... 35

Table 1 Some previous studies about Hospitality in Homer or Antiquity

Author(s)	Year	Focus
Harsh	1950	Discusses the encounter between Penelope as the host and Ulysses, the beggar
Kakridis	1963	Studies the notion of friendship and hospitality in Homer
Benveniste	1969	This work about the Indo-European languages has become a turning point concerning some specific words. Hospitality is among them
Edwards	1975	From the concept of type-scenes that help explain the possibility for ancient rhapsodes to recite such lengthy poems, the authors try to establish what a hospitality scene would be in Homer
Herman	1987	Explains the term *xenia* or guest-friendship in opposition to other kinds of relations in Ancient Greece
Hoces de la Guardia and Bermejo	1987	The authors offer a more general study about hospitality in Homer
Reece	1993	Another turning point. The author individualises all hospitality scenes in the Odyssey and in the Iliad, and proposes a pattern
Konstan	1997	Studies friendship in all of Greek and Roman authors, contributing to the understanding of guest-friendship
Pedrick	1998	Focuses on the noble women of the Odyssey and the role they play in hospitality

(continued)

Table 1 (continued)

Author(s)	Year	Focus
Finley	2002	This original work from 1954 is also a turning point because it offers a wide description of the era in the actions of Homer's poems are set. Taking to consideration archaeological findings, as well as philology and history, the study revisited by the author in 2002 is very comprehensive
Schérer	2005	It is a philosophical essay about the religiosity embedded in hospitality
Guevara de Álvarez	2006	Tries to establish the typical formulae used by Homer in relation to hospitality
Marco Pérez	2003	A thorough study of the concept *xenos* in Homer, Hesiod and Pindar
Marco Pérez	2006	The author concentrates on the character Aeolus
Marco Pérez	2007	A brief description of how hospitality articulates the entire poem of the Odyssey
Amadei Sais	2011	Emphasises the role of Penelope as host and the implications of a woman assuming that role
Santiago	2013	A study based on the double translation of the Greek term *xenos* as both stranger and guest-friend
Saúl	2019	An analysis of all the scenes presented by Homer in the Odyssey and the description of what constitutes the typical Homeric hospitality

2 The Essence of Hospitality Extracted from the Odyssey of Homer ...

Action Prompts

Keep spaces clean and cosy, aiming to resemble the ambiance of a home, as a good host. Get the maintenance and cleaning service personnel, if any, or your family if they can, to contribute to this. For hospitality professionals: endeavor to develop attitudes that express hospitable sensitivity.

When you are a guest, define the duration of your stay.

Study Questions

1. How can a poem written more than twenty-eight centuries ago have any relevancy for a study of hospitality today?
2. What can be learned from the way hospitality was practised in Ancient Greece?
3. What are the essential elements of hospitality according to the author?

Chapter Summary

It seems an undeniable fact that hospitality as the generous action of receiving someone, usually a stranger, in the home has been a millenary practice. This may have to do with the fact that man possesses the capability to move around the Earth, and therefore when he is in a foreign land, he may need shelter or refuge.

In this context, many authors have considered Homer's poem the *Odyssey* a good place to study this phenomenon, since it is the remotest testimony in Western Literature of a great journey, the one in which Odysseus takes 10 years to return home.

An author that complements the study of Homer is Aristotle since his theory of virtue offers a possible conception of hospitality as a human trait that is acquired through effort and models a person's moral character towards the good. This chapter tries to unite both Greek authors to find

> the essence of hospitality and from there, the possible implications for the hospitality professionals nowadays.

References

Amadei Sais, L. (2011). Penelope Anfitriã. Letras Clássicas. *Universidade de São Paulo, 15*, 62–77.

Aristotle, *Eudemian Ethics* 1227a. http://www.perseus.tufts.edu/hopper/text?doc=Perseus%3Atext%3A1999.01.0049%3Abook%3D2%3Asection%3D1227a

Aristotle, *Politics* 1253a. http://www.perseus.tufts.edu/hopper/text?doc=Perseus%3Atext%3A1999.01.0058%3Abook%3D1%3Asection%3D1253a

Autenrieth, G. (1967). *An homeric dictionary*. Macmillan.

Brotherton, B. (2019). Conceptualising, defining and theorising hospitality. *Tourism Today, 18*, 25–53.

Chirinos, M. P. (2002). *Antropología y trabajos: Hacia una fundamentación filosófica de los trabajos manuales y domésticos*. Servicio de Publicaciones de la Universidad de Navarra.

Finley, M. (2002). *The world of Odysseus*. The Folio Society.

Harsh, P. W. (1950). Penelope and Odysseus in Odyssey XIX. *The American Journal of Philology, 71*(1), 1–21.

Herman, G. (1987). *Ritualised friendship and the Greek City*. Cambridge University Press.

Kosman, L. A. (1999). Being properly affected: Virtues and feelings in Aristotle's Ethics. In N. Sherman (Ed.), *Aristotle's ethics: Critical essays* (pp. 261–275). Clarendon Press.

Liddell, H. G., Scott, R., & Jones, H. S. (1996). *Greek-English lexicon*. Clarendon Press.

Morrison, A., & O'Gorman, K. (2008). Hospitality studies and hospitality management: A symbiotic relationship. *International Journal of Hospitality Management, 27*, 214–221.

Reece, S. (1993). *The stranger's welcome: Oral theory and the aesthetics of the Homeric Hospitality scene*. University of Michigan Press.

Saúl, F. (2019). *La hospitalidad en la Odisea*. Panorama-UP.

Telfer, E. (1996). *Food for thought, philosophy of food*. Routledge.

Works of Table 1 Not Referenced in the Chapter, in Alphabetical Order

Benveniste, E. (1969). *Le vocabulaire des institutions indo-européennes*. Éditions de Minuit.

de la Guardia, H., & Bermejo, A. L. (1987). La hospitalidad en Homero. *Gérion, 5*, 43–56.

Edwards, M. W. (1975). Type-Scenes and Homeric Hospitality. *Transactions of the American Philological Association, 105*, 51–72.

Guevara de Álvarez, M. E. (2006). Formulación Gnómica del deber de hospitalidad en Homero. *Revista De Estudios Clásicos, 33*, 54–63.

Kakridis, H. (1963). *La notion de l'amitié et de l'hospitalité chez Homère*. Doctoral dissertation, Université de Paris.

Konstan, D. (1997). *Friendship in the classical world*. Cambridge University Press.

Marco Pérez, A. (2003). *La hospitalidad en la poesía épica arcaica. Análisis y valoración del concepto* ξεῖνος *en Homero, Hesíodo y Píndaro*. Diego Marín.

Marco Pérez, A. (2006). La respuesta de Eolo a Odiseo (Od. X 72–75). *Koinòs Lógos:, 2*, 581–587.

Marco Pérez, A. (2007). Funciones de la hospitalidad en la Odisea de Homero. *TONOS: Revista Electrónica De Estudios Filológicos* (Vol. 14). Retrieved October 18, 2021, from https://www.um.es/tonosdigital/znum14/secciones/estudios-16-odisea.htm

Pedrick, V. (1998). The hospitality of noble women in the Odyssey. *Helios, 15*, 85–101.

Santiago Álvarez, R. A. (2013). La polaridad «huésped»/«extranjero» en los Poemas Homéricos. *Faventia Supplementa, 2*, 29–45.

Schérer, R. (2005). *Zeus Hospitalier*. La Table Ronde.

3

Hospitality in Indigenous Nigerian Cultures

Ezinne Ukagwu

E. Ukagwu (✉)
Atlantika Cultural Centre, Lagos, Nigeria
e-mail: ezinneukagwu@gmail.com

© The Author(s), under exclusive license to Springer Nature
Switzerland AG 2022
K. Ogunyemi et al. (eds.), *Humanistic Perspectives in Hospitality and Tourism, Volume II*, Humanism in Business Series,
https://doi.org/10.1007/978-3-030-95585-4_3

1 Introduction

The hospitality industry is important in the development of any society, not just because of its economic importance but also because being hospitable is part of what makes us human. It is one of the few industries that is highly lucrative at the same time that it is very clearly linked to human traditions. Travel and tourism alone provide 25% of new jobs created all over the world; 10.6% of all jobs[1] and 10.4% of global GDP[2] (World Travel & Tourism Council, 2021). Yet even though the hospitality industry has been this successful, we should always keep in mind that its very roots lie in human nature. This is because man is a social being with the capacity to be in continuous interaction with other people. According to Aristotle, "Man is by nature a social animal; an individual who is unsocial naturally and not accidentally is either beneath our notice or more than human. Society is something that precedes the individual. Anyone who either cannot lead the common life or is so self-sufficient as not to need to, and therefore does not partake of society, is either a beast or a god" (Politics Book 1, 1253a).

Since man is a social being, he necessarily must interact with other men. The history of this interaction is the history of families, communities and environments where each person can give freely to the others without thinking of getting back anything in return. The custom of providing food, clothing and shelter to visitors and strangers has engendered many generations of bonds of reciprocity and friendship. When we examine our own cultural and societal roots, we discover that the traditional setting which forms the life and ambit of many people has favoured the continuous need to be hospitable. In many circumstances, these habits of engaging in hospitality are not acquired through formal learning but passed on from generation to generation orally and by example. They could almost be said to be natural to every civilisation.

---

[1] 334 million.
[2] 9.2 million USD.

3 Hospitality in Indigenous Nigerian Cultures   43

For instance, among the oldest traces of traditional hospitality are the Lascaux caves in France, which were developed to accommodate members of other tribes; the caves date back to 15,000 BCE (Hollander, 2019). Also famous is the standard social ritual from ancient Greek culture, where hospitality was also known as "guest-friendship" and was a basic expectation. When a stranger arrived, he would be taken in as a guest: he would be welcomed, offered a bath, invited to sit and usually offered the best seat at the table (Johnston, 2018). Afterwards, the guest would be given a place to sleep, and offered a bath; then he would exchange gifts with his host and be offered a light departure meal. In fact, the hospitality rules of Greek culture bound the host to complete care for their guests: people could be counted on to provide visitors with food, a bath, gifts, safety and a safe escort when they were leaving (O'Gorman, 2007).

In ancient Rome, public hospitality meant that all homes in the city would open their doors and place miscellaneous items in the courtyard for all passersby to enjoy, whether they were strangers or known to the family (O'Gorman, 2007). Additionally, they exhibited private hospitality in a manner like that of the Greeks, but more defined in that the character of a *hospes*, that is, a person linked to a Roman through ties of hospitality, was held sacred. The person's claim on the host was stronger than that of a blood relative. The hospitality bond created with a stranger gave the Roman host several obligations. He or she had to treat them with courtesy and consideration and he or she also had duties of protection towards that stranger (O'Gorman, 2007).

2   Hospitality and Culture

Hospitality in the traditional setting aimed at giving guests excellent care and an enjoyable experience—a beautiful and comfortable room, a delicious meal, beautiful sights and sounds as they move around, clean surroundings, etc. The encounter between the host and the guest passed from a mere experience of spending time together to an action that embedded human values. Whether or not the host had complete knowledge of the guest, hospitality by its very nature required that the host enter into a cordial relationship of peace and harmony with the guest, shown by services rendered to provide comfort. Every human being endowed with freedom can take decisions that enhance the wellbeing of those they encounter through being hospitable. In the traditional setting hospitality became a basic facet of life and it established bonds between individuals from different villages through the provision of food and accommodation to 'foreigners'.[3] There was a widespread belief that caring for strangers brought good luck and the gratitude for the services was a blessing—several African folkloric traditions attest to this. This fostered in many the spirit of solidarity and empathy which then evolved to the economic plane where hospitality is practised as a means of earning a livelihood. Thanks to a similar evolution in tourism, today we speak of cultural tourism, where people travel from one place to another for cultural motivation such as study tours (immersion in nature, folklore or art), tours for performing arts, festivals and other events, visits to interesting sites and monuments and religious pilgrimages. According to the definition by the United Nations World Trade Organisation, UNWTO General Assembly, at its 22nd session (2017, https://www.unwto.org/tourism-and-culture), cultural tourism happens when the visitor's main purpose is to get to know and experience (through sights, sounds and tastes, for example) the services and products typical of a place.[4] The attraction could be art, music, literature, theatre, crafts, architecture, business, history, nature (flora and fauna), geography, culinary arts, etc. or just people (lifestyles, value systems, and traditions).

Hospitality is closely linked with culture. Some early civilisations show how hospitality determines the lifestyle of the community or group of individuals. One can consider how Persian hospitality is ingrained in Iranians, such that it is evident in their traditional architecture. Historically, in Iranian homes, a room was set aside particularly for visitors, and this room would be bigger, more comfortable, and more lavishly decorated than the family rooms; they gave the best to their guests (Elmira, 2019).

---

[3] Travellers from other villages.
[4] General Assembly, 22nd session.

The culture of an ethnic group is not static but is in continuous development through policies laid down by the governance structures and the elders in response to the events in the life of the people. The historical path of hospitality is one of the contributors to such events and the resulting policies and has therefore broadened the culture of the people who make up every society. As an aspect of life geared towards the achievement of a common good which binds people with a common ideal together, hospitality to an extent can be said to foster the development of cultures. This is evident in developing countries and countries that rely heavily on tourism, such as the Caribbean Islands, Seychelles, Maldives, etc., where hospitality has led to the development of these islands. The reason is that the tourism sector is easily accessible worldwide and it is made up of lower skilled jobs. Evidence also shows that many other sectors benefit from the hospitality and tourism sector, further enhancing the countries' GDP and human development index (Toronto School of Management, n.d.).

Culture cannot exist without hospitality also because hospitality directly impacts its development by providing the humane factor, which is a key element of any normal society. Every sector of society has unique features that distinguishes it from the others, in food, arts, music, literature and technology, and it is around this field that the hospitality sector is built.

We have said that hospitality influences culture, but it is also true that the culture of a region can influence hospitality development in that region. For instance, a study by Omotoba and Oluwatuyi (2016) shows how Ekiti State, a Yoruba State in southwest Nigeria has a lot to offer culturally. Like most Yoruba States, they have many festivals held throughout the year in the various towns and villages. During these festivals, more people visit Ekiti State. Apart from the actual festivities, tourists love the attractive delicacies, especially pounded yam with vegetable soup which is the staple food. Then there are artwork and crafts: exquisite mats and products made of mat material (laptop bags, table mats and coasters, purses, caps and hand fans, etc.)—all these draw visitors to the Ipole-Iloro, Ogotun and Ipoti districts within the

State. In other districts,[5] ceramics are the draw—shaped into cups, jugs, plates, cutlery, pots, candlesticks, and other decorative items of very good quality. Several historical and cultural sites in the area also promote the influx of visitors: Olosunta rocks, Esa cave, Erin-Ayonigba river, and Ikogosi cold and warm water springs. A cultural trend of filling palaces with artifacts also prompts hospitality. Among these, the palaces of the Ewi of Ado, the Oore of Otun, the Elekole of Ikole, and the Alawo of Awo-Ekiti stand out (Omotoba & Oluwatuyi, 2016).

Thus, an enormous world of hospitality is built around culture such that hospitality brings culture to the foreground and to the attention of both outsiders and insiders of that region, providing beautiful elements that foster the sector's growth and practices. Each time, technological advancement also means that a better understanding of human cultural heritage around these cultures is conveyed.

3 Discover Hospitality in Some Indigenous Cultures in Nigeria

The enriching experience of welcoming strangers is something that one fully appreciates when studied in the context of a particular culture. Hence, having discussed the relationship between hospitality and culture, we now look at hospitality in sone indigenous cultures in Nigeria. Through observation, interviews and inquiry, this chapter looks at how strangers and family members are welcomed in four Nigerian ethnic groups[6]—Yoruba, Igbo, Hausa and Edo, chosen from the main geographical regions of the country. The purpose of the interviews, questionnaires and observations was to find out how hospitality impacts the lifestyle of people. One limitation of the study is that age range and number of respondents varied for each of the ethnic groups. To initiate the discussion about each ethnic group, a brief historical background there will first be given. Understanding the background will help give a

---

[5] Isan, Ara-Ijero, and Ire.

[6] Though the practice is worth investigating in other ethnic groups because each group is unique and has its own hospitable traits.

clear view of why the people take great care to be hospitable both to relatives and strangers. Tracing roots through describing history could help to highlight the core of the practice of hospitality in these cultures.

4 The Yoruba Culture

4.1 Brief Historical Background of Yoruba People

The Yoruba are said to come from Ile-Ife. Since the eleventh century, they have almost always been in south western Nigeria but at some point, they were spread as far as some part of the north central region. According to oral tradition, their ancestor, Oduduwa, migrated from Mecca in Saudi Arabia centuries ago (Mullen, 2004). They have established and lived in urban settlements for over 1500 years, says Ogunbitan (2007). According to him, they farmed, traded, produced art and craft—in bead, metal, textile, glass, wood and clay media (Ogunbitan, 2007); this last set of activities continues to attract tourism and prompt hospitality till date. Yoruba can also be found in Togo, the Republic of Benin, Brazil, Cuba, the Caribbean and the United States.[7] Then again, many are currently in Europe, especially in the UK, living among 'strangers' while continuing to maintain their cultural heritage and an openness to hospitality in their social interactions with people from various countries.

4.2 Hospitality in Yoruba Culture

The Yoruba have traditionally been among the most skilled and productive craftsmen in Africa. They are also known for their hospitality towards family, friends and strangers. This virtue is shown in their greetings, food, respect, family life and entertaining their guests. That is why Yoruba people are called Omo kaaro-oojire (which means 'the children of [those who greet] "good morning, did you awaken well?"). Yoruba culture has greetings for almost every occasion, situation or condition.

---

[7] Descendants of those taken there from West Africa during the slave trade.

This easily attracts strangers. For instance, when making hair in the salon, they may greet you 'eku oge' (congratulations on [the work of] beauty). When someone gives birth, eku ewu (congratulations [on overcoming] the danger of birth), when sitting, eku joko (well done [for] sitting), eku isinmi (congratulations on resting well), eku odun (congratulations on the festive occasion). Growing up, children are taught these greetings; they pick them up automatically since they hear them a lot and they also learn to respond appropriately to them. If they do not respond, not only do their parents correct them but even their neighbours. These greetings unite the people and are a sign of good manners and respectfulness.

Showing respect is very important in Yoruba culture, including to strangers. The traditional way to greet is that ladies kneel down to greet while the gentlemen prostrate. Okebukola (2021) in her response to the questionnaire administered, explained that this means that one is "greeting both the person and the little god in the person, as the traditional belief is that everyone has their individual deity". That is why each person has an *oriki*[8] that relates to the deity of the person. When this is applied to visitors (relatives and strangers) it is easy to understand the welcoming attitude and the readiness to be hospitable by default.

Hospitality is expressed in various ways in Yoruba culture. For example, it is a belief among the Yoruba that one does not eat alone. They are so hospitable that they readily invite people to eat with them, with the expression '*e wa ba wa jeun*'[9] or '*e ba mi re*',[10] the reply to which is '*aa gba 'bi 're o*'[11]. Also, Ladun Adediji explained in her questionnaire that it is a custom for every family to store water in "clay pots called *amu* which keep it cold and refreshing, and ever ready to be offered to visitors along with seasonal food like fresh corn, dodo *ikire*, *adun*, garri and dried fish, *ikokore* and *egbo*". In one instance, "a group of friends got stranded while on a long journey and sought shelter in a home along their way. The family received them warmly and offered them first water as a sign of welcome and then dinner. When the family had made the

---

[8] A paean; calling someone with *oriki* or chanting *oriki* at a special event, for example, wedding ceremonies, funerals, birthday celebrations, is a way to honour the person.

[9] Come, eat with us.

[10] Well met.

[11] It will find a good path.

strangers comfortable, they set about preparing another dinner since it was their dinner they had offered to the unexpected visitors!" The family made this sacrifice with all pleasure because for the Yoruba, anyone who knocks on your door brings good luck if you treat them kindly. If the visitors are relatives, apart from making them comfortable, they must make them feel welcome for as long as they are there or want to be, as it is considered impolite to ask them when they are leaving.

Majayi, F., in an interview, also narrated a story from her grandmother about the importance of always having water in the clay pot for any stranger who passes by. It happened that "once upon a time, a stranger on the way to a far place approached a family for shelter. A little boy was sent to bring some water for the stranger who looked worn out and thirsty. While trying to get water from the pot, the bowl scraped the sides because the pot was almost empty, and the boy grumbled to himself, 'there is no water'. The stranger overheard the statement and told the boy that he (the stranger) will make him continue uttering that complaint. The boy continued as predicted, grumbling nonstop, until the family begged the stranger to undo the curse". Brought up hearing this story, as a child she always made sure there was enough water in the clay pot for visitors.

5 The Igbo Culture

5.1 Brief Historical Background of Igbo People

No one knows where the Igbo people came from, nor does anyone know the etymology of the word (Afigbo,[12] 1975; Onwuejiogwu, 1996). In the last fifty years, a greater amount of scholarly effort has been invested into tracing the origin since the people are indeed interested in their history, contrary to what scholars like Ottenberg (1971) had perceived. Evidence from history, archaeology and linguistics is yet non-conclusive evidence (Ilogu, 1974; Shaw, 1975, 1988). The Igbo people live chiefly in south eastern Nigeria. During the late nineteenth century, Igboland

---

[12] An Igbo historian.

50 E. Ukagwu

became part of the Southern Protectorate of the colony.[13] Among the different ethnic groups in Nigeria, the Igbos are known to be social and friendly people. They integrate easily with strangers because they learn their language, which fosters communication and friendship.

5.2 Hospitality in Igbo Culture

Hospitality is an outstanding feature among Igbo people. In their individual homes, workplaces and at ceremonies and cultural exhibitions, they manifest a spirit of hospitality. They welcome visitors with kolanut and *ose oji*, pepper and red oil ground into a paste, to symbolise an offer of goodwill, friendship, respect and good wishes directed at the visitor. Usually, prayers are offered for the good health and prosperity of the people who will eat the kolanut, since *"onye wetera oji, wetera ndu"*.[14] The presentation of the kola nut establishes a bond of love and trust among them all. If the guest is an important visitor, he will be offered one to take home. This gesture reflects a connection forged between the host and the guest. Regina Akosa explained in her response to the survey that, apart from the kola nut, palm wine is offered: "in some traditional setting, the elders offer gin, spirits and palm wine to entertain important guests. Before drinking, a libation is poured in thanksgiving and petition to the gods. Assorted food items especially pounded yam, fufu made from cassava - a starch root similar to sweet potatoes - is offered with soup and other delicacies". Dance troops are used to welcome guests for important occasions.

In the interview with Ogbozor, N., she recounted an experience with her mother. A palm kernel trader who was stranded during a trip approached her mother for shelter. Her mother took her in, fed her and invited her to sleep in their room. The next day, before continuing her journey after having had breakfast, the trader formally thanked her mother for her hospitality. Since then, she would pass by on her business journeys to greet the family that had been so kind to her. Gradually, she became a close family friend.

---

[13] All parts amalgamated into the entity called Nigeria in 1914.
[14] An Igbo proverb meaning "one who brings kola brings life".

Onoh, M. narrated a story that took place in her hometown Ngwo in Enugu State many years ago. The son of a prominent village chief who had gone to England to study was coming home with a friend[15]: "The best dancers in the village prepared cultural dances called *atilogwu* and *akunechenyi*. The young maidens in their native attire danced *ugobueze* and *nnem ezigbonnem*.[16] The big town square was decorated with Igbo musical instruments like *udu, ekwe, opi* and *ogene*. On arrival, they were presented with three varieties of kolanut – *ojiigbo, ojiugo, ojigwolo* – and *ose oji* in a dish of native clay. An elaborate meal of pounded yam with melon soup, *isiewu, nkwobi* and tasty *abacha* all in wooden dishes was served. They prepared gifts of native fabric (*akwuete*) and tropical fruits for his return trip to England". The visitor was happy and grateful for the hospitality and left eager to tell the story to his people. He promised to return in the near future.

Onoh, M. also described how her elderly mother once received a group of European and Australian ladies[17] to their family home: "being a poor widow, she welcomed them with many smiles, and with groundnuts and banana; this was all she could afford. After the visitors had left, her mother would often nostalgically recall them as friends and praise their "attractive and friendly appearances and the goodness showing on their faces"—she had taken her guests wholly into her heart even in that brief encounter.

6 The Benin Culture

6.1 Brief Historical Background of Benin People

The Edo empire (1440–1897) made up a large region in precolonial times and is still now presided over by a ceremonial *oba* (king) with regard to culture and, for some, religion. The empire is in the southwestern area of Nigeria and Benin City is its capital and the home of

---

[15] Commander Alexander Billy.

[16] Also typical Igbo traditional dances.

[17] Charo Bastera, Maria J. Marco, Imelda Wallace and Joan Gilmartin.

52   E. Ukagwu

most of the Edo. Tourist attractions include artwork, especially bas-relief sculptures, in wood, ivory and brass. Their plaques depicting historical scenes and life-size head sculptures made Benin art famous globally. They farm the oil palm, yam, melon, pepper, beans and okra.

6.2   Hospitality in Benin Culture

The richness of the Benin culture includes their special way of welcoming strangers in such a way as to give the feeling of being at home. Kristi-noba Olotu, one of the interviewees, explained the different ways of manifesting hospitality: "when Benin people have visitors, they receive them first by greeting them, '*obokhian*', translated as 'welcome' in a general way. However, greetings in Benin language depend on the age grade of the visitors and where they are from. If they are from Benin, we greet them with the 'family greeting' (each family in Benin has their own unique family greeting, that tells other Benin people their background). If they are old, they will be greeted '*wa domo eniwaren*' which means, 'hail/greetings, our elders'". When they are strangers, the initial greeting '*obokhian*', suffices. "Then they say, 'we thank God for journey mercies' and offer them seats. After this, they serve them drinks, usually a variety of alcoholic and soft drinks. Then they present them with kolanut and or bitter cola and get on with the business of the day" (Olotu, K., interviewee).

7   The Hausa Culture

7.1   Brief Historical Background of Hausa People

Northwestern Nigeria is home to the Hausa, who are mostly found there and the southern part of the neighbouring country, Niger, around the River Niger and Lake Chad. They constitute the largest ethnic group[18]

---

[18] Same language, laws, and customs.

in the area[19] and have traditional rulers called Emirs. Their main religion is Islam. Typical occupations traditionally included extensive farming, leather craft, salt-mining, blacksmithing, trading, fishing, and hunting. The Hausa economy has grown due to craft products and the farming of onions, tomatoes, sorghum, guinea corn, millet, and maize. Their leather goods—bags, hand fans, satchels, shoes, bracelets, wall hangings—are popular items with tourists and other visitors.

7.2 Hospitality in Hausa Culture

The Hausa people are simple and welcoming. Like the Igbo and the Edo, they also welcome visitors with the kola nut, which they call *gworo*. A guest could ask the host, '*ina Sallah gworo?*' during one of their celebrations and it would be promptly and generously provided, perhaps together with delicacies like *tuwon shinkafa*, *tuwon masara* and a traditional drink, *burukutu*.

8 Welcoming Strangers: An Enriching Experience

The tradition of a place distinguishes the locality from others and usually has certain traits which are unique and pedagogical for understanding the people. The modes of addressing guests and opening one's doors to others, who form part of the family or are strangers, portrays the amiable qualities of that particular tradition. This way of acting comes from an instinct of human beings to recognise and protect their own species, and it is a pity that it is dying out in many modernised places. Each tradition has its own way of receiving people—specific welcoming words, greetings, and gestures; yet warmth is common to them all as well as joy at the presence of the guest. That joy makes the guests feel comfortable and able to reach out to the host for their needs rather than keep their concerns to themselves, which could lead to misunderstandings or a bad

---

[19] The other large population in the region is the Fulani.

54   E. Ukagwu

experience and therefore to dissatisfaction and disaffection. Modern and formal hospitality establishments need to train their staff in this level of deep welcoming.

Sometimes, guests are reluctant to ask for things because they do not want to be seen as demanding or imposing. Perhaps this is why in the ethnic groups explored, the hosts go out of their way to anticipate guests' needs and also repeatedly ask if they need anything else, more food, more water, more palm wine, etc. Again, hospitality staff in modern establishments need to be trained to ask guests if there's anything else that they need or want. This does not mean that everything a guest asks for must or should be provided. It only means that the interest in doing what is realistically, legitimately and morally possible to make them happy is expressed.

In all the cultures discussed, they end by making the guests feel that they are welcome to return in the future. This attitude makes the guests realise that their presence was appreciated, even in these homes where they did not pay anything and in fact felt themselves the receivers of all the benefit of the interaction. In a commercial setting, it would be even more important and impactful to the guest or tourist.

9   Conclusion

From the above data and discussion, one can glimpse that the practice of hospitality has changed the way of life of many cultures, incorporating virtues in the host and the guest. These hospitality-oriented virtues have evolved as customs and expressions and continue to constitute a feature of the ethnic groups. Culture is a progressive phenomenon that cannot make any significant impact in any society without the hospitality which establishes and strengthens connections among individuals and groups and eases their interaction for business or pleasure. This study thus celebrates the beauty of a service which continues to create long-lasting bonds among people of various backgrounds and beliefs. We understand that a more humane society can only be nurtured, developed and sustained through the practice of hospitality.

3 Hospitality in Indigenous Nigerian Cultures   55

In addition, hospitality has deepened the cultural roots of many ethnic groups over the centuries through creating a uniting force of love, peace and harmony among them. It fostered a sense of belonging and respect for cultural practices which enhanced the identity of the people.

To develop a more humane society it is important that those who influence the trends and decisions regarding the growth of the industry continue to help the stakeholders to remain in business. As this industry contributes largely to the economic growth both in rural and urban sectors, everyone concerned, including traditional elders and ethnic group rulers, should uphold the practices of hospitality in the traditional ways since these continue to contribute to developing the industry.

Action Prompts

1. Recognise the various expressions of hospitality among the traditional cultures around you.
2. Use a phrase that expresses hospitality from one of the four ethnic groups or one from your own ethnic group, when next you are addressing or entertaining guests.
3. Be alert to ways to show respect for other people's culture.

Study Questions

1. How did the practice of hospitality influence the development of indigenous cultures in Nigeria?
2. In what ways do you think that hospitality could foster the growth of cultural and traditional practices?
3. The Yoruba are known to have many greetings. How does this practice foster hospitality?

Chapter Summary

The chapter discussed the relationship between culture and hospitality. It shows how both culture and hospitality leans on each other heavily. The indigenous cultures may have different ways of expressing hospitality, but they all show the primordial nature of this human quality. In the last part, we looked at the common elements and expressions that should be present while welcoming strangers and entertaining guests. In indigenous cultures, though the expression of hospitality may be different, they all have some key features that are key for hospitality. These features are expressed in gestures, words and the various elements of receiving a guest. These features are dealt with in the last part of this chapter. Entertaining guests has been in existence from the moment people had the need to move around for reasons of necessity, leisure or luxury. In a traditional setting, hospitality is primordial, and it established bonds between individuals from different villages through the provision of food and accommodation. Indigenous Nigerian cultures show the key elements of hospitality. It demonstrates that the entertainment of guests has engendered lifetime bonds among strangers and their hosts. We also that this relationship provides humanity with service, charity and with people with magnanimous hearts.

References

Adediji, O. (2021, August 20). Personal communication through questionnaire.

Afigbo, A. E. (1975). *Prolegomena to the study of the culture history of the Igbo-speaking peoples of Nigeria*. Oxford University Press.

Akosa, R. (2021, August 4). Personal communication through questionnaire.

Aristotle. (n.d.). *Politics*. http://www.perseus.tufts.edu/hopper/text?doc=urn:cts:greekLit:tlg0086.tlg035.perseus-eng1:1.1253a

Elmira. (2019, June 15). *Iranian hospitality: You are never an outsider!* Iran Tourismer. https://irantourismer.com/iranian-hospitality/

Hollander, J. (2019, October 22). *Modern history of the hospitality industry: The last 100 years*. Retrieved November 30, 2021, from https://hoteltechreport.com/news/modern-history-hospitality-industry

Ilogu, E. (1974). *Christianity and Igbo culture* (p. 12). Nok Publishers Ltd.

Johnston, P. (2018). "All strangers and beggars are from Zeus": Early Greek views of hospitality. *Pacific Journal, 13*, 103–113. https://fpuscholarworks.fresno.edu/bitstream/handle/11418/1252/PacJournal2018-8.pdf?sequence=1&isAllowed=y

Majayi, F. (2021, August 2). Oral Interview.

Mullen, N. (2004). *Yoruba art and culture: Phoebe A*. University of California.

Ogbozor, N. (2021, August 8). Oral interview.

O'Gorman, K. (2007). Dimensions of hospitality: Exploring ancient and classical origins. In *Hospitality: A social lens. Advances in tourism research*

Ogunbitan, F. W. (2007). *Creation story of the Yorubas*. X libris Publishers.

Okebukola, O. (2021, August 15). Personal communication through questionnaire.

Olotu, K. (2021, September 2). Personal Communication through questionnaire.

Omotoba, N., & Oluwatuyi, O. (2016). Cultural tourism and community involvement: Impacts on sustainable tourism development in Ekiti State, Nigeria. *Donnish Journal of Geography and Regional Planning, 2*(1), 1–18. http://www.donnishjournals.org/djgrp

Onoh, C. (2021, August 7). Oral interview and questionnaire.

Onwuejiogwu, M. (1996). An Igbo civilization: Nri kingdom and hegemony, London, Ethiope Pub. Corp.1981. In J. I. Okonkwo (Ed.), *Nri Myth of Origin: An Aro Problem Review* (p. 81), in: AAP, Nr. 48, Dec. 1996, Universität Köln.

Ottenberg. 1971. p. 40: In: ibid. 9.

Shaw, T. (1975). *Discovering Nigeria's past*. Oxford University Press.

Shaw, T. (1988). *Africa and the origin of man*. Ibadan University Press.

Toronto School of Management. (n.d.). *Hospitality and the development of a country*. Toronto School of Management. https://www.torontosom.ca/blog/hospitality-and-the-development-of-a-country.

World Travel and Tourism Council. (2021, April 6). *Economic Impact Report*. World Travel and Tourism Council (WTTC). https://wttc.org/Research/Economic-Impact

4

Celebrations and the Cultural Aspects of Hospitality

Adaora I. Onaga

A. I. Onaga (✉)
Institute of Humanities, Pan-Atlantic University (PAU), Lagos, Nigeria
e-mail: aonaga@pau.edu.ng

60   A. I. Onaga

1   Introduction

The word, celebrate, from its Latin origins *celebrare* signifies 'to assemble to honour'. These assemblies or celebrations have been a part of human existence since the earliest civilisations. They have taken place with many different rites, in diverse places, and for a variety of reasons. Why is it necessary to celebrate? What do these assemblies honour? How do celebrations relate to the human condition and inform the cultural aspects of the hospitality industry? Can cultural aspects of the hospitality sector be oriented to individual and organisational flourishing? These are some of the questions the chapter addresses.

1.1   Why Celebrate?

Celebrations are multidimensional, experiential, ontological, and ethical. They are multidimensional because they cut across cultures and geographic locations. This is one indication that all peoples share basic conditions and needs which celebrations meet. It is important to note that this concept includes political gatherings, business meetings, social or religious conventions, academic and professional reunions, festivities of all types, etc.[1] Hotels and restaurants serve as venues but also set the human tone and determine the quality of sociality that will take place. This makes them a vital aspect of celebrations.

The ability to celebrate with its rhythms, traditions, and interactions requires cognitive and affective abilities. This makes it a true subjective experience even though it is objectively shared by all the participants. Celebrations, therefore, are *human* activities. As Handelman notes, 'celebrations are culturally designed forms that select out, concentrate, and interrelate themes of existence—lived and imagined—that are more diffused, dissipated, and obscured in the everyday' (Handelman, 1990, pp. 15–16).

---

[1] Although there are societies or cultures in which parties as a manifestation of celebration are part of the life of human beings and others in which they are regarded as bad or at least unnecessary, these latter societies have their own ways of celebrating.

4 Celebrations and the Cultural Aspects of Hospitality   61

Celebrations become part of the ontological structures of a person's life as an individual and as a member of a given society. This is because they can link past and future and break the continuous rhythm of the present. There is an impact on the identity of those who celebrate. Therefore, to celebrate fulfils certain social, psychological, moral, and spiritual needs of the human being.

The social dimension is fairly obvious from the meaning of celebration itself. Assemblage refers already to a collection, in this case, of individuals. However, the idea of assembly does not necessarily indicate that there are social bonds among these individuals. A celebration ought to manifest and strengthen already existing bonds. These events can foster a sense of one's place and reaffirm identity even when that is not the focus. All this is possible because of the social nature of the human being which cannot be considered in isolation from his cognitive status. They are topics that will be discussed subsequently in more depth because the foundations of human sociality are crucial to the understanding of both the cultural aspects of the hospitality industry and the anthropology of celebrations.

Some psychological needs are met by feasts and celebrations. These needs have been made particularly poignant with the lockdowns experienced in some pandemics. In the year this chapter is being written, many gatherings and celebrations were cancelled due to a viral pandemic.[2] It has been found that such restrictions, over time, result in low moods, reduced zest for life, and higher rates of hospitalisations (Ceban et al., 2021). It is another affirmation that the need to interact socially is a normal part of the human *psyche*.

A key part of the right functioning of the hospitality industry is determined by its contribution to the tone of celebrations and festivities. The hospitality industry takes its etymological root from *hospes* which means 'guest'. An essential aspect of welcoming a guest in all cultures with differences in modality is entertainment so that the visitor finds rest and recovers strength. This is a 'celebration' of his arrival and is related to the essence of events and festivities.

---

[2] This brings to mind that at times there are reasons for having "no celebration" at the individual level or at the social one.

Celebrare, with its assemblage of individuals, is directed to giving honour to persons and shared events. In this way, it gives tribute to the culturally and personally meaningful activities that humans engage in and fulfils the emotional need for meaning and belonging. With celebrations, a certain aspect of ordinary life and relation is brought out as a point to re-focus on. New meaning can be given, or old meanings remembered, and this affirms individuality and fosters cooperation among persons.

Celebrations also serve an educative role. People tend to commemorate what they consider important. The more solemn the celebration, the more value is placed on the event (Lombo & Russo, 2017). In this way, the event and its format point to what is significant and provide informal education to the members of that community. For this reason, people celebrate births, marriages, funerals, harvests, the beginning of the year, the coming of age, promotions, graduations, family anniversaries, and religious events. All these are cross-cultural events and indicate the moral compass that directs one's life. It points to what one considers fundamental to individual and communal flourishing.

Religious events are often the cause of feasts and celebrations. They respond to the spiritual dimension of human beings. There is a human requirement to transcend oneself, everyday life, and even the community. Commemorating religious events leads to another plane that gives meaning to one's existence and sense of belonging. The spiritual dimension speaks to the origins of the human being and what defines ultimate happiness. Thus, particular importance and solemnity are given to the celebrations that remind one of the cycles of life, one's origins, or divine providence.

The hospitality industry needs to be able to measure its performance in providing adequate services commensurate with the diversity of events. There is a reciprocal impact of celebrations on the hospitality industry in terms of economy, culture, tourism, and social policy. A 'balanced score card' has been tried as a measure of hotel performance for the financial, customer, internal business, and innovation and learning perspectives (Elbanna et al., 2015). The specific concept of celebrations has not been added as an indicator in most performance scales assessing the hospitality industry. Its incorporation will likely enrich the evaluation of services and uplift the perception of the industry in the future. A good scorecard ought to go beyond financial indicators and complement operational practices and long-term objectives so that personal and industry performance improve (Ribeiro et al., 2019). This will make it an ethical guide for optimal services of hospitality industries in the future.

Celebrations are, therefore, multidimensional, experiential, ontological, and ethical. The plethora of reasons for celebrating universally focus on characteristics and qualities shared by all humans. There will always be reasons to mark events and acknowledge diversity while appreciating the generalisable aspects of feasts and celebrations which make them human events.

2 Celebrations Manifest Human Sociality and Individuality

As we have seen, the uniqueness and shared qualities of human nature provide a basis for the similarity of experiences despite the wide variety. These stable ontological elements need to be remembered and fostered through shared events. Human sociality is the foundation for human interactions and is different from sociability as skill sets that make these interactions effective. It counts on the fact that each human being is a subject with faculties and abilities to decide and act as an individual.

Language and communication are important aspects of intersubjectivity or human sociality. Language is anchored in verbal and bodily expressions which form a good part of celebrations. They provide the inherent symbolism and capture meanings that may not be apparent to one who does not belong to that group. The public manifestations of shared meanings through language and bodily expressions make a phenomenology of celebrations possible. What does it feel like to live through this particular celebration or to celebrate with this group of people? These are the questions that a phenomenology of celebrations will be interested in. Answers will come from intersubjectivity which is the most basic quality of human existence, constitutive of each subject, and his interactions with the objective world.

A strong bond for human sociality is provided by love. It offers the capacity to be in the other's place and share deeply in the events he finds significant and worth celebrating. Love inclines towards the good in general and therefore to one's good and the good of the other. It seeks out that good and celebrates it actively. In phenomenology, the natural world becomes the shared location for a world of experience. With the stable elements in human nature, we can have a special mode of participation in events. Thus, one has the possibility of experiencing the world through one's subjectivity and through the other in that bond of love. In this understanding, presence is just as important as language and communication.

This does not mean that all the participants in a celebration are bonded in love, presence, and perfect communion. In fact, many celebrations are attended by strangers, competitors, or even enemies. Our consideration here is to discourage celebrations that lack the foundation in the promotion of human sociality as a good for the individual and the community. It should be oriented to the true well-being of all the participants for it to be a human event worth encouraging.

An important part of a celebration should, therefore, be the quality of assemblage since these events can foster and manifest social virtues and aspects of intersubjectivity. They, in their turn, can be translated to the wider society and strengthen communal bonds. Celebrations with this understanding cannot be occasions to show off economic or political power neither should they be an opportunity to dishonour or disrespect any individual or community.

If celebrations are going to serve their aim of bonding individuals and communities in love and respect, there are personal and social habits that need to be fostered. These habits will refer to physical presence, the dispositions of space and time, and relations with others. For every celebration, human bodies are the first manifestations of one's physical presence. These bodies exist in space and function in time making these coordinates important for a well-oriented attitude towards feasts and celebrations.

With physical presence, one needs to dress appropriately for the event. This shows respect for the one celebrating and gives value to one's presence. The dispositions of space are just as important in indicating

4 Celebrations and the Cultural Aspects of Hospitality 65

the significance of the event. Therefore, the venue, decorations, and arrangements of material objects for the event should be harmonious and pleasing. The questions of time motivate respect for the people's time. This means that events should start punctually and should be designed to achieve their aims with the most effective use of time. Yet, a good part of celebrations should be respectful of the aims of achieving rest and social bonding. It ought not to be a frenetic line-up of activities but a plan that encourages harmony, peace, and bonding. With considerations of physical presence, time, and spatial dispositions for celebrations, we begin to approach an important aspect of human culture and the role of the hospitality industry in these celebrations.

Since human sociality is related to human individuality with rationality and freedom, it is different from the interaction of animals. It can be directed to the acquisition of good or bad habits, virtues, and vices while building culture (Lombo & Russo, 2017). Classical philosophy, especially Aristotelian philosophy, already developed reflections about a group of social virtues which encompass those that recognise ties and dependence on one's origins, *pietas*, those that respect legitimate authority, *observantia*, those that honour merit and excellence, *dulia*, and those that follow commands and keeps the norms, *obedientia*. Others facilitate reciprocity and friendship such as gratitude, sincerity, affability, and generosity (Aristotle, 2014).

For this topic, I would like to emphasise the virtues of generosity, authenticity, and friendship. Generosity perfects the tendency to give a part of what we possess to others. It is an important part of the cultural aspects of celebration and hospitality. With personal growth, one moves from simply sharing gifts, wealth, or objects to the giving of oneself. This means that one is truly present to the other and honours them for *who* they are rather than for *what* they have. It becomes an exchange of personhood even though this occurs to different degrees depending on the relationship and the occasion. Authenticity is necessary for that true self-giving because it involves manifesting oneself as one is. Authenticity is shown in the use of language, bodily expressions, and the sharing of one's talents, gifts, and self. The hospitality industry must check its ability to foster these virtues periodically and assess practical means to recover lost ground.

Finally, these virtues deepen the bonds of friendship which is the true reason for celebrating others. They orient towards love and seek the common and individual good while keeping up the efforts to perfect one's possibilities. Are these virtues possible and necessary in a hyper-connected world? One of the lessons from a pandemic such as recently lived has been the realisation of the necessity for personal interactions even when there are virtual relationships. Virtual relationships are those that dispense with physical bodies and operate solely on the connections provided by the internet and cyberspace. The physical, psychological, moral, and spiritual dimensions of the human being are not completely satisfied by virtual relations nor are celebrations sufficient simply as online events. The human celebration, therefore, comprises formal properties such as repetition and order, presentation of cultural symbols, entertainment, and active physical participation (James, 1985). The material and non-material aspects already discussed are important as an integrated whole to ensure the success of celebrations.

A discussion on human sociality is therefore not a nod to uniformity. It is respectful of the different personalities and preferences regarding celebrations and feasts. It requires a solid basis in the individuality of each one, yet it does not degenerate into egoism. It accepts that some prefer large and boisterous events while others will rather have small, quiet celebrations. Regardless of the form and type, there can be no celebration without others. To celebrate alone is a misnomer and an abnormality. The ordinary human being needs to share sorrows and joys, and this is founded on a shared social nature. These inclinations can be directed to personal growth when an effort is made to develop the virtues that promote them.

3 Hospitality as a Cultural Phenomenon; Relation to Sociality and Celebrations

Since the definition of culture given by Edward Burnett Tylor, the concept has been understood to encompass all the learned traditions and lifestyles of the members of society including material and immaterial aspects (Tylor, 2010). This means that culture is acquired, not innately present at birth. It derives from one's social environment and is always a collective, not emerging from one's genes (Hofstede, 2011). Human beings adapt to their environment because they are rational and relational. The adaptation to the physical environment constitutes the material aspects of culture. It includes artefacts, technology, clothes, architecture, food, etc. The non-material aspects are intangible like linguistics, knowledge, customs, beliefs, norms, laws, etc.

Why is hospitality regarded as a cultural phenomenon? The meaning of 'hospitable' is universal and intercultural. There are expectations in all social environments for the reception of a visitor and how he is made welcome. It is a consequence of living in the world and interacting with one's surroundings. The environment does not only include inanimate objects but living creatures which make hospitality not only social but ecological as well. There are a variety of ways to show warmth, friendship, and openness to the visitor/client even if he is a stranger. Therefore, one can distinguish between gestures or expressions that convey antisocial tendencies and others that are universally gratifying. Hospitality is thus a cultural phenomenon with a double sense. It is the social adaptation to a visitor or guest situated in a specific environment and it is the totality of expressions and gestures which are universally comprehensible.

There is a blend of general expectations and personal preferences which define the hospitality industry. One of the functions of this sector is to create or promote relationships among people. It facilitates the exchange of goods and services that go beyond the material and become symbolic (Selwyn, 2001). Since hospitality is a human tendency, the industry, with its professionalism, takes on an important meaning for intersubjectivity. This does not mean that those who work in the industry cannot become receivers of hospitality. In fact, the dynamicity of these relations is that the professional description of hospitality workers is as hosts who are capable of being gracious guests when the occasion demands. They teach others to be good hosts by themselves being professionally competent hosts and good guests.

In this way, the industry connects inter-relationality, an inherent human quality, to culture, a learned adaptation to the environment. It can become transformative for society when it plays an active part in human socialisation and respects the particular culture in which it is located. Irrespective of the service that it offers; lodging and accommodation, food and beverage, recreation, travel and tourism, or education, it needs to find the human face behind a request. It needs to be host to that guest who asks for food, drink, shelter, or rest.

With this dynamic interchange of roles, the hospitality industry is set to be relevant for all times. Hosts and guests have been a part of society since ancient civilisations and continue to be important despite the present cultural and technological changes. Ritzer (2007) has traced the origin of hospitality services to micro-households in ancient times. They shared their homes with strangers while accepting responsibility for their safety and well-being. Others have acknowledged that the intensity of service depends on cultural backgrounds and varies from childhood to adulthood (Hausler, 2017).

A good part of receiving guests is to aid their physical and psychological recovery. Play as opposed to work becomes a central theme for the guest. Play is not just an expression of the need for physical repose, distraction, or entertainment but involves the human capacity for creativity regarding ordinary reality (Lombo & Russo, 2017). Play can also be a part of celebrations. To really achieve their aims, both play and celebrations should focus on the persons that are involved as ends rather than means to some utilitarian goal of self-interest or material gain.

There is a deep relationship between work and play and a lack of balance between these two can be a source of emotional, moral, and spiritual crises. When there is a misunderstanding of the different roles of the two, not only will there be a crisis in hospitality, in the conceptualisation of what it means to be a good host, but also in knowing how to receive graciously and gratefully. This is why it is essential to reflect on the meanings of work and rest especially in the hospitality industry where work can become overwhelming, and play is sacrificed.

Work is a gift that needs to be treasured as a space that makes personal and social growth possible. The hospitality industry particularly provides this opening for one to develop one's talents and relish the ability to give joy and service to others. Gradually, with the frenetic pace of life especially in this industry, one begins to lose the habits of receptivity which makes it possible to be with others in silence, wonder, contemplation, and mutual appreciation. These qualities have been gradually replaced by the frenzy of just constantly doing and ticking off or the measurement of productivity in material objects. Again, there is the return to the idea of presence as the nucleus of celebration which values the *being* of the other above the *doing* or *having*.

Feasts and celebrations are still at the heart of leisure and play. Regarding the hospitality industry, the much-needed value for feasts and celebrations motivates organisational climate, the orientation of service, and lived experiences of both the hosts and guests. This informs the internal and external culture of hospitality organisations.

4 Cultural Types/Models for the Hospitality Sector

When considering the work–rest balance, the hospitality industry is not only charged with providing rest for its guests or clients but with looking inwards to the internal customers who create the work ambience. The hospitality sector is often characterised by low pay, long working hours, and low job security which leads to a high labour turnover (Akanpaadgi & Matthew, 2014). Therefore, while the provision of services to the clients is critical for the development and perfection of human sociality, the industry must be concerned for the well-being of those who serve as service providers or hosts.

The sector must find persons with the qualities that promote intersubjectivity while maintaining professionalism and the capacity to fit into the national or regional culture. When the organisation can maintain a group culture where the persons are of primary importance, there will be motivations to work harmoniously and in ways that promote teamwork and individual flourishing (Hausler, 2017). It is when these are in place that the customer's overall enjoyment of the product is assured. The industry meets the needs, persons, and circumstances appropriately so that organisational culture and personal culture interact.

There have been studies about the best models for promoting such interactions. These models are based on the adaptations to the materiality of objects that need to be worked with and the technicalities of practice. As culture includes the adaptations to the total environment, these become cultural types that influence human behaviour as it shapes both the perceptions and the attitudes of people. Thus, the systems, processes, and businesses that are established and the interactions that take place among the clients are culture-bound (Erdogan, 2020).

Some of these types as adapted by Cameron and Quinn (1999) include adhocracy which breeds a sense of entrepreneurship. It rewards energy and creativity but can engender urgency in a dynamic environment. The clan culture type prioritises family and the 'we' above the 'I'. It is structured to develop a collaborative environment with humane work, loyalty, commitment, and participation. The hierarchy culture is characterised by an authoritarian structure. It values rules, regulations, and processes. It has distinct lines of communication and accountability with the maintenance of tight control of smooth operations. Finally, the market culture is goal-focused, highly competitive, and geared towards productivity (Pizam & Haemoon, 2008; Tesone, 2008). Certain elements of each cultural type are essential for running the ideal hospitality environment which promotes interpersonal relations, collaboration, creativity, and unity while not neglecting technical efficacy. Each organisation has to closely study the cultural environment it wishes to promote.

These organisations need to focus on both the internal and external cultures as important. The external culture is dependent on the location of that organisation and the culture of the people it services. The adaptation to the physical environment is shown in the architectural designs and interior decoration. It also affects the dressing, foods, and services offered. They are done in the spirit of hospitality which means that the distribution of objects is done in a welcoming way. The hostesses and hosts also need to adopt attitudes that are open, inclusive, and welcoming. In this way, they transmit a culture that does not only have an external impact but is internalised within the individual and the organisation.

The internal culture refers to the organisational mores which has been defined by Davidson (2003) as the shared beliefs and values that are passed on to all within the business. It is a system of shared meaning held by members that distinguish the organisation from others because there is a set of key characteristics that are valued. The ability of the members of staff to understand customers' and other employees' cultures and integrate these accordingly is referred to as *intercultural sensitivity* (Erdogan, 2020). The internal culture, therefore, encompasses the customs, traditions, gestures, and behaviour, symbolic elements, and communication of those who work in that service industry.

Finally, the cultural aspect of hospitality should respect the spiritual dimension of the human being. It should make it conducive for arriving at transcendence and worship of God if desired. The services, ambience, internal, and external culture ought not to be contrary to this desire for establishing an intimate relationship between the bodily sphere and the spiritual. It is in this union that the human being finds his fulfilment so that the hospitality industry becomes a place for human flourishing.

5 Celebrations and Hospitality Culture Directed to Flourishing

An important theme that has run through this chapter is how the hospitality sector is well-positioned to help human beings achieve some of their goals. They have a special task of caring for the well-being of human beings while being concerned for the balance of all creation since the material and non-material elements of the environment are vital to the good functioning of the hospitality industry. In a globalised consumer economy with frenetic work habits, the balance of sociality and individuality that the industry can provide is particularly relevant.

Hospitality workers cater to the physical, psychological, social, and spiritual dimensions. How well this is done is subject to the principles that guide the industry and the relevance they give to what is truly important. This is why performance matrix scales which can evaluate non-financial indicators such as the quality of celebrations and the culture created are relevant for the long-term improvement of the industry.

In respecting and building their culture, it is good that attention is given to excellence. This means that the creative and cognitive aspects are directed to excellence but not for its own sake. It must keep intersubjectivity in view and foster an active relationship with transcendent realities. It is more than ever necessary given that we exist in societies that are being transformed into secular, individualistic aggregations of people.

The hospitality industry must promote an ambience where the giver and the taker live authentic human lives with individual and communal fulfilment. It requires a correct image of the human being as a model and point of reference. This model includes character development, constant perfection of the faculties, unity between the body and spirit, and an intimate relationship with God manifested in divine worship. It is in addressing these varied dimensions of the human being that happiness can be achieved. These are general indications that the leaders and managers in this industry need to translate into specific, measurable, achievable, relevant, and time-bound (SMART) objectives for their businesses.

There are character traits or virtues that working in the hospitality industry can help promote. In the earlier sections, we referred to the virtues of generosity, authenticity, and friendship which facilitate relationships with others. Since this chapter is on the cultural aspects of hospitality and celebrations, we have limited the discussions to habits that facilitate these specific areas.

The concept of celebrations can only be well directed to flourishing when the concept of work is understood, when there is a work ethic that guides decisions and actions i.e. when one works a lot and well for the common good. There is a real danger that work becomes simply drudgery because of the rhythm and pace of manual work required. When this happens, the workplace is transformed into an unfriendly space with a culture that breeds competitiveness and egoism. For the employers, there is an obligation to provide an ambience where the individual can thrive through work and can maintain the needed distance to develop other areas of life. Celebrations are at the root of well-being when there is a work–rest balance that is conducive to personal growth.

Meaning and transcendence can be found in the daily tasks and even celebrated. The culture that pervades the industry should celebrate the persons and their healthy relationships. This reaffirms personhood and situates people in their past, present, and future. With a personal biography, one celebrates in communion and there is a close network of relationality that satisfies the unquenchable desire of all humans to love and be loved. This desire is, however, never fully satisfied on earth so that there is always a cycle of ordinary events, celebrations, hospitality, and receptivity.

The future hope for the hospitality industry is that it fosters relations among workers and clients that promote personal and industry growth while adapting effectively to the changes that time inevitably brings. Growth understood as not limited to productivity but as an increase in societal appreciation for its relevance in fostering a cultural climate that is conducive for human flourishing. It needs to tailor its physical adaptations to that of the local culture it finds itself in while striving for personal and professional excellence. It needs to be situated in that culture while open to diversity and differences. It requires that the persons who offer services have the personal capacities to make this hope a reality and those who are clients or guests can receive the gift of the hospitality industry in the spirit it is given.

6 Conclusion

This chapter has addressed celebrations as human events related to the cognitive and social abilities of human beings to function as individuals, live in communion with others, and draw attention to events worth commemorating. These events or celebrations give significance to persons and occurrences which are considered relevant to the individual and communal life of the people involved. For this reason, human sociality has been considered a key concept that requires a deeper understanding of the cultural aspects of the hospitality industry and celebrations to be better understood.

The hospitality industry deals with the physical dimensions when it adapts to the material environment through its architecture, interior decor, food, and clothing. It is also a psychological necessity for the human being who needs rest, play, and festivity to work better. Celebrations and feasts are at the heart of human play and the hospitality industry through its services can provide these in a way that facilitates personal growth. The social dimension refers to the celebratory meetings that need to manifest and strengthen the bonds of love and friendship. It should not be a place for hostility but of welcome and warmth. Finally, the spiritual dimension can be promoted by an industry that motivates the search for transcendence and celebration of religious events.

It is when the different dimensions of the human being are provided for that cultural differences are enriching. Culture manifests diversity yet binds in openness, authenticity, and acceptance when these are fostered. The industry needs to build a culture that reflects the customs and traditions of the place it is located in yet maintain an ethical guide to what is right for human and industry flourishing. It needs to promote an ambience where individual and organisational cultures coincide in orienting towards the good of the person.

Action Prompts

Find time for rightful celebrations because celebrating fulfils certain social, psychological, moral, and spiritual needs of the human being.

Orient every celebration so that it is for the true well-being of all the participants.

Avoid using celebrations as an opportunity to dishonour or disrespect any individual or community.

Study Questions

1. Why is intersubjectivity a stable basis for the concept of celebrations?
2. What role does the hospitality industry play in the work–rest balance?
3. What challenges can virtual celebrations pose to human sociality manifested through feasts and events?

4 Celebrations and the Cultural Aspects of Hospitality

Chapter Summary

The chapter is a descriptive study of the position the hospitality industry holds in promoting celebrations through the culture it models. Celebrations bring into prominence little breaks in the rhythms of ordinary life. Individual and communal commemorations are attended to through feasts and events. The need to celebrate is an essential manifestation of human individuality and sociality.

Celebrations are multidimensional, experiential, ontological, and ethical because they cut across cultures and transverse space and time. They require cognitive, emotive, and physical capacities which immerse one in an experience that can be guided and evaluated. Therefore, it is a *human* activity that fulfils material, social, psychological, and spiritual needs.

The bonds forged through celebrations must originate and end in friendship. Though this is not always the case, when a culture of love, social cohesiveness, and communality is created it becomes possible to foster friendships. This is where the hospitality industry is relevant for creating an ambience that can facilitate this. It is a sector that, through its various departments, can foster attitudes and virtues that encourage human flourishing.

There are challenges to the creation of such a culture. The chapter proposes that a deeper understanding of human sociality and its requirements, a phenomenology of celebrations, and the appreciation of a work–rest balance will aid practitioners to serve better and create a culture of love and friendship. Developing an adequate performance measure is also a useful tool in directing the industry towards personal growth and the flourishing of its internal and external customers.

References

Akanpaadgi, E. V., & Matthew, A. C. (2014). An assessment of the effects of leadership on the motivation of employees towards the achievement of organizational goals: A case study of the hospitality industry in the Bolgatanga municipality. *European Journal of Business and Management, 24*(6), 32–37.

Aristotle, (2014). *Nicomachean ethics in complete works of Aristotle, Volume 1: The Revised Oxford Translation*, books 8–9. Princeton University Press.

Cameron, K. S., & Quinn, R. E. (1999). *Diagnosing and changing organizational culture based on competing values framework*. Addison Wesley.

Ceban, F., Nogo, D., & Carvalho, I. P. (2021). Association between mood disorders and risk of Covid-19 infection, hospitalization, and death: A systematic review and meta-analysis. *JAMA Psychiatry*. https://doi.org/10.1001/jamapsychiatry.2021.1818

Davidson, M. C. (2003). Does organizational climate add to service quality in hotels? *International Journal of Contemporary Hospitality Management, 15*(4), 206–213.

Elbanna, S., Eid, R., & Kamel, H. (2015). Measuring hotel performance using the balanced scorecard: A theoretical construct development and its empirical validation. *International Journal of Hospitality Management, Elsevier, 51*, 105–114.

Erdogan, K. (2020). *Cross cultural aspects of hospitality and tourism: A services marketing and management perspective*. Routledge.

Handelman, D. (1990). *Models and mirrors: Towards an anthropology of public events* (pp. 15–16). Cambridge University Press.

Hausler, N. (2017). *Cultural due diligence in hospitality ventures; A methodological approach for joint ventures of local communities and companies*. Springer International.

Hofstede, G. (2011). Dimensionalizing cultures: The Hofstede model in context. *Online Readings in Psychology and Culture, 2*(1). https://doi.org/10.9707/2307-0919.1014

James, W. C. (1985). The celebration of society: Perspectives on contemporary cultural performance. In F. E. Manning (Ed.). Bowling Green University Popular Press, 1983. pp. x + 214. *Studies in Religion/Sciences Religiousness, 14*(2), 268–268. https://doi.org/10.1177/000842988501400234

Lombo, J. A., & Russo, F. (2017). *Philosophical anthropology: An introduction*. Midwest Theological Forum.

4 Celebrations and the Cultural Aspects of Hospitality 77

Luboshitzky, D., & Gaber, L. B. (2001). Holidays and celebrations as a spiritual occupation. *Australian Occupational Therapy Journal, 48*, 66–74.

Montgomery, K., & Tansits-Wenze, G. (2002). Science, religion, and celebrations: A paradigm for teaching holidays. *The Educational Forum, 66*(2), 170–178.

Pizam, A., amp; Haemoon, O. (2008). *Handbook of hospitality marketing management*. Elsevier.

Ribeiro, M. L., Vasconcelos, M. L., & Rocha, F. (2019). Monitoring performance indicators in the Portuguese hospitality sector. *International Journal of Contemporary Hospitality Management, 31*(2), 790–811.

Ritzer, G. (2007). Structuration theory. *Contemporary Sociology, 36*(1), 84–85. https://doi.org/10.1177/009430610703600154

Selwyn, T. (2001). *An anthropology of hospitality in 'In search of hospitality': Theoretical perspectives and debates*. L. Conrad & M. Alison (Eds.) (pp. 18–37). https://doi.org/10.1016/B978-0-7506-5431-9.50006-8

Tesone, D. (Ed.). (2008). *Handbook of hospitality human resources management*. Elsevier.

Tylor, E. B. (2010). *Primitive culture: Researches into the development of mythology, philosophy, religion, art, and custom*. Cambridge University Press.

5

Harnessing Technology for Hospitality and Tourism

Ngozi Nnamani

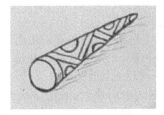

N. Nnamani (✉)
Lagoon School, Lagos, Nigeria
e-mail: ngozi.nnamani@gmail.com

© The Author(s), under exclusive license to Springer Nature
Switzerland AG 2022
K. Ogunyemi et al. (eds.), *Humanistic Perspectives in Hospitality and Tourism,
Volume II*, Humanism in Business Series,
https://doi.org/10.1007/978-3-030-95585-4_5

1 Introduction

Hospitality is a centuries-old traditional activity which has developed very dynamically since the beginning of the twenty-first century (Ivanov & Webster, 2019). It is an industry that offers services in all countries and cultures of the world. In addition, it is an industry with perpetually growing competition. This challenge leads to a need to want to stand out to remain relevant. Hospitality providers and enterprises who have learned how to integrate technology to provide higher-level services at a reasonably affordable rate seem to stand out and survive.

One of the concrete aspects of technology that has redefined our lives today and is changing the future is Artificial Intelligence, which is very much at the backend of the design of Robots and process automation. There is no doubt that this has improved processes, making them faster and raising the quality of services provided in the hospitality industry.

On the other hand, these inventions have influenced and redefined the role of humans in the hospitality industry, raising lots of questions and concerns. AI is also challenging some of the basic principles of life, causing many to wonder about human nature and what makes us distinct from the rest of creation (Thacker, 2020).

The purpose of this chapter is to highlight significant moments in the history of technology in hospitality, highlighting the concerns raised by this development, especially the role of robots and AI. Solutions based on humanistic principles are suggested by way of solutions and answers to these questions and concerns. Although technology's influence was already noted before the 1900s, the chapter's focus is from 1941 to 2020. From the studies and research available, the most significant technological advancements have been noticed in the hotel and airline sectors but do not exclude the proliferation of technology in other aspects of the hospitality industry.

From the origins of humanity, man has always been guided by norms, principles, and customs to orient all man's activities. The advancement in technology and the growth, especially of AI, needs some guidance and orientation. Technology, especially AI, will continue to evolve, opening up new and maybe unimagined possibilities for man. There is a need for regulators, managers, tech designers, and decision-makers within the hospitality to always "Do the right thing". How do we know the "right thing"?

Current AI initiatives, especially when adopted in scientific institutions or companies, embrace a principle-based approach, deontological approach. This approach has its origin in the Greek word "*deon*", which means: "duty" or "obligation" (MIttelstadt, 2019). It, therefore, bases its correctness or not of man's actions on a sense of obligation or duty. Consequentialist moral theory, often manifested in utilitarianism, is another ethical theory. Utilitarianism bases its decision on its usefulness, practicality, and results.

Deontology is adequate for setting guidelines and principles. Utilitarianism helps decide especially between two conflicting principles. However, recent studies and research have shown that these approaches fail (MIttelstadt, 2019), because they either fail to consider the limitations of the human mind or cannot encompass cases in absolute.

For this reason, in this paper, Virtue Ethics is given the centre stage. Although not very prevalent, it dates back to the time of the Greek philosophers and is primarily attributed to Plato and Aristotle. Plato developed the four cardinal virtues (justice, temperance, prudence, and fortitude), while Aristotle expanded them into the moral virtues, adding some intellectual ones, like wisdom. This classical view on virtues holds that ethical, moral principles should be based on what is good for the person (the acting subject), and in cases, applicable on what is good for the persons influenced by this action. It is important to note that "good" as stated here, is not equivalent to pleasurable nor convenient but instead speaks more to what perfects the human person. Virtue ethics weighs the consequences of actions (like utilitarianism) as well as their agreement with rules (like deontology) (Sison et al., 2018).

This work proposes that decision-makers in the design and adoption of technology and AI for hospitality adopt the virtue-ethics principle. Since hospitality is a field that serves the human person, what better approach to adopt than the principle that focuses on perfecting the person?

2 A Journey Through the Evolution of Technology in the Hospitality Industry (1940–1960)

2.1 Reservation Systems: 1940–1960

1945 marked the end of World War II following the dropping of the Hiroshima bomb on Japan and other events in other parts of the world. At the University of Pennsylvania, the first programmable computer was unveiled called the ENIAC (Electronic Numerical Integrator and Computer). That same year, Westin established the first hotel reservation system called HotelType and allowed credit cards for payments, thereby kickstarting the reservation revolution. Before then, hotels solely relied on a series of books, papers, and pages for reservations. American Airlines installed a booking system in the airline industry, which was still at the experimental stage.

In 1947 Roosevelt Hotel NYC installed guest room Television for the first time. Subsequently, in 1951, Hilton Group made televisions mandatory in all bedrooms.

Sheraton Hotels introduced an improvement on the reservation system introduced by Westin in 1958, called Reservation. It was the first automated electronic reservation system in hospitality and the first toll-free reservation system. At around this time, American Airlines and IBM were making progress in the experimental airline reservation system. The project will continue till about the mid-60s.

2.2 Boost in Reservation Systems and Other Technologies: 1960–1980

The online reservation system, SABRE, developed by IBM and American airlines, was finally completed in 1964. It is known that SABRE could process about 7000 bookings per hour with almost zero error rate. It was also fascinating because it was the first time a reservation system could store a passenger's information in its memory. Many other airline companies got interested in this and began to contract IBM to develop similar

5 Harnessing Technology for Hospitality and Tourism   83

systems. At the beginning of the 1970s, almost all United Stated Airlines had built their reservation systems. With time, airlines collaborated to develop consolidated reservation systems.

Although World war II had ended, the 1960s was dominated by other wars, killings, and assassinations. A space race began that culminated in a moon landing. At the same time, there was a growth in technological inventions. Intercontinental Hotels and Resorts introduced lots of inventions that facilitated and improved hotel services. The guest corridors provided ice vending machines, retractable drying lines in guest showers, and others.

Between 1973 and 1976, many hotels in the United States started to introduce movies and TV-paid subscriptions. In 1976, two Florida hotels were the first to offer HBO in their bedrooms, going a step higher than just having Television in the rooms.

2.3   Personal Computers, In-Room Phones, Credit Cards, and Keycards: 1980s

It was not until the 1980s that things started to get a bit more technical. Without the invention of the 80s, life and work as we experience today would have been much more different. In July 1980, IBM introduced Personal Computers into the mainstream market. Although it was costly at the time (over $1500), it was still a significant development from where we were. Shortly after that, in 1983, Apple announced the Macintosh. Motorola announced the cellphones that same year, and two years after, in 1985, Microsoft was launched, and the World Wide Web was born.

As these technologies influenced virtually all industries, hospitality did not remain untouched. Some of these changes were boosted by the Personal Computer revolution, and others were technological advancements that just happened simultaneously.

In 1983, Vingcards invented the Optical Keys. That same year, Westin was the first hotel to offer reservations and checkouts using credit cards. In 1986, Teldex Corp introduced the first telephone designed especially for hotel guestrooms. Teldex allowed for room service, chargeable calls, and interaction with families and friends. Although other brands have been developed since then, Teldex remains the most popular brand in the market and has been installed in more than 125 countries.

This invention paved the way for the Smartphone technologies used today to improve the guest experience in every aspect of hospitality.

The custom of tracking guest data and information started in the 1980s. Today data is being tracked differently and in a more sophisticated manner. Customer Information tracking has evolved to CRM systems, customer engagement, and tools for marketing. It is currently building the basis for the present and future technology: Artificial Intelligence.

2.4 Laptops, Mobile Phones, and Internet Boom: 1990s

With the boom of Personal Computers and other related technologies in the 1980s, IT became a primary global industry. Around the mid-90s, computers started to manifest themselves as almost indispensable in daily life and work. Job seekers in all with computer skills stood at an advantage over those without these skills. This applied to all the industries, and hospitality was not wanting at all.

With the internet, communication and retrieval and delivery of information were made much faster. In 1994, Travel web was launched—the first online hotel catalogue. That same year, Hyatt Hotels and Promus Hotel Corporation broke the record as the first hotel industry to launch a website. This indeed created a novelty in the cataloguing system. However, research still shows that hotel customers and travellers still appreciate the printout of hotel brochures.

Although the reservation system was already in existence before now, Choice Hotels and Promus Hotels were the first to introduce online access to the reservation system. Choice Hotels also introduce a PC in the hotel room for the first time as one of the amenities for their clients. From the 1990s, there was also a boost in the online travel agency business.

2.5 Wireless Internet and the iPhone: 2000s

Hotel WIFI was invented in the 90s. Nevertheless, by 2003, its use became more widespread, and over 6000 hotels and inns made it available to their guests and customers.

On January 9, 2007, Apple Inc. CEO Steve Jobs unveiled the iPhone—a touchscreen mobile phone with an iPod, camera, and Web-browsing capabilities, among other features—at the Macworld convention in San Francisco, marking a change in mobile technology and apps (History.com, 2020). This invention gave a spur and push to application developers in the hospitality industry. By 2009, Intelity built the first mobile application that improved guest service and hotel operations. Hotels did not seize the moment to take advantage of all of these. Apple Inc., however, did not stop developing; by 2010, the iPad was launched. That same year was the first in-room iPad released, in the Plaza NYC Hotel, thus setting new standards for technology in hospitality.

In 2012, Conrad Hotels & Resorts, through a partnership with Intelity, introduced the first service-enabled hotel brand app; this development caused the industry to question and change its view of mobile technology as a bridge to guests (A Brief Look at the History of Hotel Technology, 2016).

2.6 Robots in Hospitality and Artificial Intelligence: 2016

In 2016, the first world robot hotel was launched in Nagasaki, Japan, and the Henn-na Hotels. At the launch, it was considered a remarkable feat and looked upon as the future model. Unfortunately, resulting from customer feedback and other issues experienced, some of the robots were gradually discontinued and replaced with human employees (Fig. 1).

Fig. 1 An overview of the history of technology in the hospitality industry

3 How Various Technological Inventions Have Influenced the Hospitality Sector

3.1 Mobile Technologies

With mobile accessibility via smartphones and tablets in hotel reservations, there is almost no limit to what a customer can do. A potential customer can within a short time have access to the number of hotels available and can, at the click of a button, compare options and make reservations. In addition to making hotel reservations, a customer can select specific preferences desired with the mobile application, such as an extra pillow, a specific drink, laundry services, and much more. With mobile phones, one can easily order a complete menu with any desired combinations and additions and have food delivered on the go. Almost everywhere you go, it is widespread to come across a QR code that enables you to scan for some service to be provided. With mobile scanning, electronic payments in all areas of hospitality have been simplified. You can scan to pay, scan to discover the age of the wine, scan to find out the ingredients, among other features. Mobile technology has improved the lives of service receivers and has gone a long way in simplifying processes for service providers.

3.2 Digital Kiosks

The Digital kiosk is a technical invention that speeds up processes at hotels, restaurants, and airports. It makes the normal processes more efficient. With this invention, individuals can register themselves, pick a number on the queue, make payment for services, self-board, and much more without the usual delays because of back-and-forth communication between the client and the service provider. Digital kiosks, when used in hospitality, improve customer experience by eliminating delays. For hotels, the implementation of digital kiosks provides a potential opportunity to increase revenue through up-selling and one-to-one marketing offers of additional revenues (Ivanov & Webster, 2019).

3.3 Social Media

Social Media has changed the way people around the globe communicate with one another (Seth, 2012). With the invention of mobile phones and the improving conditions of people in developing countries, there is an increase in the number of people accessing the internet. On any day in the last five years, there were on average 640,000 people online for the first time (Roser et al., 2015). According to Broadbandsearch.net, global internet usage increased by 1266% from the year 2000–2020. With websites like Tripadvisor, Expedia, Kayak. Skyscanner and Opentable, many more people, make their choices and decisions based on what people say on the digital media and the ability to request such services through that channel.

In 2017, Facebook (now Meta), rolled out its online ordering feature for restaurants, making it easier for customers to order food from their favourite restaurant using the application (Sachs, 2020). The most exciting thing about this is that customers did not need to navigate to a particular restaurant or a delivery service. Shortly after, Instagram followed suit, and gradually most Social media applications are seeing the need to use their platforms to offer consolidated hospitality services.

4 Artificial Intelligence in the Hospitality Industry

The term "artificial intelligence" refers to the part of computer science whose tools renounce algorithmic constructions and analytical data processing in favour of heuristics and a global approach (Yousra & Khalid, 2021). The terminology was used for the first time at a seminar held at Dartmouth College in the United States in 1956. Artificial intelligence has its roots in machine learning, which is the ability to analyze data to discover valuable patterns to make predictions. This process of prediction is similar to the process of learning in humans. The more we repeat actions or process information, the more predictions we make about events, and the more they inform our future actions.

4.1 Robots

In 2016, the world's first all-robot hotel was launched in Japan. Robots are systems that have been programmed to move within a determined location and carry out tasks, just like humans do but based on a programme and algorithm. Some of them can talk, move, dance. Robots are being used in many aspects of hospitality to deliver a high level of service at an objective standard, perform monotonous tasks, and reduce high employee turnover. Bear Robotics is a company that builds Robots and specifically designed Penny, which is used in hotel services. In an interview with Juan Higueros, Co-Founder and Chief Operating Officer, he talks about a test that was carried out when Penny was launched. The staff of the particular restaurant where Penny was initially tested were required to wear pedometers. In his words: "We discovered that in a typical 8–12-hour shift, a server walks between 5 to 9 miles in a small restaurant". He notes this could lead to physical exhaustion, prevent some from carrying out such jobs, and maybe eventually wear them down altogether. He believes that Penny is a solution to this human problem. By delegating some tasks to our robots, servers can redirect their time to more value-added steps involving customer service (Ivanov & Webster, 2019)(Fig. 2).

5 Harnessing Technology for Hospitality and Tourism   89

Fig. 2 A receptionist robot greets a hotel employee, demonstrating how to check-in at the new hotel, aptly called Weird Hotel, in Sasebo, south-western Japan (Photograph: Shizuo Kambayashi/AP)

4.2 Chatbots

For several years, chatbots have been an emerging hospitality technology trend, but their value is just expanding, especially as clients want quick answers to questions at all hours of the day. Hotels and restaurants will frequently receive inquiries from customers in different time zones, making it challenging to have employees available. Chatbots are programmed to answer the most common questions without the assistance of a person. In more complex scenarios, they can gather information from the client and quickly forward the query to an actual staff member while also giving them access to what the customer has said. Chatbots have a clear, positive impact on both the consumer and the hotels that use them. This technology allows hotels to give a better client experience while also saving money on staffing. Again, since the answers provided by a chatbot depends on the pre-provided algorithm and data, the same chatbots could provide different answers as shown in Fig. 3.

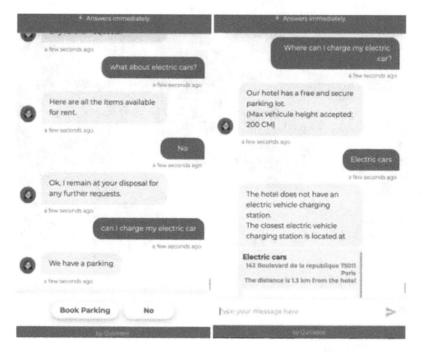

Fig. 3 The same chatbot can give excellent or poor answers depending on the information the hotel made available (*Source* www.hotelhero.tech)

4.3 Smart Rooms

A rising number of hotel corporations, including Hilton and Marriott, are adopting the notion of the smart hotel room. The most basic argument is that it can enhance a hotel's real experience by increasing convenience. A smart room utilizes "smart" electronic gadgets fueled by the Internet of Things (IoT). This IoT innovation implies that what were once conventional gadgets are presently fitted with internet connectivity, permitting them to send and get information and, viably, communicate with one another. For hospitality providers, this is a plus as it enables them to create a high level of service and streamlined user experience. One of the major concerns for the guest who no doubt enjoys this service is their data security and intrusion to their privacy rights.

5 Designing Technology for the Future and the Ethical Consequences/Concerns

As more technologies continue to emerge, it becomes imperative to ask questions like: "Is this good or bad?" Therefore, there is a need to give some sort of orientation, a compass to this exciting development and evolution. Such questions are classified under the subject study of ethics—a discipline of philosophy that evaluates the morality of man's actions (goodness or badness). This aspect of philosophy is also known as Moral Philosophy.

Before raising suggestions about designing future technologies, we will quickly review some of the ethical concerns technology, and AI poses in the hospitality industry. AI presents three major areas of ethical concern for society: privacy and surveillance, bias and discrimination, and perhaps the most profound, most difficult philosophical question of the era, the role of human judgement, said Sandel, who teaches a course in the moral, social, and political implications of new technologies (Pazzanese, 2020). Specifically, in the hospitality industry, the primary concern is the loss of employment, the lack of human touch and emotions inherent in the nature of hospitality, and the possibility of failures or mistakes.

5.1 Human Labour and Employment

Implementing Technology has an obvious implication of downsizing human personnel. "The future of the restaurant industry will not only be characterized by dynamism as it continues to metaphorically evolve but will also be eminently auspicious for virtual restaurateurs even though it will present fewer job opportunities" (Sachs, 2020). When Japan opened the first Robot-only hotel, it started with personnel of 30 human staff for a hotel that could take 300 guests. With time, as things improved, they brought it down to 7. This left 23 humans unemployed or in search of new employment, with the ripple effects of the families dependent on them for sustenance.

5.2 Human Touch

Another big challenge is that these machines do not have emotions, human intelligence, and will. They perform many tasks that they have been programmed to perform following commands designed by human beings. Some of the reviews of customers who visited the Henn-na Hotel in Japan were concerned about this. One of them in her blog had this to say about Churi-Chan, the bedroom assistant: "The conversation between Churi-Chan and I did not go smoothly. Although she looks cute, the chemistry was really never there". According to Oracle's report in 2019, 50% of restaurant patrons find robot service invasive, and 40% will avoid visiting restaurants serviced by robotic staff.

Experts in the AI industry are developing robots and AT machines with emotions, but is this possible? Even if this is achieved, consciousness and self-awareness cannot determine self-worth and personal responsibility. Humanity cannot be defined as a computer programme because the being of a human person is not composed of a set of fundamental instructions. Humanity is founded on something higher and spiritual, the intellect and the will, which cannot be programmed.

5.3 Cost of Implementation and the Poor

Another growing concern about building technology for the future is the cost of implementation and accessibility by the "common man". The terms inclusivity and equity have become very widely used in this century. Nevertheless, we continue to witness so much human inequality among nations and people.

5.4 Data and Privacy

When Sergey Brin and Larry Page founded Google in 1998, they brought in a new dimension to how we searched for things on the world wide web, expanding it. They devised a new algorithm that crawled to the ends of the internet and ranked pages based on how many times another site referenced (Thacker, 2020). Recently, an Alexa disclosed

5 Harnessing Technology for Hospitality and Tourism   93

personal information in error, and some smart refrigerators ended up taking the internet down.

5.5   Is AI That Smart and Accurate?

One of the growing concerns of managers of the hospitality and service-providing industry is the lack of confidence in these systems. The room assistants at the Henn-na Hotel were intelligent and accurate but could not identify exceptions when they arose. For instance, it would confuse the sound of a snore, thinking the customer needed something. Customers complained of the inability of the front-desk droid to identify their passports correctly, thereby necessitating human intervention every so often.

In 2018 a self-driving Uber Volvo SUV hit and killed a woman that was riding her bicycle. The car could not recognize the pedestrian cross-walk that the cyclist was using (Board, 2018). The algorithm failed, or better said, the algorithm was not developed enough to identify an object as a pedestrian unless the object was near a crosswalk. In cases like this, these issues are noted, and subsequently, an upgrade was installed. However, these remain a growing concern. How many unprogrammed human scenarios will technology and AI be able to cater for?

5.6   Covid-19

COVID-19's brutal spread across the globe is, first and foremost, a human catastrophe that has harmed the health of hundreds of thousands of people. The global economy is being impacted by the implications of efforts made worldwide to combat the pandemic. Due to the migratory nature of the hospitality industry and a forced pause on global travel, public restaurants, and tourism, lots of impacts were felt. Many people lost their jobs due to the economic burden on the industry and because the concept of social distancing forced the introduction of robots and machines to minimize human contact.

6 An Objective Moral Compass for Tackling the Ethical Issues Raised by Technology and AI in Hospitality

Some peoplebelieve that social conventions create morality; That culture, feelings, pain/pleasure, rationality alone, etc., should determine what is permissible and impermissible. This has a rather limiting and pessimistic implication. A society of morally sick individuals will be ruled by egoism, greed and arrogance, and their institutions which should check this would definitely be unable to prevent its failure in the long run (Argandoña, 2008; Melé et al. 2011). Perhaps a more objective hinge should exist on which human beings can base every action or decision to act, which is not dependent exclusively on culture or time that is subject to change. Also, arriving at that which is socially or culturally acceptable is highly dependent on a value framework. People make rules based on experiences, convictions, and traditions. This makes it clear that consistent values, norms, and moral concepts always play a significant role when people organize themselves in social communities (Vieweg, 2021). These norms and values are usually what determine the answers to questions about justice, solidarity, care of the people, and the distribution of goods and resources.

However, there is a minimal consensus of fundamental values that have proven themselves for the coexistence of people and which therefore remain untouched (Vieweg, 2021). This minimum axis for orientation is deeply rooted in human nature and has been formally expressed in different forms and simply referred to as natural moral law.

Thomas Aquinas is universally recognized as a leading exponent of a natural law approach to ethics (Elegido). By natural law approach to the study of ethics, he refers to the fundamental principles and values that should guide human beings to act rightly or wrongly. He says that it is a natural law because he argues that these principles and norms have a binding force for us by nature: no beings could share our human nature yet fail to be bound by the precepts of the natural law (Elegido).

According to him, these principles are inherent in man's nature. Therefore, by sharing human nature, all human beings have the essential awareness of the precepts of natural law.

In 1948, the United Nations made a Universal Declaration of Human Rights, one of the significant milestones in the history of humanity since it was the first time that people from all regions of the world agreed on rights that are universally human and therefore should be protected as such. The general assembly with representatives from all over the world agreed on 30 Articles, some of which are highlighted below:

1. All men are born free with equal dignity
2. Everyone has a right to life, freedom, and security of person
3. Everyone has the right to work, free choice of employment, just and favourable work conditions, and protection against unemployment.

These universally acceptable principles are also well-grounded in the essence of virtue ethics, attributed mainly to the ancient Greek philosophers Plato and Aristotle. Plato developed the idea of the cardinal virtues, following the line of his master Socrates, affirming that every human person should excel in good acting and that the cardinal virtues determine what is good. Among Artistole's many conclusions on what it means to be virtuous or to act virtuously, one is when he contends that what makes you virtuous is what makes a thing function well or what an object is. Hence when applied to humans, it is that which perfects human nature.

In other for policymakers, managers, and designers of technology for hospitality to make decisions that perfect the human person, one may consider basing these decisions on some of the virtues inherent in the teachings of these Ancient Greek philosophers.

1. **Justice:** The habit of rendering to the other his/her rights (Stedman, 2010). This will push technology creators and AI designers to be fair to all, avoiding excluding certain kinds of persons based on who they are or where they come from. Justice will ensure that decisions are made looking beyond algorithms and extended to foster respect for social and religious beliefs, equity, and diversity, particularly the

marginalized's inclusivity. When applied in making decisions about adopting or designing a technology for the hospitality industry, it will help the decision maker look beyond the machines or the mechanistic process. The decision maker will consider the biographical aspects of the worker that will be related to this technology and its outcome on the well-being of the worker (Bertolaso & Rocchi, 2020).

2. **Temperance:** The habit of moderation in the use of pleasurable things (Stedman, 2010). Applying this virtue in decision-making will help design and build technology that avoids direct, and in cases possible, indirect harm to the human person and the rest of creation. This will also guide the implementation and the use of AI and technology with moderation at all times.

3. **Prudence:** The habit of choosing the right means to achieve worthy ends (Stedman, 2010). It confers the ability to make the proper judgement.

4. **Fortitude:** Habit of restraining fear or moderate behaviour in the face of danger or difficulty (Stedman, 2010). When applied in decision-making for the design of technology for hospitality, fortitude will allow the subject to stick to its ideals or responsibilities against all odds. This has several implications, like speaking up when confronted with problems against one's moral conscience.

Action Prompts

Suppose virtue ethics is applied in the design, adoption and use of technology in the hospitality industry, the human person will continue to remain at the centre of every technological decision. The focus will move from solving material problems to deep reflection on what is worth adopting (Bertolaso & Rocchi, 2020).

•The hospitality industry's focus will remain on delivering quality service to human persons, in particular, not in abstract. Human persons understood as having their narratives and historicity, which are aspects that machines cannot precisely identify with because they lack those qualities. They are unable to synthesise things like perceptions, emotions and thoughts (Bertolaso & Rocchi, 2020).

> •Education in the hospitality industry: Perhaps an adoption of an anthropocentric curriculum in educating hospitality industry professionals, decision makers and technology designers will ensure that the objective good of human person remains at the Centre of the practice.
>
> •Although it may appear evident and obvious that machines cannot replace humans, however, there is need for more in-depth research carried out by the hospitality professionals on the ethical consequences of technology.
>
> • Chose technology while conscious of the need to protect human dignity.
>
> • Practice virtue ethics when deciding on adopting AI—"Do the right thing".
>
> • Ask for guidance and orientation when it comes to technology, especially to AI, this is needed.

Study Questions

1. What aspect of technological development(s) would you consider the most influential in the current technological trends in the hospitality industry?
2. How will Artificial intelligence redefine the future?
3. What ethical compass can leaders and policymakers in the hospitality industry apply when designing/adopting new technology?
4. How would you analyse a hospitality management team's decision to reduce its staff strength, replacing them with Robots and other technological innovations, based on feedback that many customers complained about human errors? Discuss this from the deontological and consequentialist point of view?

Chapter Summary

There are very few areas of our daily lives and operations that have not been impacted by technology. While not being an exception, the hospitality industry appears to have been affected as much or more than other aspects of life. Maybe a few years ago, some people still considered it impossible, given that most of the operations of this industry are related to activities that are very human and that involve the five senses: the ability to look and to see; to hear and comprehend; to feel; to perceive and to taste. Despite the very human desire to maintain these aspects, it will be futile to attempt to halt the influence of technology in any industry or remain at the level of reminiscing what had been. Certain basic things will always remain. People will always need to sleep in a bed, eat for sustenance, desire to travel the world, and experience nature. However, technology has redefined and will continue to redefine the process of rendering these services. For a discipline as entrenched in humanity as hospitality, many queries and issues have been raised regarding the utilization of technology in its various aspects.

The automation of tasks and processes presents several implications at all levels. In the hospitality industry, technology is no longer a "new invention" to be put up with because of its use in printing receipts, generating invoices, etc. It has become indispensable and, in a broad sense, can be described as the backbone of the industry. Technology continues to permeate and revolutionize the hospitality sector. In doing so, these technological innovations appear to modify current delivery practices. Hence, hospitality managers, policymakers, and hospitality tech designers need to consider the possibilities of striking a balance between the efficiency of established processes and the fulfilment of staff/customer expectations.

While technology is generally beneficial to the hospitality industry, many long-standing concerns and problems have been raised, primarily related to ethics, privacy, and security. In making choices about adopting technology, hospitality industries could focus on protecting one core aspect of human dignity—work. The main concerns raised about adopting technology and AI relate to human work and privacy or security. To constantly manage these things in a balanced and objective way, hospitality industry leaders, decision-makers, and tech creators need virtue ethics as a guide. At the legislative level, the government must establish and enforce laws and policies founded on universal human

> rights to ensure that these devices and future technologies are secure enough. Virtue ethics could also guide the education of technology creators and hospitality professionals.

References

(n.d.). *A brief look at the history of hotel technology*. (2016, May 16). Retrieved from Intellity: https://intelity.com/blog/a-brief-look-at-the-history-of-hotel-technology/

Argandoña, A. (2008). Integrating ethics into action theory and organizational theory. *Journal of Business Ethics, 78*(3), 435–446. https://doi.org/10.1007/s10551-006-9340-x

Aristotle. (350BCE). *The Nicomachean ethics of Aristotle*. Retrieved from http://classics.mit.edu//Aristotle/nicomachaen.html

Bartneck, C., Lutge, C., Wagner, A., & Welsh, S. (2021). An introduction to ethics in robotics and AI. *Springer Briefs in Ethics*.

Benveniste, E. (1973). *Indo-European language and society* (Vol. 12). University of Miami Press.

Bertolaso, M., & Rocchi, M. (2020, April 11). Specifically human: Human work and care in the age of machines. *Business Ethics, the Environment and Responsibility*. https://doi.org/10.1111/beer.12281

Board, N. T. (2018, March 18). Collision between vehicle controlled by developmental 1–10. Retrieved from https://www.ntsb.gov/investigations/AccidentReports/Reports/HAR1903.pdf

Chirinos, M. P. (2007). Hospitalidad y amistad en la cosmovisión griega. In Acerbi, M.-D'Avenia, M., φιλία: *Riflessioni sull'amicizia* (pp. 43–48). Edusc.

Chirinos, M. P. (2017). Cooking and human evolution. In M. B. Stefano (Ed.), *The handbook of studies in applied philosophy* (pp. 147–161). Springer.

De Beauvoir, S. (2010). *The second sex*. Knopf.

Derrida, J. (2002). *Acts of religion*. Routledge.

Descartes, R. (1998). *Discourse on method* (D. A. Cress, Trans.). Hackett Publishing.

Devisme, B. (2020, September 28). *Chatbots in the hospitality industry*. Retrieved from Hotel Hero: https://www.hotelhero.tech/blog/chatbots-in-the-hospitality-industry

Dikmen, F. B. (2017). The role of service culture in hospitality industry. *International Journal of Business and Social Science, 8*(5), 85–98.

Elegido, J. M. (n.d.). *Introduction to ethics.*

Etherington, D. (2018, March 19). Uber self-driving test car involved in accident resulting in pedestrian death. *Tech Crunch.* Retrieved from https://tec hcrunch.com/2018/03/19/uber-self-driving-test-car-involved-in-accident-resulting-in-pedestrian-death/

Finaly, S. (2021). *Artificial intelligence and machine learning for business. A no-nonsense guide to data driven technologies.* Relativistic.

Friedan, B. (2010). *The feminine mystique.* WW Norton & Company.

Galvan, J. M. (2003/2004). On technoethics. *IEEE-RAS Magazine*, 58–63.

Gilligan, C. (1993). *In a different voice: Psychological theory and women's development.* Harvard University Press.

González, A. (2004). La dignidad de la persona, presupuesto de la investigación científica. Concepciones de la dignidad. In J. Ballesteros & Á. Aparisi (Eds.), *Biotecnología, dignidad y derecho: bases para un diálogo* (pp. 17–41). EUNSA.

González, A., & Iffland, C. (2014). *Care professions and globalization: Theoretical and practical perspectives.* (A.González, Ed.). Palgrave Macmillan.

Grönroos, C. (1990). *Service management and marketing: Customer management in service competition.* Lexington Books.

Grönroos, C. (2007). *Service management and marketing: Customer management in service competition.* Wiley.

Hagendorff, T. (2020). AI virtues. The missing link in putting AI ethics into practice. *Cluster of excellence "Machine learning: new perspectives for science" International Center for Ethics in the Sciences and Humanities".* https://dblp.uni-trier.de/db/journals/corr/corr2011.html#abs-2011-12750

Hamington, M. (2010). Toward a theory of feminist hospitality. *Feminist Formations, 22*, 21–38.

History.com (Ed.). (2020, January 7). *Steve Jobs debuts the iPhone.* Retrieved from History: https://www.history.com/this-day-in-history/steve-jobs-deb uts-the-iphone

Ivanov, S., & Webster, C. (Eds.). (2019). *Robots, artificial intelligence and service automation in travel, tourism and hospitality.* Emerald.

Kant, I. (2020). *Groundwork of the metaphysic of morals.* Routledge.

Kittay, E. F. (2014). The completion of care—With implications for a duty to receive care graciously. In A. M. González & C. Iffland (Eds.), *Care professions and globalization* (pp. 33–42). Palgrave Macmillan.

Lashley, C. (2000). In search of hospitality: Towards a theoretical framework. *International Journal of Hospitality Management, 19*(1), 3–15.

Lashley, C. (2008). Studying hospitality: Insights from social sciences. *Scandinavian Journal of Hospitality and Tourism, 8*(1), 69–84.

Lashley, C. (2013). *In search of hospitality.* Routledge.

Lynch, P. M. (2011). Theorizing hospitality. *Hospitality & Society, 1*(1), 3–24.

MacIntyre, A. (1985). *After virtue: A study in moral theory.* Duckworth.

MacIntyre, A. (1999). *Dependent rational animals: Why human beings need the virtues.* Open Court Publishing.

MacIntyre, A. (2006). *The tasks of philosophy: Selected essays* (Vol. 1). Cambridge University Press.

Mayer, D. (2006). *Setting the table: The transforming power of hospitality in business.* HarperCollins.

Mboya, E. (2020, June 5). *Business Daily.* Retrieved from Kenya overtakes Angola as third-largest economy in Sub-Saharan Africa: https://www.businessdailyafrica.com/bd/economy/kenya-overtakes-angola-as-third-largest-economy-in-sub-sahara-africa-2291948

Melé, D., Argandoña, A. & Sanchez-Runde, C. (2011). Facing the crisis: Toward a new humanistic synthesis for business. *Journal of Business Ethics, 99*(1), 1–4. https://doi.org/10.1007/s10551-011-0743-y

MIttelstadt, B. (2019). Principles alone cannot guarantee ethical AI. Nature Machine Intelligence 1. *Nature Machine Intelligence,* 501–505. https://www.nature.com/articles/s42256-019-0114-4

Murdoch, I. (1986). *The sovereignty of good.* Ark Paperbacks.

Noddings, N. (2002). *Starting at home: Caring and social policy.* University of California Press.

Pazzanese, C. (2020, October 26). *The Harvard Gazette.* Retrieved from Great promise but potential for peril: https://news.harvard.edu/gazette/story/2020/10/ethical-concerns-mount-as-ai-takes-bigger-decision-making-role/

Post, S. G. (2005). Altruism, happiness, and health: It's good to be good. *International Journal of Behavioral Medicine, 12*(2), 66–67.

Redgrave, K. (2014). "Moved by the suffering of others": Using Aristotelian theory to think about care. In A. González (Eds.), Care professions and *globalization* (pp. 63-86). Palgrave Macmillan.

Robot Hotel in Japan, the Coolest and Weirdest Hotel Experience Ever. (n.d.). Retrieved from FlitterFever: www.flitterfever.com

Roser, M., Ritchie, H., & Ortiz-Ospina, E. (2015). *Our world in data.* Retrieved from https://ourworldindata.org/internet

Sachs, D. H. (2020). *The future of the restaurant industry, how technologies will revolutionize The restaurant industry and cause more dark kitchens to emerge, and the benefits of leveraging robots in restaurant industry.*

Sennett, R. (1998). *The corrosion of character. The personal consequences of work in the new capitalism.* WW Norton & Company.

Seth, G. (2012). *Analyzing the effects of social media on the hospitality industry.*

Sison, A. G., Ferrero, I., & Guitian, G. (Eds.). (2018). *Business ethics. A virtue ethics and common good approach.* Routledge.

Slote, M. (2007). *The ethics of care and empathy.* Routledge.

Stedman, J. M. (2010). Aristotle's cardinal virtues: Their application to assessment of psychopathology and psychotherapy. *Practical Philosphy, 10,* 59.

Stossel, S. (2013). What makes us happy, revisited. *The Atlantic Magazine.* Retrieved from http://tony-silva.com/eslefl/miscstudent/downloadpage articles/behappy-atlantic.pdf

Thacker, J. (2020). *The age of AI. Artificial intelligence and the future of humanity.* Zondervan Thrive.

The Evolution of Hotel Technology-from Legacy to Mobility. (2016, June 30). Retrieved from StayNTouch: https://www.stayntouch.com/blog/hotel-technology-through-the-ages-1960s-2016

Tronto, J. C. (1993). *Moral boundaries: A political argument for an ethic of care.* Routledge.

United Nations. (n.d.). Retrieved from Universal Declaration of Human Rights: https://www.un.org/en/about-us/universal-declaration-of-human-rights

Vieweg, S. H. (Ed.). (2021). *AI for the good.* Springer.

Wijesinghe, G. (2013, January). Reimagining the application of sustainability to the hospitality industry. *Journal of Sustainable Tourism.* https://doi.org/10.1080/09669582.2013.819875

Wrangham, R. (2009). *Catching fire: How cooking made us human.* Basic Books.

Ybaraa, O., Burnstein, E., Winkielman, P., Keller, M., Manis, M., Chan, E., & Rodriguez, J. (2008). Mental exercising through simple socializing: Social interaction promotes general cognitive functioning. *Personality and Social Psychology Bulleting, 34*(2), 248–259.

Yousra, M., & Khalid, C. (2021). Analysis of the variables of intention of the adoption and acceptance of artificial intelligence and big data tools among leaders of organizations in Morroco: Attempt of a theoretical study. *European Scientific Journal, ESJ, 17*(29), 106. Retrieved from https://doi.org/10.19044/esj.2021.v17n29p106

Part II

Customer Care Perspectives

Having reflected on cultural perspectives, the next chapters look at customer care, starting with a discussion on service as gift-giving and leadership. This is followed by a discussion on internal customers as the asset in a humanistic workplace: needed to achieve delightful service for the external customer. Case studies of two hospitality schools depict the importance of high-quality training to achieve employee empowerment and development and excellent customer care, and the importance of person-centred care for nursing home residents is also highlighted. Luxury hotel customers are not left out of the discourse, as this part's final spotlight turns to how guest relations affect brand loyalty.

6

Hospitality as Gift-Giving and Leadership

Ebele Okoye

E. Okoye (✉)
Afara Leadership Centre, Lagos, Nigeria
e-mail: ebele.okoye@afaraleadershipcentre.com

1 Introduction

By nature, the human being is a social being. In his books on politics, Aristotle states that an individual who is unsocial naturally and not accidentally is either beneath our notice or more than human (Aristotle Pol. 1.1253a). This statement confirms that no human can live alone without entering into relationships with other human beings. This simply means that life in society is important for humans to survive, flourish, and achieve fulfilment. We need to cooperate and be of service to one another (Elegido, 2018, p. 90). Serving others and receiving service from them manifests the many ways humans enter into relationships with other humans. Relationality is an originary quality; that is, it lies at the very origin of human beings to relate with others (Lombo & Russo, 2007).

One way humans relate with others is through work. Indeed, every kind of work is a form of service to others. In the case of hospitality, it is a service industry par excellence. It provides essential intangible services that touch lives directly (Team ProMiller, 2020). This is seen from the very definition of hospitality. According to the Oxford English Dictionary, hospitality is the friendly and generous reception and entertainment of guests, visitors, or strangers. It has to do with providing the guest a place to stay, food, entertainment, and other facilities to make the guest comfortable. Hospitality defines the relationship between a guest and a host where the host serves the guest with warmth and courteousness. Different types of establishments offer hospitality services, e.g., hotels, motels, lodges, resorts, bars, restaurants, and furnished apartments. We discover that hospitality refers mainly to businesses that provide food, drink, or a place to sleep (Cambridge English Dictionary). These are basic human needs that must be met in the life of every person. Whether these needs are met in the ambit of the home or in a commercial setting, they greatly impact every man's life. Humans are social beings who need the attention and care of others from infancy till death, albeit in varying degrees and different intensities throughout life. Thus, humans have many more years of real dependence on others, even before birth, compared to other animals. This is evident in the life of feral children, also known as wild children or wolf children, who have grown up with minimal or no human contact (LaPointe, 2005). Having had little human care, no human language, and no human behaviour experience, these children find it difficult to act human.

Every human being needs to develop around others as an imperative for total wellbeing—psychological, physical, and moral. Human beings are open to reality and to others, and this is related to their rationality. The ability to relate to others, i.e., relationality, is the ability to establish relationships, orient oneself towards others, and give of oneself (Lombo & Russo, 2007). Human beings need other human beings for their normal functioning and flourishing. Experiments in psychology show that a lack of care in the life of humans can be devastating, but even more so in the life of a child. Children, if left to grow up without adequate care, are likely to become a burden to family and society.

The Care Effect Report highlights the cost to society when children don't receive the love, care, and support of a family. This includes cognitive, social, and learning difficulties; lack of coping skills for emotional resilience; a higher rate of depression, substance abuse, and attempted suicide; lack of preparation for the transition to adulthood and employment, resulting in greater difficulty in finding jobs and becoming contributing members of society (SOS Children's Villages International, 2017). But, according to the SOS report, all these negative effects are reversed in an atmosphere of love, care, and attention, which is hospitality.

2 Theory of Service

Humans need others to succeed not only because of what they get from them; but also because of their self-realization and self-transcendence. The fullest expression of self-transcendence consists in love and in giving of self (Lombo & Russo, 2007). The flourishing of human beings thus depends on good social relations, a part of which is rendering service and receiving the service (Bielskis & Mardosas, 2014). Service can be simply defined as a way of showing love and giving oneself to others.

Helping others in different forms gives joy and leads to human flourishing (Baltazzi, 2019). It could be volunteering in an organization, helping a colleague or friend, working in an older people's home, etc.

Many human relationships involve one person rendering service to the other person, as when a mother happily takes care of her children. These activities give joy and fulfilment (Titova & Sheldon, 2021). Humans experience joy in other essential activities like eating and procreation. There is a need to eat because life depends on food. The great taste attached to food makes us want to eat. If nobody can live without eating, perhaps we could also suggest that nobody can be fully human without serving others and receiving service in return. Science shows that using functional MRI on people's brains shows that serving others hits the same parts of the brain as food and sex (Gunderson, 2020).

Since service demonstrates the ability human beings possess for self-transcendence which in turn leads to self-realization, hospitality should not be used as a tool of oppression, where a set of second-class citizens slave for an upper class. Similarly, it should not be seen as a servile activity. It is an essential part of human value, development, and flourishing and therefore benefits from a firm humanistic foundation since humanism pays attention to human values and their manifestations (Manalu, 2020).

For instance, care is a fundamental human concept; hospitality provides that care we all need as persons. We easily understand the care needed by strangers, guests, or foreigners because they are away from home, and we may have been in such situations of special need. They show how fundamental these services are to human lives. However, hospitality may be lost even in such situations if attention is concentrated solely or mostly on the drive for profit. The familial nature of hospitality is often forgotten, and attention easily goes to the enormous commercial potential of the industry. We need a paradigm shift in the industry that will look beyond the financial benefits it offers. The profit maximization mandate should be balanced with compassion, generosity, and real care for the guest. The hospitality industry should not be run only as a profit-orientated venture, although this is undeniably one of its features, but above all as a service that perfects humans. Without its services, humans would not be so different from animals. In fact, genuine hospitality is offered without any concern for repayment or reciprocity (Lashley, 2015) since, strictly speaking, hospitality services cannot be given a monetary value. How do you pay a mother for nursing her child and caring for her home or a father for organizing a restful holiday for his family and doing repairs around the house?

As one study rightly argues, when people try to derive an estimate of the monetary value attached to the unpaid work women do, this is meant not to conclusively demonstrate what the work is worth and certainly not to demand a wage in return for it. Instead, the value is meant to demonstrate the magnitude of the value of the work women do without pay and to give women the recognition they deserve for their contributions (Efroymson, n.d., p.13).

Genuine services to others are a key part of hospitality. If you remove the concept of service, then there is no hospitality. Nevertheless, hospitality has been separated from service in certain spheres to highlight aspects differentiated from mere service delivery. Within this context, service is defined as the action of helping or doing work for someone, while hospitality refers more to the emotional connection one makes with the customers (Hasa, 2016). The latter is genuine service and real hospitality since there should be a deeper connection between the host and the guest. This connection may go beyond mere superficial connection and may probably reach deeper emotional levels, which may result in more benefits to the person as services get tailored to their needs.

Since hospitality is defined as friendly interaction and generous reception of guests, visitors, or strangers, this means it must go beyond a mere "cold" service delivery. Hospitality means that the reception of a guest will include a warm greeting and a question or two about their travel plans before proceeding to the check-in process. Guests want to be recognized, respected, validated, and appreciated. Hospitality has the enormous possibility of making the world a better place by bringing out the best in others. Everyone loves attention, respect, and kindness, and most respond by giving back the same to others. As highlighted above, rendering service leads to self-realization and self-fulfilment, which means that services should be carried out with the idea of contributing to the perfection of others. Likewise, serving perfects the one that serves because serving others gives meaning and direction to one's life. It is difficult to find someone who has decided to live for others who is not purpose-driven and happy in life.

110   E. Okoye

3   Service as Gift-Giving

When we think of the concept of giving a gift to another person (gift-giving), what comes readily to mind is the idea of parting with a tangible object. Hospitality and all associated services in the industry are gifts in the form of tangible and intangible goods and they involve both tangible and intangible services. In the case of tangible services, it refers to products that one can taste, see or touch. In the case of intangible services, one cannot see, taste, or touch the product, but it can be felt. A service is mostly a form of intangible product that cannot be touched. It is produced and consumed at the same time. When a hospitality professional shows empathy to guests, listens to them patiently, has a positive attitude, etc., she makes a gift of herself to her guest. Hospitality involves the giving of oneself to others in an intangible way. Of course, the person rendering the service may part with material goods in exchange for payment made. But the emphasis here is on those intangible and priceless services to the client that goes beyond a "cold" and mere service delivery. Herein lies the giving of oneself to another in hospitality.

Receiving a gift often causes a good feeling in the recipient. This is one of the many genuine reasons why people give gifts to others: they want to make a good impression on the other person. Genuine hospitality, in making a gift of self to another, simultaneously makes a good impression. In this way, the service delivered is imbued with human values. The guests are recognized, respected, and appreciated as human persons. The Merriam-Webster Dictionary describes humanity as referring to the state of having a compassionate, sympathetic, or generous behaviour or disposition. It is also the quality or state of being humane. Being human is to love, show understanding, be kind, have compassion, and show empathy. All these human qualities are implied in hospitality. Indeed, hospitality can transform society and make the world a better place to live, where man is **not** a wolf to man.[1]

---

[1] "Man is a wolf to man" (*Homo hominis lupus*) is a Latin proverb used to describe those situations where humans have behaved in a way comparable in nature to a wolf, i.e., predatory, cruel, inhuman, and uncivilized.

Gifts are usually an invitation to give something in return or at least to show kind consideration towards the giver. Guests reciprocate such excellent service by giving positive recommendations and returning to the same establishment to repeat the experience. Merriam-Webster Dictionary defines "gift" as something "voluntarily transferred" and "without compensation". Indeed, the amount paid for a hospitality service can never really be commensurate with the invaluable service rendered: a service that makes us more human, thereby making us more who we are.

Hospitality has to do with the relationship between the guest and the host. For a high quality of service delivery, some soft skills and virtues are needed by the hospitality professional. For instance, hospitality professionals should possess the readiness to understand others. Understanding others makes it easier to serve them and, if necessary, go the extra mile to provide for their needs. Other virtues they require include good listening skills, patience, tolerance, and above all helpful. Organizations, especially hotels, often monitor their employees to make sure they consistently keep to all the rules for customer service delivery, many of which include soft skills (Ibraheem & Iwuagwu, 2015). To be a good professional in hospitality requires certain dispositions, expressed in practising hospitableness. It is not based only on competencies and task proficiency or specific technical expertise and job aptitude (Gebbels et al., 2019). We will consider some of these soft skills at the end of this chapter.

Hospitality professionals are called to give themselves to others the same way a mother or caregiver is called to give herself to the family. In hospitality, the quality of customer service is translated into customer experience. The experience could be in the form of feeling valued or heard. These intangible components of service usually make a guest prefer one tourist agency or hospitality provider to another. There is something about quality of customer service that you often cannot put your finger on, but you know it is there (Hinck, 2015).

This "*something*" is that gift in service, which should be a feature of every hospitality service. It is that authentic spirit of service that emphasizes the person over any other benefits. A hospitality professional needs to see persons, fellow human beings, to show love through service. This critical factor contributes to hospitality and tourism success, both as a means of satisfying ever-increasing customer expectations and as a way to achieve business profitability (Erdly & Kesterson-Townes, 2002).

4 Receiving as Service

We have seen that hospitality is a form of gift-giving. It is a gift of self to another. Every giving implies a receiver. If not, there is "no giving". From experience, we see that generally people like receiving gifts and, when it is a surprise gift, it is sometimes even more appreciated. A gift is also appreciated when it is very special to the receiver either because he or she has always dreamt of it or because of the role it will play in their lives. In hospitality, there are some similarities between gift-giving, as used in normal parlance, and services delivered. In the case of hospitality, the gift is the gift of self in the form of services. Since hospitality is a warm and generous welcome towards the guest, this action could include many elements or surprising details that warm the guests heart.

In giving and receiving gifts, it is not necessarily the content that matters but the kind thoughts of the gift-giver. In like manner, even when service delivery is not optimum, it would have achieved the invaluable and intangible service that sometimes is more important than mere or cold service delivery. The service industry is a real gift because of the way it makes us more human. Of course, not every gift is appreciated in the same way, but there is no doubt that every gift that makes us human is appreciated since this is what we are. We identify with it fast, and we are comfortable in that space.

It is important to consider that receiving is as important as giving. When hospitality is at its best, it makes us feel special, showing that we are in another person's thoughts. In turn therefore, how hospitality services are received is important. Thoughtfulness should accompany the reception of every gift together with appreciation and kind regard towards the giver. A gift from another person should not be received with scorn or derision, especially since it is not only the gift in itself that matters but the thought behind it.

6 Hospitality as Gift-Giving and Leadership   113

There is a popular saying that it is better to give than to receive, but we can only give what we have (Baker, 2020). The person who gives can only do so because they have first received it. According to Albert Einstein, we must exert ourselves to give in the same measure as we have received and keep receiving (Einstein, 1954, pp. 8–11). We can give precisely because we have received, and we keep receiving. In a way, therefore, receiving enjoys precedence over-giving. Life itself is a gift received so it can be given to others. This gift of self to others is important so that we do not lose our humanity. Even in commercial relationships, the principle of gratuitousness and the logic of gift as an expression of fraternity can and must find their place within a normal economic activity (Benedict XVI, Charity in Truth, p. 36).

Receiving entails courtesy even when feedback on poor service delivery has to be communicated. The feedback should be given in such a way that it respects the dignity of the person. Though sometimes it is difficult to separate service from the one rendering the service, in the same way, that it may be impossible to separate the gift-giver from the gift-given. The giver is always associated with the gift they give. For this reason, it is not surprising that both the giver and the gift are so closely linked. But to receive a gift gracefully, it is important to make a mental separation between the gift and the giver. This is important, especially in cases where the gift falls below expectation.

We must look beyond the gift and see the person presenting the gift. Focusing on the person that is providing the service makes it easier to provide useful feedback in a dignified manner to the hospitality professional. Giving feedback should always be positive and constructive. It should be reassuring, constant, and positive in an atmosphere of true friendship. Corrections and feedback should never be given in a demeaning or condescending manner. Good professionals would always like to improve their work and, they realize that feedback is necessary to achieve this.

Receiving must be graceful for it to reflect respect for the person rendering the service. It, therefore, should include personal interactions between the customers and employees. Personal interactions are interpersonal relations that may include, exchange of pleasantries, warm gestures, courtesy, friendliness, and respect (Ennew & Binks, 1999). These interactions are part of the role customers play in quality customer delivery. Friendly words and gestures should not be coming from only the tired host who has been on his or her feet all morning, nor from the tired mother who has juggled many things during the day, nor from the waiter who has attended to all sorts of clients during the day, etc. Customers should also facilitate the warm ambience that makes service delivery run smoothly. It should happen often that a customer takes the time to write a "thank you" note or post positive online reviews to show appreciation for a nice service.

5 Service as Leadership

Following on the discussion so far, we now turn to consider that service in hospitality implies a certain form of leadership. What is the right attitude with which to deliver hospitality services? In other words, what soft skills are needed for a good hospitality service delivery? Hospitality professionals need leadership skills because true service has a lot to do with leadership (Gaitho, 2017). Hospitality professionals are true leaders because they constantly remind us about our humanity and because service requires leadership. Self-leadership is an important part of effective service leadership, a prerequisite for consistently providing quality services to others (Shek et al., 2015). Through their acts of service, hospitality professionals are people who remind others what it means to be human. For this important role they play in human lives, they need to possess a good and deep knowledge of both technical and soft skills (Gebbels et al., 2019).

5.1 Leadership Skills Required in Hospitality

We will now examine some leadership skills that are needed to achieve quality service delivery. This chapter will concentrate only on three leadership skills: people skills, critical thinking skills, and problem-solving skills.

People Skills

People skills refer to the ability to interact with others effectively, i.e., in a friendly way. They include interpersonal or social skills. In a fast-paced world like ours today, it is very easy for each person to be lost in their things. Today, we find that connecting with others is more difficult, and gradually, people are beginning to forget its importance. With the pandemic and the resulting requirement to connect more virtually rather than physically with many others, it is becoming increasingly difficult to make real-life connections. (Nunes et al., 2021). In hospitality and tourism, connection with others is important. It aids in understanding their needs. It is true that, with technological advancement, there is a possibility that machines may replace humans in some aspects of the service industry. This means that, though it is not likely human touch could be completely replaced by machines, the role of human beings in service delivery could change. Human beings are still needed to keep the "hospitality" in hospitality (Harkison, 2017).

A good hospitality professional should foster the ability to connect with others irrespective of age, cultural, and economic background. Skills such as the ability to listen to others and empathize with them are key skills. Demonstrating empathy is a key part of emotional intelligence and it improves human interactions. In general, empathy leads to more effective communication and positive outcomes (Leading Effectively Staff, 2020). Understanding the guest is crucial in delivering customer-centred services. For services to be personalized and meet the needs of each client, a good relationship must be established between the customer and employer. A hotel brand needs to understand the needs of its clients to deliver accurate services. Only then can employees go beyond customer expectations to deliver outstanding services (Zendesk, n.d.).

Hospitality professionals understand the importance of taking care of little details. Attention to detail requires magnanimity, which is greatness of soul. It makes it easy to be in the big picture and yet not forget the little details that make service special. Magnanimity is therefore important in hospitality, combined with a dose of kindness, humility, and self-forgetfulness. Other key skills include adaptability, friendliness, cheerfulness, courtesy, readiness to take up difficult and unpleasant tasks, etc. A good professional in this field should be able to adjust to changes and not easily lose composure even when under pressure. All these qualities enhance leadership capacity.

Communication Skills

Models for measuring service delivery aim to identify guests' needs and provide accurate services to meet those needs. One of the most effective ways to grasp the particular needs of each guest is to communicate effectively. With effective communication skills, it is easy to build trust and confidence. As a result, clients are more confident in the services provided. Responsiveness requires good communication skills, keeping customers informed about when services are to be performed. Good communication is important to keep information clear and avoid irritation, anger, and unnecessary annoyances. Effective communication must include good listening skills that take non-verbal aspects of communication into account. Communication should be accurate, clear, and concise. Communication should be personalized as much as possible, always with an open mind, confidence, and conveying respect for the other person. Since we are in a digital age, online communication also must consider the features of good communication.

Critical Thinking and Problem-Solving Skills

There is a wide variety of needs and problems, as many as there are people on earth. Studies have shown the importance of teaching critical thinking to hospitality professionals (Stone et al., 2017). In their studies, Stone et al. developed the California Critical Thinking Skills Test (CCTST) to determine the extent to which hospitality and tourism students acquired critical thinking skills.

The CCTST provides an overall measurement of reasoning and the measurement of five critical thinking subdomains using five parameters. The parameters for measuring critical thinking include analytical skills, inference skills, evaluation skills, deduction skills, and induction skills. The **analytical** skill is gathering, organizing, synthesizing, and scrutinizing information on a particular issue. This will help the professional decide what is relevant to a particular issue or problem and draw up effective possible solutions. **Inference** skill is the capacity to draw up solutions with the information gathered using sound judgement. **Evaluation** skills represent the ability to critique the quality and credibility of information, argument, opinions, etc. **Deduction** skill is the ability to trace reasoning from the original information presented to a proposed solution that is logical and justified. Finally, **induction** skills represent the ability to make decisions in complex situations where all the facts may not be available, with many other perspectives to consider. It is the ability to make educated guesses based on limited information (Stone et al., 2017) (Table 1).

Table 1 California Critical Thinking Skills Test (CCTST)

Skills	Definition
Analytic skills	Ability to identify assumptions, reasons, and claims. It is a skill used to gather, organize, synthesize, and scrutinize information. Analysis is used to gather information from charts, graphs, diagrams, spoken language, and documents
Inference skills	Ability to draw conclusions from evidence, offering thoughtful suggestions and hypotheses. It is the capacity to generate solutions to a problem and use the information to make sound judgements and draw logical conclusions
Evaluation skills	Ability to assess the quality and credibility of sources of information, arguments, opinions, and the claim they make. It enables us judge the strength or weakness of an argument. Applying evaluation skills we can judge the quality of analyses, interpretations, explanations, inferences, options, opinions, beliefs, ideas, proposals, and decisions
Deduction skills	Ability to trace reasoning from the original information presented to a proposed solution that is logical and justified. Deductive reasoning moves with exact precision from the assumed truth of a set of beliefs to a conclusion which cannot be false if those beliefs are true
Induction skills	Ability to make decisions in uncertain and complex situations, with many perspectives to consider and all the facts may not be available. This skill is used when we draw inferences based on analogies, case studies, prior experience, statistical analyses, simulations, and patterns recognized in familiar objects, events, experiences, and behaviours

5.2 Measuring Customer Experience

With the right kind of skills, service delivery quality is assured. For the measurement of service quality experienced by customers, the most extensively studied model is SERVQUAL. It is a framework that uses ten dimensions (Reliability, Responsiveness, Competence, Access, Courtesy, Communication, Credibility, Security, Knowing the customer, Tangibles) to measure the gap between the customer's service experience quality and the expected service quality. One derivative of SERVQUAL is the RATER (Saleh & Ryan, 1991) model, which highlights five dimensions that customers consider when using a service. It is like a condensed version of the original SERVQUAL model. According to the RATER framework, customers evaluate a business based on five metrics. These include Reliability, Assurance, Tangibles, Empathy, Responsiveness. We will now discuss each of these parameters.

Reliability

This simply means that you deliver the service at the agreed time. Reliability means readiness to overcome any possible obstacles that may prevent the agreed product from reaching the guest at the right time. Reliability implies that the service offered is trusted, and this can be achieved when the service is delivered on time, regularly, and accurately (Javed, 2020). Under reliability, what every customer is looking out for is integrity, honesty, and efficiency.

Assurance

This has to do with credibility and trust. Customers should feel safe in the hands of the staff because they know they are competent. It shows how informed the employees are about the services they deliver (Mulder, 2018). All employees should be able to give accurate information to a customer. This parameter measures trust, and this is key in any customer relations.

Tangibles

This is the total of the environment, materials, and the employees' appearance. The physical appearance of everything that has to do with the establishment. The office, website, equipment, and employees should all look clean and reliable (Mulder, 2018).

Empathy

This defines how the host understands and attends to the need of the customers. That ability to understand the needs of others is key in hospitality, and it is a key feature of a leader. To provide attention and care to another person successfully requires an understanding of the person's plight.

Responsiveness

The timely delivery of services is what responsiveness is all about. Giving timely responses. One study carried out in a hotel showed that the clients demanded: offering or providing assistance that goes above and beyond without being asked, going out of the way to assist the call of duty, displaying a positive mental attitude (Czaplewski et al., 2002) (Fig. 1).

6 Conclusion

Hospitality is a human quality. It is a form of gift-giving where the host makes a gift of self to the guest and, by doing so, reaches self-fulfilment and self-realization. Since it is a form of gift-giving, it should be received with gratitude. Hospitality reminds us that we are human, and for

Fig. 1 The RATER model (*Source* Carroll et al., 2017)

this reason, hospitality professionals are leaders. They are constantly reminding us and, in a way, orienting us towards those qualities that make us human. Their task is to preserve humanity and those human qualities that make it up. Hospitality professionals possess certain soft skills that enable them to achieve this role. With certain leadership skills, they deliver accurate services. We can apply the concept of servant leaders to hospitality professionals. This concept is important in the service industry. As the name implies, a servant-leader is first a servant, then a leader. Good hospitality professionals must be servant leaders with the primary aim to serve. Precisely by rendering these human services, they lead humanity in preserving its human qualities.

> **Action Prompts**
> Every time someone performs an act of service for you, receive it with gratitude.
>   Serving others is an essential feature of our lives as human beings; seek ways to serve others in order to live a fulfilled life.
>   Always "connect" with the guest in order to give him or her a personalized service.

6 Hospitality as Gift-Giving and Leadership

Study Questions

1. Is receiving a service better than rendering a service?
2. What are the leadership skills required by a hospitality professional?
3. What is RATER?

Chapter Summary

The Hospitality and Tourism industry has grown enormously over the past decades, and it is currently a million-dollar business worldwide. According to the 2021 report of the World Travel and Tourism Council, before the pandemic, travel and tourism provided about 10% of the world's GDP, and annually it accounted for 1 in 4 of all new jobs created globally. A close look at the various models of services offered by the industry shows that it is a service industry par excellence because it directly offers innumerable intangible benefits to the human person, whether it is accommodation services, food, and beverage, tourism, entertainment, travel, health, recreation, etc. No matter the angle from which we approach hospitality, it always has to do with high-touch customer services. Therefore, customer experience and customer service delivery is the real game in the industry. Quality service gives an unforgettable customer experience. Hospitality is made possible because of the many acts of service rendered to a guest. Therefore, understanding service from an anthropological perspective is important to guarantee a sustainable service delivery that inspires guest satisfaction. From a humanistic perspective, service delivery and receiving service have a lot in common with giving gifts and receiving gifts. Although, in a service industry like hospitality, there may not be any physical or tangible goods delivered nevertheless, service is a gift of self to the other. True service has a lot to do with leadership, and so there are some key leadership skills needed by a hospitality professional to be able to deliver quality service i.e., give the best of self. There are models such as RATER that are very useful in measuring the quality of this service.

References

Baker, W. (2020). *Why giving isn't always better than receiving*. Linkedin. https://www.linkedin.com/pulse/why-giving-isnt-always-better-than-receiving-wayne-baker-1

Baltazzi, M. (2019). *Why science says helping others makes us happier*. Thrive globe. Retrieved July 8, 2021, from https://thriveglobal.com/stories/why-science-says-helping-others-makes-us-happier/

Benedict, XVI (2006). Encyclical letter *Deus caritas est* of the Supreme Pontiff Benedict XVI. Ottawa: Canadian Conference of Catholic Bishops. XVI.

Bielskis, A., & Mardosas, E. (2014). Human flourishing in the philosophical work of Alasdair MacIntyre. *International Journal of Philosophy and Theology*, *2*(2), 185–201. http://ijptnet.com/journals/ijpt/Vol_2_No_2_June_2014/12.pdf

Carroll, N., Travers, M., & Richardson, I. (2017, March). Connecting multi-stakeholder analysis across connected health solutions [International Joint Conference on Biomedical Engineering Systems and Technologies]. https://www.researchgate.net/publication/314203429_Connecting_Multistakeholder_Analysis_Across_Connected_Health_Solutions

Crane, G. (Ed.), (1985–2021). *Perseus Digital Library & Tufts University Aristotle, Politics*. https://www.perseus.tufts.edu/hopper/. Accessed October 18, 2021.

Czaplewski, A., Olson, E., & Slater, S. (2002). Case in point applying the RATER model for service success five service attributes can help maintain five-star ratings. *Marketing Management, 11*, 14–17.

Efroymson, D. (n.d.). Women, work, and money: Studying the economic value of women's unpaid work and using the results for advocacy. In *Gender Summary Report*. https://healthbridge.ca/images/uploads/library/Gender_summary_report_final.pdf

Einstein, A. (1954). Ideas and opinions. In C. Seeling (Ed.), *Mein weltbild* (pp. 8–11). Bonanza Books.

Elegido, J. M. (2018). *The nature of human beings*. Pan-Atlantic University Press. ISBN-978-978-967-615-6

Ennew, C. T., & Binks, M. T. (1999). Impact of participative service relationships on quality, satisfaction, and retention: An exploratory study. *Journal of Business Research, 46*(2), 121–132.

Erdly, M., & Kesterson-Townes, L. (2002). *Experience rules, IBM Business Consulting Services' vision for the hospitality and leisure industry.* IBM Business Consulting Services.

Gaitho, P. R. (2017). Leadership qualities and service delivery: A critical review of literature. *Saudi Journal of Business and Management Studies, 2*(6), 643–653. https://doi.org/10.21276/sjbms

Gebbels, M., Pantelidis, I. S., & Goss-Turner, S. (2019). Towards a personology of a hospitality professional. *Hospitality & Society, 9*(2), 215–236.

"Gift". Merriam-Webster Dictionary. Accessed 15 Oct 2021. https://www.merriam-webster.com/dictionary/gift

Gunderson, G. (2020). Serving others is as important as food and sex. *Forbes.* Retrieved October 19, 2021, from https://www.forbes.com/sites/garrettgunderson/2020/09/08/serving-others-is-as-important-as-food-and-sex/?sh=596c94827ede

Harkison, T. (2017). The importance of the human touch in the luxury accommodation sector. *Research in Hospitality Management, 7*(1), 59–64.

Hasa, (2016). *Difference between service and hospitality.* Difference Between.com. Retrieved July 28, 2021, from https://www.differencebetween.com/difference-between-service-and-vs-hospitality/

Hinck, A. (2015). *Introduction to tourism and hospitality* (M. Wescott, Ed.). BCcampus Open Publishing. https://opentextbc.ca/introtourism2e/part/customer-service/

"Hospitality". Oxford English Learner's Dictionary. Accessed 15 Oct 2021 https://www.oxfordlearnersdictionaries.com/definition/english/hospitality?q=hospitality

"Hospitality". Cambridge Dictionary. Accessed 15 Oct 2021. https://dictionary.cambridge.org/dictionary/english/hospitality

Ibraheem, A., & Iwuagwu, C. (2015, March). Service delivery and customer satisfaction in hospitality industry: A study of the Divine Fountain Hotels Limited, Lagos, Nigeria. *Journal of Hospitality, 6*(1), 1–7. https://doi.org/10.5897/JHMT2015.0139

Javed, S. (2020). *What is the RATER model? Customer service quality framework.* emojics. Retrieved July 8, 2021, from https://www.emojics.com/blog/what-is-rater-model/

LaPointe, L. L. (2005). Feral children. *Journal of Medical Speech-Language Pathology, 13*(1), VII–IX.

Lashley, C. (2015). Hospitality and hospitableness. *Research in Hospitality Management, 5*(1), 1–7. https://doi.org/10.1080/22243534.2015.11828322

Leading Effectively Staff. (2020). *The importance of empathy in the workplace.* Centre for Creative Leadership. https://www.ccl.org/articles/leading-effect ively-articles/empathy-in-the-workplace-a-tool-for-effective-leadership/

Lombo, J. A., & Russo, F. (2007). *Philosophical anthropology: An introduction.* Midwest Theological Forum Downers Grove. ISBN 978-1-936045-76-1

Manalu, R. (2020). Humanism in the hospitality industry. *Universitas Gadjah Mada.* https://www.researchgate.net/publication/346030833_HUM ANISM_IN_HOSPITALITY_INDUSTRY

Mulder, P. (2018). *RATER model.* Retrieved September 8, 2021, from tool-shero: https://www.toolshero.com/marketing/ratermodel/

Nunes, G., Thais, R. S. d. O., Teixeira, M., Ribeiro, I., Santos, J., & Torres, Y. (2021). Social isolation and quarantine in the COVID-19 pandemic: Impacts on mental health and quality of population life. *Research, Society and Development, 10.* https://doi.org/10.33448/rsd-v10i2.12535

Saleh, F., & Ryan, C. (1991). Analysing service quality in the hospitality industry using the SERVQUAL model. *Service Industries Journal, 3*(11), 324–345.

Shek, D., Ma, C., Liu, T. T., & Siu, A. M. (2015). The role of self-leadership in service leadership. *International Journal on Disability and Human Development, 14*(4). https://doi.org/10.1515/ijdhd-2015-0455

SOS Children's Villages International. (2017). *The care effect: Why no child should grow up alone.* sos-childrensvillages. Retrieved July 26, 2021, from https://www.sos-childrensvillages.org/

Stone, G. A., Duffy, L. N., Pinckney, H. P., & Templeton-Bradley, R. (2017). Teaching for critical thinking: preparing hospitality and tourism students for careers in the twenty-first century, *Journal of Teaching in Travel & Tourism, 17*(2), 67–84. https://doi.org/10.1080/15313220.2017.1279036

Team ProMiller. (2020). *Hospitality industry—From the view of Abraham Maslow.* ProMiller. https://www.promiller.in/post/hospitality-industry-from-the-view-of-abraham-maslow

Titova, L., & Sheldon, K. M. (2021). Happiness comes from trying to make others feel good, rather than oneself. *The Journal of Positive Psychology.* https://doi.org/10.1080/17439760.2021.1897867

Zendesk. (n.d.). *Making guests feel welcome.* zendesk.com. Retrieved July 8, 2021, from https://www.zendesk.com/service/ticketing-system/hotel-cus tomer-service/

7

Internal Customers: The Asset of the Humanistic Workplace

Adaeze Eloka

A. Eloka (✉)
Pan-Atlantic University, Lagos, Nigeria
e-mail: aeloka@pau.edu.ng

1 Introduction

The hospitality and tourism industry is a human capital intensive industry that cannot function independently of people to achieve their goals (Ahmady et al., 2016; Concern, 200 C.E.). The knowledge one has of any of these hotels or tour operators might be limited to the external architectural structure and to interaction with a particular service. If one obtained a sharper focus as to the inner workings of any of these organizations, one could see that what defines it goes beyond the external architectural structure. Depending on the size of the company, one would witness a beehive of people, activities, projects, etc., all interconnected and aimed towards achieving a goal, which is often external customer satisfaction. These activities make service delivery possible.

External customers take for granted that services will get delivered and they will get value for their money. Nevertheless, the quality of these services depends on the quality of the internal network of people and activities within the organization. This internal network of people are the internal customers who are the employees of the organization (Al-Zoubi & Alomari, 2017). In hospitality and tourism, more emphasis must be placed on the importance of the internal customer for the success of the organization (Kumar & Indu, 2015). Organizational culture sets the tone for internal customer satisfaction. It will significantly influence the internal customer's creativity, innovation, sense of belonging, and participation in organizational undertakings (Mosoma, 2014).

The culture of an organization is the expression of shared beliefs and values within the organization. This is usually manifested in what is known as unwritten rules. Culture is pervasive and is not restricted to any level within an organization but cuts across multiple levels and applies broadly. People who first come into an organization react instinctively to the culture because the ability to sense and respond to culture is universal. What they sense shapes their perception of the organization and their judgement as to whether the beliefs and values are in alignment with their personal beliefs and values. Those who do not find themselves aligned to the culture tend to leave over time (Groysberg et al., 2018).

Leaders in hospitality have an important role to play in the shaping and promoting of their organization's culture. The smaller the organization, the easier it is to shape and maintain a culture. However, this task gets more difficult as the organization grows. Nevertheless, research has shown that there is a strong relationship between organizational culture and customer satisfaction. The values of an organization play out in its organizational culture, so, the more stakeholders share in these culture values, the higher the customer satisfaction. This includes internal customer satisfaction (Groysberg et al., 2018; Ward & Osho, 2006). Culture helps to shape organizational climate which in turn influences productivity and customer satisfaction (Ward & Osho, 2006).

Therefore, management needs to drive a culture that is conducive to the success of the internal customer in accordance with the external environment and consider individual customer satisfaction as a key factor (Ward & Osho, 2006). Each individual within the organization also has a responsibility to accept, assimilate and further diffuse this culture and make it a reality. Examples of cultures that are conducive to success are those that emphasize integration, managing relationships and coordinating group effort, as well as those that prioritize innovation, openness, diversity and a longer-term orientation (Groysberg et al., 2018).

2 Practical Aspects and Dimensions

Organizational structure influences organizational culture (Janicijevic, 2013). The organizational structure of businesses across the hospitality and tourism industry are mostly functional. These structures organize tasks around specific functions which then operate as departments within the organization. For example, the typical organizational structure of a hotel would include five department heads that report directly to the general manager. The departments are administrative and include rooms, food and beverage, accounting, sales and personnel. These departments are subdivided into smaller organizational units that further refine the tasks according to the knowledge and skills of the people in each subunit (O'Fallon & Rutherford, 2010).

Research has shown that organizations that have a structure based on functional departments are unable to establish a strong relationship with their internal customers. Organizations in hospitality and tourism are no exception (Øgaard et al., 2008). On the other hand, organizations whose structure is based on business processes are known to have better internal customer relationships. The business process structure allows for a certain level of communication and cooperation across process departments (Eichorn, 2004). This makes it possible for everyone in the organization to be involved in achieving the aims and goals of the organization, and in the case of hospitality, this would be the total well-being of their guests.

Operating processes, management processes and supporting processes are business process structures that could be adapted in hospitality and tourism organizations. Operating processes could include:

- The process of hotel housekeeping, for example, hygiene of hotel rooms, bed making, laundry and cleaning, hygiene of hotel public areas, safety and security, interior decoration of the hotel, technical maintenance.
- The process of supplying necessary inputs, for example, selecting and certifying suppliers, purchasing food and beverage, receiving food and beverage, storing food and beverage, issuing food and beverage.
- The process of guests' arrivals and departures, for example, ease of making reservations, guest arrivals, occupancy, departure, and post-arrival.
- The process of producing and serving food and beverage, for example, preparation and pre-treatment of food, thermal processing of food, preparation of cold appetizers, cold dishes and salads, preparation of sweet dishes and desserts, serving food and beverage.

Supporting processes could include:

- The process of understanding markets and consumers, for example, determining customer needs and wants, measuring customer satisfaction and monitoring changes in market or customer expectations.

- The process of developing vision and strategy, for example, monitoring the external environment, defining business concept and organizational strategy, designing the organizational structure and relationships between organizational units and developing and setting organizational goals.
- The process of designing hotel products and services, for example, developing new product or service concept and plans, designing, building, and evaluating prototype products and services, preparing for production and managing the product/service development process.
- The process of marketing and selling, for example, marketing product or services to relevant customer segments and processing customer orders.

Management processes could include:

- The process of developing and managing human resources, for example, performance management and development, employee coaching, mentoring, succession planning, organizational development.
- The process of managing Information Technology (IT), for example, determining business requirements for IT systems, managing IT budgets and costs, monitoring safety and compliance, controlling system and network security, implementing new software, hardware, and data systems, providing technical or help desk support.
- The process of managing financial and physical resources, for example, obtaining physical resources such as machine equipment or facilities, facilities planning/management, financial management, budgeting.
- The process of managing reputation, quality and change, for example, monitoring reputation, addressing negative content or customer feedback, monitoring changing beliefs and expectations.

Individuals can then be appointed to own these processes (Krstic et al., 2015). This structure flattens the hierarchy of the organization thereby promoting creativity, innovation, faster decision-making, cross-functional coordination, shared responsibility for overall-performance and more training opportunities. This is because a range of skills is required to ensure the success of each process as opposed to the specific and limiting skills required in the case of functional structures.

As already mentioned, business process structures promote cross-functional coordination. This means that an individual will most probably have to relate with an array of supervisors, peers and subordinates. Each supervisor, peer or subordinate is an internal customer, and their needs, concerns and requests should be taken seriously. Doing this well takes a combination of both skill and experience. Internal customers want to be helped to succeed, no matter their position in the organization (*Guide to Managing Up and Across*, 2013).

Humanistic management places an importance on the good and the dignity of the human person in an organization (Melé, 2016). This dignity should be upheld in relating with supervisors, peers and subordinates. The reason for treating an individual with respect should not necessarily be because one gets something out of it, instead it should be because treating an individual with respect is good in itself and right.

2.1 Relating with Supervisors

In relating with supervisors, it is important to know their goals and objectives. One must be attentive and able to read between the lines in conversations. Most times the expectations the supervisor sets for the supervisee reflects his or her own goals and objectives (*Guide to Managing Up and Across*, 2013). This would be the case, for example, in a situation where one is expected to implement a process of baking bread in-house as opposed to getting from suppliers, to improve the quality of menu items, reduce cost and reduce supply risk. If one reads between the lines, one probably will discover that the driving factor for this decision is the goal to increase competitive strength by developing or improving the business capabilities of the hotel. Knowing this helps one to better understand the expectations that have been set. If one does not know the goals of one's supervisor or one is having difficulty finding out, then one can enlist the help of one's mentor in the hotel who most likely is on the same organizational level as the supervisor (*Guide to Managing Up and Across*, 2013).

Secondly, the pressure a supervisor faces at any moment probably determines his or her attitude towards supervisees. Most likely the supervisor has a supervisor, and he or she must also deliver on expectations. In every organization, there are milestones to be reached, expectations from external stakeholders, etc. These events do not happen in an isolated fashion. Often, the pressure will get to the supervisor before it gets to the supervisee. Knowing what these pressures are and understanding them, helps one to understand his or her demands better. How do you help him or her through this? One could, for example, offer to carry out tasks even before one is asked (*Guide to Managing Up and Across*, 2013).

Human beings have strengths and weaknesses, including supervisors. Knowing what these strengths and weaknesses are strengthens the relationship. Often, it is easy to see the weaknesses as opposed to the strengths. One should recognize that the supervisor has strengths and learn to appreciate them. As for the weaknesses, one can help him or her "overcome" them by filling in, seeing how one can complement the weakness and help him or her turn it into a strength rather than make it more obvious (*Guide to Managing Up and Across*, 2013).

In addition, knowing the preferred work style of a supervisor eases communication. People have different ways of working. For example, some prefer written reports while others want oral reports. Some supervisors like to use data that has been collected and make decisions based on hard facts, others might be more inclined to accept more qualitative or anecdotal evidence. A supervisor who likes to work with facts and data will tend to listen and agree with the supervisee when he or she has facts to back up arguments as opposed to sentiment (*Guide to Managing Up and Across*, 2013).

Finally, if one is going to help one's supervisor succeed, one must be able to perform well on tasks that are assigned, be proactive and, if possible, exceed expectations (*Guide to Managing Up and Across*, 2013).

2.2 Relating with Peers

Relating with peers is an essential part of working in any organization (Kram & Isabella, 1985). To maximize individual and team performance, one needs the help of colleagues across the organization, either to get information, resources or expertise. A person could also find that they must lead a team of colleagues from across the organization to work on a project. This can be a challenge especially when the team lead is not the supervisor. It is important to know how to relate well in these situations.

For instance, in a rapidly expanding hotel chain dedicated to the provision of hotel services, it was no longer easy to communicate with the entire team at the same time and they had begun to lose the culture of belonging that they had as a smaller enterprise. The Group had more than eight hundred employees and seventeen geographically dispersed hotel units with an average growth rate of 24% in four (4) years. To cope with this growth, the Group needed a space where information could be shared rapidly and efficiently with the entire team. They believed this would improve communication and increase the feeling of belonging.

The solution was to build a single intranet site that would be viewed by all the companies in the Group and constitute a gateway to the most important information, enable access to the collaborative spaces of hotels and central services and increase employee productivity by making the solution available anytime, anywhere and on any device. The Group's IT manager was tasked with executing this project and a cross-functional team was created, as input from internal stakeholders across board was necessary.

To successfully execute this project, the IT manager needed to help the new team create a shared vision and realize that vision with individual and mutual accountability. This is referred to as the discipline of teams (*Guide to Managing Up and Across*, 2013). The discipline of teams entails:

1. Shaping and owning a meaningful common purpose based on a corporate mandate (*Guide to Managing Up and Across*, 2013). The corporate mandate in this case was to provide the finest facilities and services in the industry while providing a good place to work for the employees.

7 Internal Customers: The Asset of the Humanistic Workplace

2. Creating specific goals that flow from the common purpose. These goals will motivate the team and give a sense of urgency. When goals are shared, it is easy for everyone to focus on achieving them instead of giving importance to their titles or status (*Guide to Managing Up and Across*, 2013). For example, one specific goal was to reinforce the feeling of belonging of the employees of all the hotel units and of the Group central services.
3. Developing rules of conduct (*Guide to Managing Up and Across*, 2013), for example, punctuality to meetings, collegial decision making as well as data-based decision making, not pointing fingers, substantial contribution by everyone to the project including the team lead.

2.3 Relating with Subordinates

A good relationship with a subordinate is a significant source of motivation to produce good quality work. A subordinate that feels that she has accomplished more because of the motivation she has received from her supervisor finds that her self-esteem increases. A person with a raised self-esteem can reach a state of personal fulfilment which also translates to job satisfaction and better performance (Hampton, 2019).

The relationship with a subordinate is a manifestation of how much the person is worth to the organization. Subordinates feel they are worth something when their superiors invest in their personal development, through training, coaching, encouragement, general acknowledgement, etc. This sense of value allows them to take more responsibility in their work and pride themselves in the fact that they are instrumental to the achievements of the organization (Hampton, 2019).

In a case where a superior has several subordinates, there could be a tendency to unknowingly, perhaps, develop a hierarchy of favourites. Those at the bottom of the hierarchy will perceive this and become demotivated. This demotivation will lead to unhappiness, a feeling of being less valuable thereby evoking discouragement and low job performance. A performance report can help identify subordinates that are not receiving the care and attention they need to be successful. When this

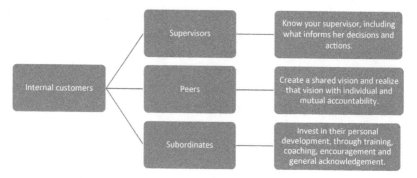

Fig. 1 The internal customer

happens, the superior needs to take steps in the right direction to ensure they provide a platform for the individual's success (Hampton, 2019).

To improve relationships with subordinates, it is important that they are not micromanaged. This gives them an avenue to showcase their creativity and grow as persons. They should be listened to and respected and their opinions should be acknowledged. An environment should also be created where they can communicate openly and honestly without being castigated or disrespected (Fig. 1).

3 Dignity and Power

The mere fact that a person is a human being means he or she possesses dignity. Dignity is part of the essence of being a human being. It is not the same as the dignity that comes with being a professional engineer for example. Professional dignity is manifested in the sense of pride that a person takes in her work and the efforts she makes within her professional framework (Branta et al., 2017). Therefore, a person can feel hurt when her profession or professional work is insulted or taken for granted. Acquiring professional dignity is a process that takes effort and hard work. No one is born with professional dignity. It is earned. Human dignity however is not earned, it is inherent (Melé, 2016).

Internal customers are human beings. Therefore, there should be that awareness that they are free and conscious beings who possess human

7 Internal Customers: The Asset of the Humanistic Workplace 135

dignity and should be treated with respect. This comes to play especially as regards how they are treated by people who possess power in the organization.

It is important to note that there is power and there is the perception of power. The first thing that probably comes to mind is the power exerted by a person in authority. However, power does not necessarily lie only with those in authority. In the organizational space, for example, there are people who possess power but are not necessarily leaders or managers in the organization. These people may not hold any formal positions of authority but are still able to leverage the bases of power that exist.

People who can exert power even when they do not hold formal positions of authority are usually natural leaders. The leader also does not necessarily have to be the boss or the highest authority in the organization. Leaders at all levels in an organization can exert some form of power whether they are supervisors, subordinates or peers. There are seven bases of power that leaders at all levels in an organization can leverage. However, of the seven of them, two are believed to be the most leveraged today. They include the power of relationships and the power of information (Bal et al., 2008).

The power of relationships primarily involves the ability to build and sustain strong networks. With the rise of social media, the importance of a strong network cannot be overemphasized. Leaders who have strong networks have more power of influence. However, having a strong network does not necessarily mean knowing many people. An effective network is one that is diverse, made up of individuals that have interests that are different from yours, colleagues from another unit, even people from outside your organization, probably from your social and family life. An ideal network is considered to comprise not more than twelve to eighteen individuals (*Guide to Managing Up and Across*, 2013). When you have a diverse network, you are exposed to views that expand your horizon. You can make better and wholesome decisions because you are not stuck with people that think like you. In addition, the people whom your decisions affect also feel that they have been treated fairly and that their concerns have been taken into consideration.

The power of information is another commonly leveraged source of power according to research (Bal et al., 2008). A person who possesses information can influence decision making, propose solutions, back up an idea or sell ideas. The information holder before exercising this power should consider how using this information could affect her colleagues or the organization, especially sensitive information. The power of information should as well not be used to promote personal agendas.

4   The Humanistic Workplace as a Venue for Human Flourishing

The humanistic workplace concerns itself with treating human beings as they deserve, with dignity and respect. This implies making business decisions based on real ethical considerations while initiating and maintaining dialogue with all stakeholders as part of its corporate responsibility (Melé, 2016). In business, the humanistic workplace addresses genuine human needs. Human beings are not seen as means to an end, profit, rather they are seen as ends in themselves. The humanistic workplace does not instrumentalize its employees, rather the employees are made to share in the values of the organization in such a way that they choose to be instrumental in achieving the goals of the organization (Kimakowitz et al., 2011).

While acting in this manner, each individual sees the goal and she sees how she fits into the big picture. She understands why she is doing what she does, and she does it because she shares these same values. This way, people will only work in an organization where they feel part and parcel, where they share the values. They will not choose to be instrumental to a goal that is not in alignment with their personal values. In this light, we can see how the humanistic workplace directly impacts the individual. The humanistic workplace is not only of benefit to the employees of the organization but to the society. It benefits the flourishing of the individual, both inside and outside the organization.

Research has shown that doing business from a humanistic point of view is very much possible, regardless of the size of the organization, the geographical location, the diversity of the workforce, etc. (Kimakowitz et al., 2011). However, management is free to choose what path they will take. It is a decision that must be adapted organization-wide, from the top, down and across.

An organization that decides to focus on creating social value instead of focusing on maximizing profits will discover that there will be an increase in stakeholder trust and stakeholder involvement in the promotion of the organization, in addition to being profitable as well. However, it should be noted that being profitable is no longer the priority, that is, it is no longer the end that is sort. This means that if the organization finds itself in a situation where it must consider compromising on social value as opposed to making profit, it will rather make a loss (Kimakowitz et al., 2011).

A humanistic workplace actively creates opportunities for personal development and individual flourishing. This is easier in decentralized organizations where employees are allowed to make decisions and assume responsibility for whatever decision they make. This makes them feel trusted, empowered and motivated to deliver good quality work. When the organization gives employees a certain form of independence to make important decisions, they should also leave room for mistakes that could occur because of the decision made. People should be helped to learn from their mistakes so they can make better and more informed decisions that will benefit the organization in future. On the other hand, if the employees are unnecessarily punished for bad decision making, then they may be afraid to make any decisions in future (Bansal et al., 2001). This will counteract the aim of having tried to create an avenue for the development of the person.

The hospitality and tourism industry relies a lot on human capital (International Labour Organisation, 2010), and as a result, should be as humanistic as possible. The needs of every individual should be considered, and people should not be made to feel like machines. An organization that does not take care of its stakeholders will find it more difficult to get everyone to share in its vision and mission, to own it and to promote it. A focus on profit maximization might seem more logical and beneficial in the short term but hardly sustainable in the long term.

5 The Importance of the Internal Customer for the External Customer

Discussions about customer satisfaction should not have a one-dimensional focus, be it internal customers or external customers. It is rather intuitive that one aspect is necessarily related to the other. However, these two aspects, considered to contribute to the success of any organization are not always considered in relation to one another (Gremler et al., 1995).

One relationship between these two aspects is that the satisfaction the internal customer experiences significantly determines the quality of service the external customer receives (Farias, 2010). An unhappy and demotivated internal customer will not be willing or able to provide superior external customer service. Company culture, as we have seen, contributes to the satisfaction of the internal customer. In addition, human resource policies in hospitality and tourism should be aligned to make possible individual personal development and flourishing. These policies should promote:

1. **Job security**
   If employees are assured that they will not be laid off even during tough economic periods, their trust in the organization increases as well as their willingness to commit themselves (Bansal et al., 2001).
2. **Extensive training**
   Trainings orient the internal customer in the direction that the organization wants to go, in its values and its culture. This way it is easier for the internal customer to buy into the global vision of the organization as well as see how they fit into that vision as regards personal and career development.

   It is not advisable to cut back on training when the organization is less profitable. On one hand, this reduces the trust that the internal customer has in the organization because they see first-hand that being profitable is a higher priority. On the other hand, it is during times of less economic activity that employees need to be encouraged to improve their skills and help pull the company out of its difficult situation (Bansal et al., 2001).

7 Internal Customers: The Asset of the Humanistic Workplace 139

3. **Rewards contingent on performance**
   We could also consider a situation where an organization gives generous rewards that are partly contingent on performance. One way of increasing stakeholder trust is by providing a higher-than-industry-average salary because this communicates the value an organization places on its employees. Other rewards could include those that allow the internal customer share in financial gains, or perhaps those that reward internal customers for exceptional customer service. This way excellent customer service behaviour is encouraged (Bansal et al., 2001).

4. **Information sharing**
   Sharing information about an organization's financial status, strategy, projects, accomplishments, etc. is another way of increasing stakeholder trust. This helps the internal customer see how her work contributes to the success of the organization. It is also proof that the organization plays fair and reduces the risk of an unfair advantage of some employees over others (Bansal et al., 2001).

   Also, when internal customers are empowered and are independent enough to make decisions, they feel like they have a stake in the business and can make smart decisions without needing to consult many levels of management. This also reduces the time it takes to solve any problems that may arise.

5. **Reducing status distinctions**
   This helps to reduce the feeling of being worth more, or less in an organization. If some internal customers feel they are worth less than their colleagues, this can affect their trust in the organization and consequently their performance. These status distinctions are usually visible in large discrepancies in salary across levels, better working conditions or better facilities for some and not for others. There should always be an effort to drastically reduce any distinctions by having as much as possible the same conditions for everyone (Bansal et al., 2001).

Adopting human resource policies such as these increases job satisfaction, loyalty to the organization and trust in management which positively impacts the way an internal customer relates with an external customer.

This will lead to improved external service quality, a higher level of external customer satisfaction and consequently external customer loyalty.

6 Implications for Leadership in Hospitality and Tourism

Leaders in organizations are key drivers of organizational culture. The hospitality and tourism industry are no exception. A strong organizational culture influences the satisfaction and loyalty of the internal customer. This translates consequently to a commitment to achieving the goals of the organization. Research has shown that internal customers in hospitality and tourism prefer organizations that have an innovative, open and diverse culture (Razali et al., 2018). Good relationship management and the ability to coordinate group effort are also important. Therefore, in driving an organizational culture, leaders must act with clear authority and responsibility together with openness and an attitude that is oriented towards the internal customer as opposed to being management egocentric.

On the average, the internal customer in hospitality and tourism is faced with low wages, low job security, long working hours which effectively disrupt work–life balance, lead to stress and exposure to risk (Concern, 200 C.E.). These conditions can never contribute to the development or human flourishing of the individual. The internal customer can only be satisfied and committed to the organization when she perceives that she is valued by the organization. This will ultimately reflect in the quality of external service delivery. To achieve internal customer satisfaction, leaders in hospitality and tourism must be more committed to individual well-being and development.

In line with humanistic management, the primary goal of leaders in the hospitality and tourism industry should not be on revenue generation. This will happen eventually if the internal customer is satisfied. The happy internal customer will be committed to the organization which will increase profit consequently.

Finally, internal customers should be treated as partners of the organization. This leads to the creation of a shared purpose and a common goal that everyone works towards. Leaders should recognize that the internal customer is impacted by the outcome of her work and the perceived value that is placed on it whether good or bad. Leaders need to also believe that internal customers have insights that are critical to the success of the organization. These insights should be incorporated into the organization's framework or institutionalized. Such recognition fosters a sense of ownership, nurtures innovation and encourages collaboration across the organization.

7 Conclusion

Internal customers make up the fibre of every organization in the hospitality and tourism industry and their trust, loyalty and commitment must be gained across all levels to achieve superior external service quality. To keep these stakeholders satisfied, they need to be helped to succeed, regardless of whether they are supervisors, peers or subordinates. Their dignity should be recognized, not as something that is earned, but as something that is inherent. This is reflected in decisions that are made by those in authority because these decisions will consider their concerns and well-being. If the personal and career development of the internal customer is met, then the organization can be assured of superior internal and external service delivery.

Action Prompts
Create a healthy organizational culture in the following ways:
Focus on the well-being and development of each individual in the organization.
Prioritize individual flourishing as opposed to revenue generation.
Treat internal customers as partners.

Study Questions

1. The satisfaction of the internal customer is key to the success of organizations in hospitality and tourism. True or false? Explain.
2. The humanistic workplace is a venue for human flourishing. True or false? Explain.
3. Good relationship management contributes to the satisfaction of the internal customer. How does this play out in the relationship with colleagues across all levels of an organization?

Chapter Summary

The hospitality and tourism industry are human capital intensive and as such highly dependent on internal customers. These customers are the employees of the organization. The organization's culture influences the way they interact with one another and how they evaluate the alignment of their beliefs and values with those of the organization. This significantly influences their satisfaction level and consequently, their productivity.

Internal customer relationships in hospitality and tourism can be improved by adopting an internal structure based on business processes as opposed to functional departments. These business processes will involve a certain level of communication and cooperation across units within the organization, such that everyone is implicated in the satisfaction of the external customer.

Practical dimensions resulting from this approach involves a holistic consideration of internal customer relations, including dignity, power handling and human flourishing. In relating with supervisors, it is important to know their goals and objectives, as this helps to understand their attitude at given moments.

Relating with peers implies relating with a wider range of people. However, when there's a specific need to work across units, for example, it is important to create a shared vision that is realized with individual and mutual accountability. Subordinates should be given an avenue to showcase their creativity and develop as persons.

> In conclusion, the human dignity of the internal customer should always be respected, and their genuine human needs addressed. The satisfied internal customer is loyal and committed to the organization and this leads to higher levels of external customer satisfaction.

References

Ahmady, G., Mehrpour, M., & Nikooravesh, A. (2016). Organizational structure. *Procedia—Social and Behavioral Sciences, 230*. https://doi.org/10.1016/j.sbspro.2016.09.057

Al-Zoubi, A. F., & Alomari, M. (2017). The role of internal customer in improving the quality of hotel services in Jordan: A case study of the Marriott International Hotel in Amman. *International Journal of Marketing Studies, 9*(6), 82. https://doi.org/10.5539/ijms.v9n6p82

Bal, V., Campbell, M., Steed, J., & Meddings, K. (2008). *The role of power in effective leadership.*

Bansal, H., Mendelson, M., & Sharma, B. (2001). The impact of internal marketing activities on external marketing outcomes. *Journal of Quality Management.* https://doi.org/10.1016/S1084-8568(01)00029-3

Branta, H., Jacobson, T., & Alvinius, A. (2017). Professional pride and dignity? A classic grounded theory study among social workers. In *Quality of life and quality of working life.* IntechOpen. https://doi.org/10.5772/68018

Concern, T. (200 C.E.). *The impacts of all-inclusive hotels on working conditions and labour rights in Barbados, Kenya & Tenerife: A human right, a global responsibility.* Tourism Concern, Action for Ethical Tourism.

Eichorn, F. (2004). Internal customer relationship management (IntCRM): A framework for achieving customer relationship management from the inside out. *Problems and Perspectives in Management, 2*, 154–177.

Farias, S. (2010). Internal marketing (IM): A literature review and research propositions for service excellence. *Brazilian Business Review, 7*, 99–115. https://doi.org/10.15728/bbr.2010.7.2.6

Gremler, D., Bitner, M., & Evans, K. (1995). The internal service encounter. *Logistics Information Management, 8*, 28–34. https://doi.org/10.1108/09576059510815691

144   A. Eloka

Groysberg, B., Lee, J., Price, J., & Cheng, J. (2018, January 1). The leader's guide to corporate culture. *Harvard Business Review*. https://hbr.org/2018/01/the-leaders-guide-to-corporate-culture

Guide to managing up and across. (2013). Harvard Business Review Press.

Hampton, C. (2019). *Supervisor-subordinate relationships and its effect on job satisfaction and job performance*. Chancellor's Honors Program Projects. https://trace.tennessee.edu/utk_chanhonoproj/2283

International Labour Organisation (Ed.). (2010). *Developments and challenges in the hospitality and tourism sector*. ILO.

Janicijevic, N. (2013). The mutual impact of organizational culture and structure. *Economic Annals, 58*, 35–60. https://doi.org/10.2298/EKA139 8035J

Kimakowitz, E., Pirson, M., Spitzeck, H., Dierksmeier, C., & Amann, W. (2011). *Humanistic management in practice*. http://www.alexandria.unisg.ch/Publikationen/71204

Kram, K. E., & Isabella, L. A. (1985). Mentoring alternatives: The role of peer relationships in career development. *The Academy of Management Journal, 28*(1), 110–132. https://doi.org/10.2307/256064

Krstic, B., Kahrovic, E., & Stanisic, T. (2015). Business process management in hotel industry: A proposed framework for operating processes. *Ekonomika, 61*, 21–34. https://doi.org/10.5937/ekonomika1504021K

Kumar, V., & Indu, B. (2015). Internal marketing: A tool for success of hotel industry. *Advances in Management, 2278–4551*, 8.

Melé, D. (2016). Understanding humanistic management. *Humanistic Management Journal, 1*(1), 33–55. https://doi.org/10.1007/s41463-016-0011-5

*International Journal of Business and Management Review, 2*https://www.eajournals.org/

O'Fallon, M. J., & Rutherford, D. G. (2010). *Hotel management and operations*. Wiley.

Øgaard, T., Marnburg, E., & Larsen, S. (2008). Perceptions of organizational structure in the hospitality industry: Consequences for commitment, job satisfaction and perceived performance. *Tourism Management, 29*, 661–671. https://doi.org/10.1016/j.tourman.2007.07.006

Razali, N. S. M., Zahari, M. S. M., Ismail, T. A. T., & Jasim, A. R. (2018). Relationship between organizational culture and job loyalty among five-star and four-star hotel employees. *International Journal of Academic Research in Business and Social Sciences, 8*(15), 14–32. https://doi.org/10.6007/IJARBSS/v8-i15/5090

Ward, S., & Osho, G. (2006). Organizational culture and customer satisfaction: A public and business administration perspective. *Business Research Yearbook, 13,* 518–523.

8

Training for Effectiveness: Case Studies of Two Hospitality Schools in Nigeria

Moyinoluwa Okunloye and Amaka Okpalla

M. Okunloye (✉)
Lagos Business School, Pan-Atlantic University, Lagos, Nigeria
e-mail: mokunloye@lbs.edu.ng

A. Okpalla
Lantana College of Hospitality, Enugu, Nigeria

© The Author(s), under exclusive license to Springer Nature Switzerland AG 2022
K. Ogunyemi et al. (eds.), *Humanistic Perspectives in Hospitality and Tourism, Volume II*, Humanism in Business Series,
https://doi.org/10.1007/978-3-030-95585-4_8

1 Introduction

Hospitality is one term in academic literature that has proven difficult to define as every attempt by past scholars left gaps for other scholars to criticise. One definition of hospitality that stands out is that of Brotherton (1999, p. 142); they say that hospitality is "a contemporaneous human exchange, which is voluntarily entered into, and designed to enhance the mutual well—being of the parties concerned through the provision of accommodation, and/or food, and/or drink". However, this definition has been criticised for only highlighting the few things that hospitality is about—accommodation, food and drink—all of which are carried out through service delivery (Telfer, 2012). Hospitality is a lot more than this attempt at capturing it. This is the reason Lashley and Morrison (2000) came up with three domains—the social, the private and the commercial environments—to grasp the broad categories in hospitality. These domains have in turn been criticised by several scholars with one of them, Slattery (1983), challenging the domains as excluding the main aspects of the industry to the extent that it reduces its initial intent for relationship. The essence of hospitality which is to establish cordial interaction and satisfaction between the guests and the hosts is said to have been reduced to a commercial notion whereby it becomes like a generic business focusing on the satisfaction of a customer/buyer by a seller. Slattery, seemingly taking a cue from the three domains that he had earlier criticised then categorises the models of hospitality under four headings: Freestanding Hospitality Businesses; Hospitality in Leisure Venues; Hospitality in Travel Venues; and Subsidised Hospitality which further divided the commercial environment domain from Lashley and Morrison (2000)'s suggestions. These two criticisms focus on the environment; while one expatiates on the commercial aspects, the other investigates the social, private, and commercial aspects of hospitality (Hemmington, 2014).

Despite the many controversies and arguments surrounding the definitions of hospitality, there appears to be agreement on skills and attributes required of a hospitality professional. Hospitality professionals are expected to be courteous and selfless individuals who prioritise creating amazing experiences for their guests at all times (Hemmington, 2007). That means that they would be people who go out of their way to ensure that their guests are excited, entertained and relaxed throughout their stay in that environment (Ariffin & Maghzi, 2012; Brunner-Sperdin et al., 2012; Hemmington, 2007). One other very important characteristic of good hospitality professionals is that they are respectful. They ensure that their guests are treated with utmost regard as well as that they are safe and protected in such a way that they leave the environment having experiences that are memorable and personal and that have improved their quality of life (King, 1995; Lashley, 2008). This implies that hospitality professionals are friendly people who endeavour to treat guests like friends and family members (Skandrani & Kamoun, 2014).

The implication is that what makes hospitality professionals effective are the attributes that they demonstrate to make guests feel comfortable and have great memories. These attributes include what professionals maintain due to their personal values (Rokeach, 1973; Tomasella & Ali, 2019) as well as what they have gotten from trainings and developments over time (Baum, 2002; Marneros et al., 2020). Many of their personal values are rooted in what had been taught to them by their families. However, they can also acquire some of these attributes through training programmes, so that they can carry out their duties and responsibilities effectively. This chapter examines the place of personal values and training in the effectiveness of hospitality professionals. The chapter attempts to understand the place of both personal values and formal training in how effective or not a hospitality professional will be at the job. While doing this, the chapter will also investigate the specific training and skills that are helpful and most needed by the professionals as well as make recommendations for how government and policy makers can pay more attention to the industry. A themed review of literature will follow this introduction, ending with some propositions, and after that will come case study data examining the propositions. These will then be discussed before a concluding segment ends the chapter.

2 Personal Values in Hospitality

Discussions on the hospitality profession have identified its pillars to be the culture and values of individuals in the profession, which are pivotal to the success or failure of the enterprise (Tomasella & Ali, 2019). When examining individuals' personal values and what they consider to be the right culture, especially as regards how they treat others around them, the family is the first point of contact from where these are developed. It is in families that we find the first point of learning right or wrong actions, developing a sense of community, and defining of what is acceptable behaviour; these become the foundation upon which other educational events build on.

Hospitality is in itself a virtue—it is a universal virtue that is reflected across different cultures all over the world. In some cultures, anyone who fails to extend an hospitable gesture to a guest is viewed as wicked or even inhumane because hospitality is seen as the minimum courtesy that is expected from one person to another regardless of place (O'Gorman, 2005, p. 144). In Africa, hospitality is engrained in the widely recognised Ubuntu concept. It is reflected in the sense of community—in seeing others as extensions of self, irrespective of their race or gender (Kiige et al., 2019). It is an essential value for Africans where hospitality is expressed voluntarily without expecting anything in return (Jacques, 1999; Gathogo, 2006; Ezenweke & Nwadialor, 2013). Hospitality to an African is demonstrated in the willingness to drop everything else to attend to a guest's need for warmth, companionship, food, accommodation and friendship (Healey, 1996). These are all core aspects that are ingrained in the sense of community and values, for Africans (Gathogo, 2006, 2008, 2013; Mbiti, 2015).

In early years, hospitality was practised beyond offering accommodation, food and drinks to strangers. It entailed showing compassion to all and translated into a "duty to protect, receive, accommodate, and feed each other, as well as receiving others, especially the disadvantaged without seeking compensation" (Höckert, 2015; Kiige et al., 2019, p. 211). The duty to be hospitable to travellers and foreigners became a lifestyle to people in modern England such that they would use whatever they had to ensure that guests were well accommodated (Heal, 1990). Beyond culture, hospitality is also developed as a personal value from religious injunctions. In fact, there have been arguments that claimed that the understanding of virtue that leads to human flourishing is based on a mixture of traditional and spiritual practices of patience, beneficence, prudence, hope, courage and other ethical virtues (Moore, 2009; Wijesinghe, 2014). It is seen as the highest of human virtue and a language that every race, age, gender, economic status and culture understands and practices (Arterbury, 2005; Bolchazy, 1977; Firebaugh, 1923; Heal, 1990; Leed, 1991; Newman, 2007).

For some, the argument on the practice of hospitality as a function of personal values stem from the understanding that it is a part of everyone's nature. They believe that everyone has a level of innate feeling to be hospitable to others around them, which can then be developed to become more pronounced or dominant as human beings continue to relate with one another (O'Connor, 2005). Following on this belief that hospitality is in one way or another a part of what individuals have inherent in them, organisational values in coworkers can consider this a foundation to set the tone for mutual understanding and collective efforts within the group. For this to be consistently done, hospitality has to be taught, to ensure equal exposure to what is required (Lashley, 2008; Lashley & Morrison, 2000).

3 Hospitality by Training

Despite, or perhaps because of, how essential personal values and traditions are in the hospitality industry, many academic and other studies have classified it as a low skill profile industry (Wood, 1997). It was believed that workers in the hospitality industry needed not be educated, trained or skilled, that they only needed to know how to smile and be courteous (Shaw & Williams, 1994) which needed not be taught in any formal setting. Based on these assumptions, many organisations may have made the mistake of hiring unskilled and untrained workers without paying much attention to how much excellence would accrue to the organisation from training them appropriately. Burns (1997) argued that comments about hospitality being a low skilled job are from the western communities where there is already a representation of commercial hospitality traits in their domestic practice of hospitality, where their language of communication is to some extent universal and so might not require such individuals to acquire additional technical training to perform effectively in a hospitality business. However, this might not work in an environment like Puerto Rico, Africa and other areas where there are diverse languages and cultures that would need to be harmonised. Such environments would require some level of technical, emotional and capability training to ensure effectiveness and overall success of the business, and therefore hospitality to them cannot be considered as a low skilled profession (Baum, 2002).

In any case, hospitality business, nowadays, is all about the competence of and the quality of service provided by employees. Quality of service in a hotel or restaurant is easily linked to the quality of the employees; therefore, employers are placing more priority on training in knowledge and skills so as to assure the business's survival and growth (Ahammad, 2013).

4 Training Readiness of Hospitality Professionals

Researchers testing for the training readiness of hospital professionals agreed on the importance of both employability skills as well as technical skills. Employability skills include effective communication skills, leadership skills, critical thinking skills, problem solving, creative and flexible thinking, self-management, teamwork and so on (Lowden et al., 2011; Ogbeide, 2006). These are considered as necessary skills that hospitality professionals ought to master to carry out their jobs effectively. This conclusion came from research findings regarding the effectiveness of curriculum skills on hospitality professionals in several institutions; Conradie (2012) investigates from the viewpoints of the participants and he found that specific courses in hospitality coupled with practical application in the course of learning contributes immensely to their readiness for the hospitality profession. He also found that students with innate personal values and an instinct for the profession do better during training than those who do not have such instinct (Kurniawati, 2015). While he observed from the lens of the participants, Lowden et al. (2011) and Rahman (2010) in contrast adopted the viewpoint of the employers that effective use of technology, ethical judgement and decision making, effective use of language, risk taking, effective communication skills and so on are what employers look for when scouting for hospitality professionals.

For a wholesome approach to training of future hospitality professional, it would be advisable to combine training in technical skills accompanied with practical application of these skills during training, a focus on communication skills, the use of language, teamwork and other things noted in earlier research as well as the development of their innate personal values. This means that the combination of what the participants look forward to when training for the hospitality profession and what the employers expect to find in that category of professionals should be combined in the training curriculum for a balanced training of hospitality professional. This would also mean that the participants' readiness and the market needs is matched during training thereby creating well-rounded professionals.

5 Importance of Training for Hospitality Professionals

Training for hospitality professionals inspires and motivates them to bring in their best to the job. Human Resources Management (HRM) practices and policies in most organisations put training as one of the important instruments in their development strategy (Warhurst & Nickson, 2007). It helps to increase productivity as well as assist HR in tracking progress and improvement in staff capabilities so that they can be shortlisted for promotion as and when due. Hospitality training coupled with the domestic values of hospitality helps staff to be confident in their ability and that goes on to reflect in both the quality and quantity of the output they produce. Training in the hospitality business also enables staff to work effectively with little or no supervision

(Roque & Ramos, 2019). Staff who have adequate training are also good managers of resources, materials used in service and time while limiting the frequency of accidents when working.

Based on the preceding literature review, three propositions stand out:

a. Hospitality professionals require some personal attributes and values to be effective.
b. Hospitality professionals require formal training to perform effectively.
c. Personal attributes and formal training are complementary elements of training programmes to ensure readiness for the profession.

6 Case Study

6.1 The Method

For this research, the case study method was used to get an in-depth understanding of the effectiveness of training for hospitality professionals in Nigeria. The focus on specific schools is to give a clear picture of practices, training methods, motivation for what they do and the success rate recorded in terms of how the students have thrived in their post-training careers. This method is suitable because it gives a practical meaning to what previous research had theorised in the past. It helps to see the extent to which those theories have worked in implementation and it opens up new areas not referenced in previous research. The use of interviews to back up the archival data gathered from the two schools brought in the perspectives of the students so that conclusions are not only based on the data from the case study but also from the experiences of the students.

6.2 Summarised Case Study Findings

Lantana College of Hospitality (LCH) is a project of Women's Board—Educational Cooperation Society (E.C.S.), a not for profit, non-governmental organisation registered in Nigeria for the education and development of women and the girl child. The school is one of their projects spread across the country. The school has come a long way since it first started as Lantana School of Catering in 1996. The name was later rebranded to include the word "hospitality" because it better encompassed the content of the curriculum, which they also strengthened to measure up to world class standards.

The mission of LCH is to give a total education to all women and young girls who come to the School, at the same time as giving them hospitality skills which will enable them to make an impact in their homes, their profession and in the society at large. While open to people from all faiths or of no faith, the School attends to the professional, cultural, human, and spiritual formation of the individual based on its deep root in the Catholic tradition. Skills training and personality development are two essential aspects that LCH believes help in raising the standards and for improving the quality of the service industry. Hence, their commitment to the development of the hospitality industry's most valuable resource—people.

In other words, LCH is committed to skill acquisition as well as to the education of the whole person. Through this, they are in turn doing good to families, professions and the society at large supporting a popular belief that an educated woman[1] educates the Nation. Skill acquisition is vital for an economy to compete favourably and to grow, particularly in an era of economics integration and technological change. Skills gaps are an acute issue in Nigeria, and it is one of the reasons for the growth of unemployment in the country.

St. Josemaría Escrivá, following whose inspiration many hospitality schools have been set up all over the world, defined hospitality services as the backbone of the family and society. It takes care of the essential needs of man—clothing, food, and shelter (Evans, 2012). In Lantana, they impart the professional skills needed to take care of these basic needs of man and thus help women acquire a professional approach in running their homes as well as function effectively in their businesses.

---

[1] While Lantana focuses on women and girls since that is the development goal of their NGO promoter, one must keep in view that men and boys in the hospitality and tourism industry should also have access to excellent training.

LCH understands that hospitality career is very demanding; it is not for those seeking a "9 to 5", Monday to Friday work pattern. It is an environment that this pattern does not suit, because it is an essential service that spans 24 hours, 365 days. It caters to the needs of the human person, that unique and unrepeatable creature so the profession can only become extinct when man becomes extinct. It is little wonder that there is a skill shortage when people are no longer ready to be their brother's keeper, and everyone is preoccupied with seeking a reward for every good act towards others. Yet, everyone has also been a beneficiary of some form of hospitality in the past and it is only natural or even to be expected that such acts of kindness be passed to other people around. The attitude of employers is at times discouraging but hospitality is a duty to mankind that should be promoted regardless of the economy or societal decadence.

In Lantana, the development of professional expertise is combined with an emphasis on efficient working habits, best practices and cost-saving methods, personal grooming, responsibility, management skills, and courtesy. Students learn how to handle a wide range of equipments and to work to deadlines. Graduates from Lantana are equipped for life through the combination of technical skills acquisition and fostering of social and human skills. Habits of industriousness and ingenuity are also developed by participants in the regular courses, short courses, holiday courses or the weekly Home Economics Club programmes for secondary school girls. LCH places high priority on educating the total woman in values such as regard for the human person as an individual, attention to his/her needs, service, exceeding oneself and others' expectations by giving more than what is required to ensure that a neighbour, a customer, is satisfied, and bringing a smile to one's workplace and surroundings.

The School admits a handful of full-time students annually (27 at the time of this study) because they believe in paying attention to the quality of education that they can impart to small groups. They endeavour to teach each student as though she was the only one in the school so as to impart as much knowledge as the student is capable of absorbing. This is what they call "personalised education".

LCH also believes that just like the growth of other industries is essential for economic and social sustainability in different aspects of the world, the hospitality industry also needs to be promoted, especially among youths, and they try to do this at Lantana. LCH has been instrumental to making many graduates of the school breadwinners in their homes, make them more effective at their place of work and even provide the knowledge that they need to establish their own hospitality businesses. The training they provide aligns with three (3) of the United Nations' sustainable Millennium Development Goals namely:

Goal 1: End poverty in all its forms everywhere.
Goal 2: End hunger, achieve food security and improved nutrition, and promote sustainable agriculture.
Goal 3: Promote sustained, inclusive, and sustainable economic growth, full and productive employment, and decent work for all.

Attesting to the practices and discipline of LCH, some of the students agreed that the School has helped them physically, socially and spiritually. One respondent attested that the School boosted her prowess in "etiquette and customer service", as well as her ability to "aspire" to greater feats. Another respondent, formerly a student of but now employed at the School, raved about the investment of the management into spotting talent and ensuring that they are not only well-prepared for wherever they choose to be in the hospitality industry, but also helping them scout for suitable places where they can be gainfully employed and appropriately remunerated.

The second hospitality school studied is also in Lagos. "W" School of Hospitality (WSH) derives its motivation for the training they provide their students from a recognition of the need for human capital development in Africa. They believe that just as machines are serviced and upgraded for them to function optimally, humans also need constant training, which they have tagged "Continuous Professional Development". They have observed that the ratio of hospitality outfits in Nigeria and employees is disproportionate compared to the numbers of training academies for hospitality professionals, hence there are constant complaints about low skilled personnel in the profession. Some international hotels and restaurants have attempted to curb this by arranging on-the-job training for their staff so as to ensure that their poise and performance match the standards and the brand of the business. However, this is not enough.

Training academies are needed to provide training that focuses on cognitive, people, behavioural and technical skills for professionals in the hospitality business. One other unique benefit that hospitality training provides is certification which, in the long run, helps professionals who have effectively gone through certain trainings to enjoy career growth and earn promotions. Many times, professionals who were trained on the job without getting formal certifications have been stuck in the same positions for years for the lack of recognised qualifications. This makes many of them discouraged, complacent, and irritable which can then affect effectiveness in their service delivery.

School "W" has been in existence for over 20 years, providing training of high quality to diverse participants ranging from young school leavers to adults interested in the hospitality profession. They have graduated an estimated 100 students every year since inception, with 50% going on to establish their own businesses. 30% of the students have gone into paid employment and thrive successfully in the industry while 20% of them have been retained in companies immediately after their internship. Their goal has been to train students who are employable and successful wherever they find themselves outside of the School and they have successfully done that, going by their record over the years. They focus their training on technical skills, virtue ethics, entrepreneurial skills, and people skills. Since the business of hospitality evolves and changes with new trends, they ensure they keep their faculty, their facility and equipment, and their training materials up-to-date so that their students are well groomed for the season and climate.

7 An Interesting Discussion

Several themes stood out from analysing the findings from the case studies.

7.1 Technical Skills Are Important and Complement Personal Attributes

From the two schools that were studied, the importance of training for hospitality professionals was evident. They both agreed on the need for training to sharpen the raw talents that students might already have prior to entering the programmes. They agreed on the need for technical skills, customer service skills, etiquette and other necessary skills to ensure that the students are trained to be better than their contemporaries locally as well as to compete internationally. This aligned with what previous research had documented regarding technical skills and, specifically, etiquette training especially as it relates to cultural differences, that these are needed if hospitality professionals are to thrive successfully in the global space (Baum, 2002; Burns, 1997).

7.2 Certifications from Formal Training Are Important

One unique aspect that also presented itself in the schools that were studied, as a reason why trainings are important, is what the certifications help the students to achieve in the long run after graduation. The reports and observations from the schools show that certifications from professional training help the students to successfully climb the hierarchical ladder in any hospitality outfit they find themselves in. Getting the training assures them of not getting sidelined or denied when their promotions are due, because they have the qualifications for it.

And based on the experiences they shared, the school has imparted them in fine-tuning their skills as well as opening up their minds to possibilities for them in the hospitality industry.

7.3 The Need for Government/Policy Makers to Step in

The case study also exposes the loopholes in human capital development in the hospitality industry in Nigeria. Seen as the industry contributes majorly to the reduction of unemployment, its human capital should also be invested in for sustainability and effectiveness. This is the reason the directors of the schools are calling for intervention in the industry for a quantum growth that eventually benefits all.

8 Practical Implications for Policy Makers

From findings in research and as evident in the practice at the schools that were studied, government and policy makers especially in Nigeria need to pay more attention to the hospitality industry and the impact that it is making at reducing the unemployment rate of youths. A well-trained hospitality professional would go on to be an efficient employee who in turn provides for his/her families thereby reducing unemployment as well as poverty or would go on to start a business and become an employer of labour. If the government/policy makers paid more attention to the industry by assisting with infrastructure, scholarships for some students, or provision of suitable work environments for trained hospitality professionals, then it would go a long way to make the industry thrive better in the country.

9 Conclusion

From studying the way the two hospitality training schools equip their students with the knowledge and skills to function successfully in the hospitality industry, it is clear that formal training is essential for success in the industry. This buttresses the submission of Burns (1997) that where there is a need for technical skills to function effectively, the industry cannot be categorised as "low skilled". The case studies also further show that while family background and personal values form an important context for preparation to function in the business of hospitality, it is formal training that empowers the professionals and keeps them in practice. In fact, it is the formal training that qualifies the individuals as a professional in the eyes of those assessing them; otherwise; they are just regarded as unskilled helps. Formal training is also essential for understanding how the industry works, the technicalities involved, and how to get ahead in the profession.

The study also reveals that the trainings are effective in that they provide the students the necessary certifications for them to attain hierarchical roles within the hospitality industry. It means that as much as personal values are important and the certification that formal training offers is essential for growth within the industry.

This study aimed at understanding the effectiveness of personal values and formal training in the hospitality profession in Nigeria. However, the case study highlighted the importance of training more for women more than it did for men. Also, using two hospitality schools as a case study for inferences on the effectiveness of training in the hospitality profession in Nigeria may not entirely reflect the position of all hospitality schools in the country. Future studies in the same area can expand the focus beyond two schools to different schools in other geo-political regions.

Action Prompts

Encourage friends and acquaintances who aspire to make a career out of hospitality to get the necessary skills.

Lobby government and policymakers to pay more attention to the hospitality industry, considering the vital role that it plays in reducing unemployment.

Suggest the possibility of establishing a hospitality training school or investing in training schools to an entrepreneur.

Study Questions

1. In what ways are hospitality skills necessary today?

2. In which areas in the field of hospitality do you think government policies are needed?
3. How is hospitality in itself a virtue?

Chapter Summary

The hospitality profession is an essential service that caters to the physical, emotional and psychological wellbeing of people. It is a profession in which the hosts have to be prepared to satisfy the needs of guests such that they are comfortable in the environment provided to them. Research shows that hospitality started in the family—it is a tradition that stems from the virtue of community which is interpreted in different cultures across the globe. It is demonstrated in diverse ways that include providing guests and strangers with food, drink, accommodation, and entertainment, taking the form of a virtue whose language is understood by all from different nooks of the world.

In hospitality profession, training is important. While it is essential that individuals striving to succeed in the profession need to have personal values of hospitality, it is also critical that they have some form of formal training that equips them with regard to the technicalities of the profession. There have been several arguments on this position so, in order to get a clearer understanding of the need for former training, this chapter used the case study method to examine two schools of hospitality and their experience in equipping young women with the essential knowledge and skills needed to be employable into the hospitality industry, thereby improving their financial status as well as contributing positively to their families and communities.

References

Ahammad, S. (2013). *Importance of training in hotel industry: Case study of Hilton Hotel, Cyprus. S dert rn. University* [Doctoral dissertation, Master's Thesis].

International Journal of Hospitality Management, 31(1), 191–198.

Arterbury, A. E. (2005). *Entertaining angels: Early Christian hospitality in its Mediterranean setting.*

Baum, T. (2002). Skills and training for the hospitality sector: A review of issues. *Journal of Vocational Education and Training, 54*(3), 343–364.

Brotherton, B. (1999). Towards a definitive view of the nature of hospitality and hospitality management. *International Journal of Contemporary Hospitality Management, 11*(4), 165–173.

Bolchazy, L. J. (1977). *Hospitality in early Rome: Livy's concept of its humanizing force.* Ares Pub.

International Journal of Hospitality Management, 31(1), 23–30.

Burns, P. M. (1997). Hard-skills, soft-skills: Undervaluing hospitality's 'service with a smile.' *Progress in Tourism and Hospitality Research, 3*(3), 239–248.

Conradie, R. (2012). *Student evaluation of career readiness after completing the hospitality management curriculum at the International Hotel School* [Doctoral dissertation, University of South Africa].

Sociology, 46(1), 41–56.

Ezenweke, E. O., & Nwadialor, L. K. (2013). Understanding human relations in African traditional religious context in the face of globalization: Nigerian perspectives. *American International Journal of Contemporary Research, 3*(2), 61–70.

Firebaugh, W. C. (1923). *The inns of Greece & Rome and a history of hospitality from the dawn of time to the middle ages.* FM Morris.

Gathogo, J. M. (2006). African hospitality: Is it compatible with the ideal of Christ's hospitality? Part. *Churchman, 120*(1), 39–56.

Gathogo, J. M. (2008). Some expressions of African hospitality today. *Scriptura: Journal for Contextual Hermeneutics in Southern Africa, 99*(1), 275–287.

Heal, F. (1990). *Hospitality in early modern England.* Oxford University Press on Demand.

Healey, J. (1996). *Towards an African narrative theology.* Orbis Books.

Hemmington, N. (2007). From service to experience: Understanding and defining the hospitality business. *The Service Industries Journal, 27*(6), 747–755.

Höckert, E. (2015). *Ethics of hospitality: Participatory tourism encounters in the northern highlands of Nicaragua.* fi= Lapin yliopistol en= University of Laplandl.

Jacques, D. (1999). *Hospitality, justice and responsibility: A dialogue with Jacques Derrida.*

Kiige, J. W., Selvam, S., & Njiru, L. (2019). *Correlation between African hospitality and human flourishing among young African adults in Kenya.*

King, C. A. (1995). What is hospitality? *International Journal of Hospitality Management, 14*(3–4), 219–234.

Kurniawati, R. (2015). Students' readiness to enter tourism industry. *Journal of Business on Hospitality and Tourism, 1*(1), 10.

Lashley, C. (2008). Studying hospitality: Insights from social sciences. *Scandinavian Journal of Hospitality and Tourism, 8*(1), 69–84.

Lashley, C., & Morrison, A. (2000). *In search of hospitality: Theoretical perspectives and debates.* Butterworth Heinemann.

Leed, E. J. (1991). *The mind of the traveler.* Basic Books.

Lowden, K., Hall, S., Elliot, D., & Lewin, J. (2011). *Employers' perceptions of the employability skills of new graduates.* Edge Foundation. *Journal of Teaching in Travel & Tourism, 20*(4), 237–261.

Mbiti, J. S. (2015). *Introduction to African religion.* Waveland Press.

Moore, S. H. (2009). *Hospitality and misericordia in MacIntyre.* Paper presented at the Metaphysics 2009: Fourth World Conference. http://www.metaphysics2009.org/index.php?option=comdocman&task=searchresult&Itemid=53&lang=en

Newman, E. (2007). *Untamed hospitality: Welcoming God and other strangers.* Brazos Press.

O'Connor, D. (2005). Towards a new interpretation of "hospitality". *International Journal of Contemporary Hospitality Management, 17*(3), 267–271.

Ogbeide, G. C. A. (2006). *Employability skills and students' self-perceived competence for careers in hospitality industry* [Doctoral dissertation, University of Missouri—Columbia].

O'Gorman, K. D. (2005). Modern hospitality: Lessons from the past. *Journal of Hospitality and Tourism Management, 12*(2), 141–151.

Rahman, I. (2010). *Students' perceptions of effectiveness of hospitality curricula and their preparedness.*

Rokeach, M. (1973). *The nature of human values.* Free press.

Roque, H. C., & Ramos, M. (2019). The importance of cultural training in the hospitality sector. *European Journal of Tourism, Hospitality and Recreation, 9*(2), 58–67.

Shaw, G., & Williams, A. M. (1994). *Critical issues in tourism: A geographical perspective*. Blackwell Publishers.

Skandrani, H., & Kamoun, M. (2014). *Hospitality meanings and consequences among hotels employees and guests*. Emerald Group Publishing Limited.

Slattery, P. (1983). Social scientific methodology and hospitality management. *International Journal of Hospitality Management, 2*(1), 9–14.

Telfer, E. (2012). *Food for thought: Philosophy and food*. Routledge.

Tomasella, B., & Ali, A. (2019). The importance of personal values and hospitableness in small foodservice businesses' social responsibility. *Hospitality & Society, 9*(3), 307–329.

Warhurst, C., & Nickson, D. (2007). Employee experience of aesthetic labour in retail and hospitality. *Work, Employment and Society, 21*(1), 103–120.

Wijesinghe, G. (2014). Reimagining the application of sustainability to the hospitality industry through a virtue ethics framework. *Journal of Sustainable Tourism, 22*(1), 31–49.

Wood, R. C. (1997). *Working in hotels and catering*. International Thomson Business Press.

Online Source

https://sdgs.un.org/goals.

9

Nursing Homes: The Person-Centred Care (PCC) Model

Africa Bértiz Colomer

A. Bértiz Colomer (✉)
Monteparís Mayores, Madrid, Spain
e-mail: africabertiz@gmail.com

1 Introduction: The Concept of Limitation

Attention to people in dependence has been one of the main social challenges of developed economies. In recent decades, dependence has changed from being viewed as an exclusively individual or family problem to being perceived as a problem that affects society as a whole.

In this area, one of the centres that deserve special study is the nursing home. From a demographic point of view, we are experiencing—especially in some countries where the age pyramid is being reversed—an "ageing of the ageing" phenomenon: the group of people aged 80 and over doubled in just two decades (from 1970 to 1990), which implies that, by 2025, 8% of the population—at least in Europe—will be over 80 years of age.

This has led to the professionalisation of the centres that house this sector of the population.

The contributions of the present study are two-fold:

1. An analysis of the evolution of this process of professionalisation. How could it be done.
2. The description of a new model of service focused on the person.

Hospitality services foster communication, personal relationships, education and respect. The environment—the architecture, decoration, design and distribution of spaces—and all of the sensory aspects of these facilities contribute to the well-being of their residents. The preparation of menus, the treatment of clothing and linen and the hygiene of all rooms are also important aspects of this personalised care.

For this objective of person-centred care to be achieved, the commitment and involvement of all of the staff is essential, and the figure of the Service Coordinator plays a key role. This, which may seem obvious, is not so. Often these jobs are carried out in an unselective manner, any member of the staff (without knowledge of this work) supervises them, and a value chain of staff demotivation is generated that has an impact on the dissatisfaction of the residents.

1.1 Unity: Vulnerability—Transcendence

As in any period of transition, the modern world exhibits a growing crisis that touches on the very problem of being and the truth of being. This is nothing new; where ancient and medieval metaphysics had posited a domain of formal being, modernity would establish a link with the Cartesian cogito and contemporary humanism would address the relationship of subject and object, pointing to man as the "possibility of possibility". The fact that the human being is open to growth is implicit in his own psycho-physical nature; but equally implicit is the fact of biological decay, and if we approach this from a moral point of view, there is no ethical condition that can be separated from biology.

Man is one and we cannot make distinctions with regard to his essence. We can, however, when it comes to his behaviour. This can indeed be analysed, and on various levels. Nor does this approach involve a "decomposition" but instead refers to the fact that an anthropological unity can be observed despite ontological diversity (body, psyche and the spiritual dimension). The body enables, but also limits. The discovery of both vulnerability and transcendence are effects of rationality.

1.2 Individual Responsibility: Collective Responsibility

The twentieth century–or more properly, the last third of the nineteenth—has given us a series of other connotations that shed light on this approximation to the personal being who, while bursting with possibilities, discovers his own limitations. Who is affected by this? The individual alone? Jellinek[1] tells us that the person exists a priori to the State, but also argues that the State should intervene in social and economic life to promote the socio-economic dignity of the person (Jellinek, 2019).

---

[1] Georg Jellinek (Leipzig, 16 June 1851–Heidelberg, 12 January 1911) was a German jurist and university professor of Austrian-Jewish origin. In his works on legal philosophy and juridical science, he maintained that sovereignty belongs properly to the State and not to the nation.

1.3 A Few Demographic Details

It will also serve here to highlight science that would acquire a special rigour in the twentieth century, demographics, which offers a vision of a person's behaviour both as an individual and as a member of society. Such a science does not arise by chance, but from a necessity, a reflection on one aspect of reality which for whatever reason demands a systematic and methodological analysis. The data provided by this particular science is not merely statistical but reflects such important realities as how human beings behave in relation to economic development, what decisions they make regarding procreation, how natural growth and migratory movements develop, and what concept of the family institution is adopted by each culture. A drop in the birth rate is now a reality all over the world (excepting regional and other differences) (Vollset et al., 2020). Europe is fast approaching zero growth, and in some cases, this is already negative. Birth control policy is subject to a variety of different factors and reflects the prioritisation of values other than that of the family in post-industrial society. This carries with it an important social connotation as there is now appearing a large passive population for whom care must be provided (Vollset et al., 2020). Health care, then, is no longer an individual issue, for the larger repercussions that economically supporting this older segment of the population will inevitably bring.

Since the Second World Assembly on Ageing was held in Madrid in 2002, the expressions "old" or "elderly" people (referring to those over 85) have been evolving into the current terminology of "seniors" or "older adults".

2 Nursing Homes: The Professionalisation of the Sector

Care for people in situations of dependence is now one of the main social challenges of developed economies. In recent years, however, dependence has changed from being viewed as an exclusively individual or family problem to one that affects society as a whole, demanding new public policies and a determination of the State's objectives and functions that is better adjusted to the needs of its citizens. This evolution (towards the conception of care for dependent people as an issue that transcends the private sphere, together with an awareness of the demographic situation) has led to the professionalisation of centres designed to house this sector of the population (Watson, 2009).

Nursing homes are undergoing a Copernican shift in their manner of operation. In the 1980s and 90s, professionalisation was centred on the development of work procedures for systematising processes (Brannon & Smyer, 1994; Gehrke & Wattenberg, 1981; Patchner & Patchner, 1991; Williams et al., 1992). Service became the focus of this work. The focus is now on the person and the development of his or her personal autonomy (Kloos et al., 2019; Rejnö et al., 2020).

It may seem contradictory that an approach to the care of dependent persons includes their need for autonomy. However, we must not lose sight of the fact that facilitating autonomy cannot be separated from the virtues of recognising dependency (which involve compassion and caring). Hippocrates pointed out that it is patients who must be treated, not illnesses (Yapijakis et al., 2013). Twenty centuries later, William Osler (one of the precursors of modern scientific medicine, as well as patient-centred medicine), would affirm that "it is more important to know what kind of patient has the illness than what kind of illness the patient has" (Sacristan et al., 2018, p. 22). Indeed, the need for the dependent person's own autonomy is a vital part of individualisation. It is a crucial element in the flexibilization of services, in family involvement and in the important role of hospitality for achieving the goals established.

2.1 Care from a General Services Perspective

How can general services in nursing homes be incorporated into the care process? Can some tangible activities serve to communicate the intangible reality of the sense of family and home which is the necessary substratum for accompanying this period of psycho-physical decay? The maternal bosom is man's first habitat, and after this the family. It is in the home that the process of establishing one's personality takes place. The dependent person needs to live in a home-like environment and the nursing home must create an atmosphere—and a professional area that supports it—in which the provision of food, linen, hygiene and other facilities is subordinate to its primary purpose. These are not merely technical or organisational aspects, after all. The resident is the object of all these activities. This work and those who perform it are capable of humanising this situation of vulnerability. The processes of "epimeleia" and "mimesis" have something of "production" and much of "operation". It is precisely for this reason that they "communicate", as they are not reduced to mere external actions, but are instead inserted into the sphere of operation, and serve to develop both the agent and the beneficiary of the action.

2.2 Planning Intervention and Adaptation Programs

To achieve the goal of person-centred service, it is useful to have information about the resident's family, his or her interests and hobbies, and any issues of particular sensitivity. Personal data of this kind provides essential information for designing an effective program of intervention and adaptation. By focusing the care plan in general service areas, the resident's needs may be addressed with regard to nutrition, hygiene, linen and so on. This can also be done progressively with the family so that the break with the resident's own home is made less unsettling.

This is not a merely philanthropic approach discovered by analysing our current welfare society. Florence Nightingale,[2] the nineteenth-century nurse who so decisively promoted a truly scientific, "care-based" methodology in the profession of nursing, affirmed and defined it in her Notes on Nursing in 1859. In these notes, she reflects on and demonstrates the curative effectiveness of appropriate care. Nightingale was a pioneer in this approach, arguing that hospitals should be designed by

---

[2] Nightingale gained much experience during the years of the Crimean War, in which she headed a unit of nurses in Britain's Military General Hospitals. *Notes on Nursing* was first published in December 1859 by the Harrison company and in only one month had sold 15,000 copies.

9 Nursing Homes: The Person-Centred Care ...   173

architects, nurses and administrators working in collaboration. While recognising the inevitability of illness, she also observed that there were often symptoms in the process of caring for the patient that was not inherent to the illness itself, although they might at times be perceived as such. These symptoms were easily treatable through observation and attention. If a patient complained of being cold or hot, or had no appetite, many times it was not the illness she blamed but the care-providers. She also stressed the importance of physical environment[3] (fresh air, products with a certain level of disinfection, lighting and so on). Obviously, at the time of recounting her experiences, more than 100 years ago, such physical conditions were radically different from those of today.

General services are a necessary complement to the activity of caring for the senior resident, as their purpose is to establish a pleasant, familial setting for the person who has entered into a situation of dependence. But how can this be done?

2.3   Reception: The Resident's Initial Entry into the Centre

In universal literature we have many examples of the importance that has been given to welcome. An example is the scene of Ovid's metamorphosis in which the author describes the arrival of Jupiter and his son under mortal appearance in the hills of Phrygia. Philemon and Baucis welcome them, take care of them, and facilitate their rest (Ovidio, 2003). As a contemporary counterpart is the Ulysses of James Joyce in which the protagonist wanders aimlessly and without reference.

The reception of any company begins with the presentation of its business card. In designing a plan of intervention, the centre's first contact with the resident is similarly a crucial moment. It requires an attitude of

---

[3] "On the one hand, there is the issue of the physical and aesthetic configuration of the premises, which is essential for creating a family-like atmosphere. This atmosphere is the 'air' breathed by each one of those who live there, and one of its basic elements is already in place and expressed by this configuration. Walls and planters aid or hinder the quality of life, as the case may be. The material extension of the building itself is clearly of great importance for this family feeling" (Alvira, 2007, p. 33).

humane conciliation, courtesy and friendliness in dealing with people, agility and skill in handling the various difficulties that arise on a daily basis. The reception staff, if well-trained, can make an initial analysis of the situation, on this first day or on some subsequent occasion, and inform the director, social worker or nurses of any issues they have noticed which may be relevant to the resident's integration into the centre.

A key factor in the person-centred care model is an attitude of individuality (there may be 100 people in the centre, but care is given to each one individually) and positivity. While architecture, decor, design and distribution are vital elements of larger spaces, at reception lighting, decoration, the uniforms of the staff and their welcoming smiles are especially important. This is, after all, the first truly "human" image of the centre, as prior to this one has perhaps been gathering information about it only from its website.

Throughout the seniors' stay in the nursing home, some of the reception staff may perform small services for them, such as delivering newspapers and magazines, as well as helping with the intake of new residents, sorting packages that arrive, and receiving visitors or volunteers who work at the weekends. Reception is on duty 16 hours a day in a presential capacity, and this makes it an important element of the social climate that is generated over time.

2.4 Food Service Area

The mission of the food service area is to manage the process of providing food to the residents at the standard of excellence established with regard to its nutritional, hygienic and gastronomic quality. As living in the centre implies a modification of the resident's eating habits, his or her preferences can and must be expressed to the medical staff so that an appropriate diet plan can be designed to meet each resident's current needs.

There are many ways to achieve this type of personalisation through professionalised service, for example, with menus offering choices from which residents can select what they want to eat for each meal, within the nutritional programs established for them. Diet is an integral part of the overall treatment each person receives. Residents (and especially their family members) use their own criteria regarding food to evaluate the care provided by the centre. It is a well-known statistic that the second question posed to a resident is one related to food: "Are you eating well?", "Is the food good?" A positive reply influences the resident's general satisfaction, and this is then extended to the entire rage of therapeutic services provided, which are perceived in a way that consolidates his or her trust in the staff. The fundamental objective of the food service area is one of personalised care, and this has two specific functions: dietetic (the elaboration of a manual of personalised application); and logistic (the purchasing, reception, storage, preparation and distribution of the food plans outlined in the manual). To achieve the objectives established and assure that these fulfil the functions specified an adequate coordination of the various tasks involved is essential; thus, the organisation of the food service area rests on three fundamental pillars: the total centralisation of everything related to food services; the organisation and planning of diets; and the principles of "way forward" and HACCP, which allow the level of quality to be maintained.

These technical objectives are complemented by a series of sub-points, which in all cases imply the concept of "care":

- Designing diets based on the nutritional treatment programs of residents according to their individual needs (texturized, puréed, basal).
- The dignification of the staff that performs these tasks.
- Logistics and facilities oriented to meet these objectives (and in which the most important focus is on the person).
- Effective management to maximise use and minimise cost, with enough flexibility to be adapted to individual requirements.

Finally, it is important to monitor the quantity and texture of each portion, and the garnishing and culinary techniques employed so as to assure that the diet each resident receives conforms to the established plan, that it is of adequate dietetic and gastronomic quality (i.e., it must not only fit the plan, but be well prepared), and that it is adapted as much as possible to the residents' own habits and preferences.

176   A. Bértiz Colomer

One aspect of person-centred care is the encouragement of participation, and there are many occasions (celebrations, holidays, events) on which ambulatory residents may, if they wish, help in the kitchen preparing snacks, desserts and so on (away from high-risk elements such as burners or sharp utensils). On a more regular basis, they can do this in small offices incorporated into co-living units, where they can prepare simple home-style recipes help to integrate these residents into a family-like environment. Such activities can be done in combination with those carried out by volunteer workers.[4]

2.5   Clothing and Linen: Respecting Dignity

Also in this apparently prosaic subject, literature has given us experiences of how taking care of the details collaborates in the healing of the person. In Anna Karenina, Tolstoy's masterful novel, we are shown how Kitty takes care of Levin's dying brother: taking charge of his cleaning, his clothes and leaving him in a situation of well-being within his physical decadence.

The linen supply area is responsible for managing everything related to staff uniforms, bedlinen, towels, tablecloths, napkins, bibs and, of course, personal clothing. It is very important that in this phase of the senior's life special care is given to the personal attire of both the staff and the residents themselves. Many companies opt for outsourcing this service and renting such items. In any case, a refined and personalised level of attention can be achieved in this area if several principles are kept in mind:

1. Appropriate uniform choice. Uniforms should be comfortable for working but at the same time express the idea that the centre cares about both the employees and the residents. Clothing communicates a message: a predominance of white in staff uniforms suggests an environment which is more hospital-like than familial, while warm,

---

[4] http://www.acpgerontologia.com/documentacion/guiatenciongerontologiacentradaenlapersona.pdf.

cheerful colours are more agreeable, appealing and evoke a feeling of freshness.

2. A choice of linen items that transmits a quality-price ratio appropriate for our desired standards. A "low price-low quality" ratio can be provided by any industrial linen service, and the customer often finds that such linen arrives in poor condition, generating dissatisfaction in both intermediary users (the professionals who work in the centre) and end users (the residents).

3. An RFID (Radio Frequency Identification) labelling system with a scanning antenna and reader, and at least one sorting unit. The purpose of this type of computerisation is to provide tracking for uniforms and especially for the residents' linen and clothing, and which, whether washing is done on- or off-site, allows computer-based follow-up to prevent the loss of items in the process.[5]

The linen supply area is designed to promote an atmosphere that makes the resident feel more cared for and "at home". For both internal and external services of this type, the goal is two-fold: on the one hand, an adequate disinfection of all textiles used in the centre; and on the other, a choice of fabrics and designs that provide both comfort and respect for the dignity of each person. This also implies correct washing-cycle selection in order to assure the bacteriological cleanliness of all linen and clothing items.

The design of such facilities and the training of the staff involved are important factors in achieving these objectives. Staff uniforms also play an important role, serving as another "business card" for the entity as a whole. A smart, proper uniform is not a sign of luxury but of refinement, and the correct treatment of this uniform (its washing and ironing) expresses the same respect for the person that we have established elsewhere.

Providing clean clothing at all times and in all areas of the centre will also facilitate this objective, as will the choice of adequate furnishings. Mattresses, for example, the very foundation of rest, should be orthopaedic, comfortable, of high-density hollow-fibre foam, liftable and

---

[5] https://www.merakytechnology.com/sistemas-rfid/.

designed to prevent bedsores. This is important not only for the comfort of the resident but for the healthcare workers whose job it is to tidy the rooms every day and need to make beds with a minimal back strain.

Respect for the resident's autonomy and the promotion of independence can be combined here, making it possible for residents who wish to do so to collaborate with the linen supply area in risk-free tasks whenever they choose, helping to create a more family-like atmosphere by folding napkins, delivering table linen to co-living spaces, picking up washed and ironed clothing, performing various services for less ambulatory residents and so on.

2.6 Housekeeping: Safety in the Residential Centre

While the food service area provides the residents with adequate nutrition and the linen supply area helps to make their stay more pleasant, the housekeeping area guarantees the safety of the centre. The risk of nosocomial infection, especially in immunocompromised persons, is widely known and much feared. Infection control in nursing homes is not merely a question of monitoring by an external prevention entity that visits sporadically and takes random samples (a necessary quality-control measure) but depends on the way in which the cleaning and disinfection of each area is routinely done. The training of cleaning staff is key; on the one hand, for the diversity of protocols that must be followed. Workers must be equipped with the appropriate knowledge to carry out differentiated processes in areas classed as low-to-zero risk, medium risk or high risk (as our experience with Covid-19 has shown), as well as trained in the handling and dosification of cleaning products and the chemical-biological risks that may result from their improper use and the correct protocols for these. On the other hand, if institutional training is necessary for all healthcare or administrative staff, in this area it is essential in terms of confidentiality, discretion and companionship. Like the caregivers themselves, housekeepers enter into close relationships with residents, even if they maintain the logical professional distance.

2.7 Building Maintenance

The building that houses a nursing home is not simply a box into which certain elements are fitted. It must be a home, a large one to be sure, and it has an owner. The maintenance technician is in effect this owner (although not in the economic or financial sense). Caring for a particular dwelling is what makes it a home. For this reason, the maintenance technician and the driver responsible for the mobility of people and things are key figures in any such facility. It also helps if there is an urban garden to serve as a therapeutic method in its own right. This is a hobby which is highly popular, accessible, and a valuable way for the resident to care for the natural world in this final stage of life. Such general services have the double effect of caring also for the centre's own staff, being oriented towards the "external" client (the residents) by focusing on the "internal client" (the staff).

2.8 Other Considerations

It would be impossible to include in these pages all of the many details involved in a nursing home stay. Through information provided by the nursing staff, the food service area can take note of the "celebrations" of individual residents (birthdays, anniversaries, etc.) and on those days have some small tribute given to them at mealtime. It may also happen that in moments of suffering there are life situations that call for solutions (for example, family reconciliations). It is easy to accompany such difficult times with small gestures within the basic services provided. The linen supply area can do much to contribute along these lines. Tablecloths can be used in co-living units "like at home", while residents who take meals in their rooms can opt for traditional trays rather than thermal ones. The traditional meal tray, with tablecloth and napkin, is more reminiscent of home, and allows for all the variants one might want: different table linen for holidays, Christmastime and so on. In all areas, hygiene is essential, as is a proper elimination of enzymatic odours, or the use of ozone generators that purify the air and eliminate contaminating pathogens.

3 Conclusion

In conclusion, three points are highlighted:

3.1. The crucial role of the General Services Coordinator in exercising his or her executive duties. The Coordinator acts as a bridge between directors, middle managers, staff, residents and the residents' families. Anyone with a family member in this type of care centre will want to be sure that that person is receiving proper nutrition and clean clothes, is living in a clean, sanitary environment and in a warm, welcoming atmosphere that is like "being at home". This is reflected to perfection in the Etxean Ondo project (Diaz Veiga & Sancho, 2012). The post of Coordinator, then, cannot be filled by just anyone, nor can an external company provide the level of quality required for these care-giving activities. They are tasks that are "always there" and, while they are often overlooked when they are functioning properly, they can cause an authentic "bottleneck" in the operations of a nursing home when they are not.

3.2. The importance of recruiting, training, capacitating and motivating the personnel who will be hired in the areas of food service, linen services, reception and maintenance. It may happen that, although some staff members come to their positions with little professional training or minimal people skills, they will in any case gain effective training on the job.

3.3. The significance of "opportunity cost". Many business people are reluctant to invest in these areas. Dealing with opportunity cost is a question not only of minimising resident complaints, but of achieving true well-being. If not, the "cost of not making the investment" proves high indeed. We want residents who are happy, families who are at ease and a centre that commands prestige.

Recognising autonomy is one aspect of the respect shown to a person's dignity and importance, saying in effect that *the "other" is not a possession of mine and therefore I grant that person autonomy and allow that I can never fully understand his or her situation*. Might autonomy be a path to equality? Sennett (2004, p. 128) speaks of "opaque equality"; that is, accepting in the other that which one cannot understand oneself. Also interesting in this sense is the allusion he makes to Adam Smith, who in his Theory of Moral Feelings (1759–1761) declared that "sympathy for the difficulty of another comes when someone strives (…) to put himself in the situation of the other and understands for himself all of the small circumstances of affliction that may occur to the one who suffers (…) down to the most insignificant details" (Sennett, 2004, p. 128).

Is compassion a form of respect? In the world of politics, where it is often difficult to discern the line of separation between "caring" and "controlling", or between "serving" what is "being seen in the function of serving", is it possible to care for others without compassion? Can we feel cared for by a computer in the public administration? The truth is that when care is given in an impersonal manner, the vision we have of the human condition is one that is grim and pessimistic. The result of such a vision is what may be called "compassion fatigue"; when our sympathy is exhausted by continually painful situations, a reaction of indifference occurs.

"There are places", said Leon Bloy, "that do not yet exist in our hearts and it takes suffering to bring them into existence" (Evdokimov, 1964, p. 99). We sometimes use a more colloquial expression to express the idea that "in youth one learns, in maturity one understands". Now, in the twenty-first century, we would do well to revisit the teachings of Aristotle, where he explains to Nicomachus how the virtues enable us to see every human being as a member of a reciprocal network. What follows is a question of responding to the voice of natural law.

Action Prompts

Avoid "compassion fatigue"; which happens when our sympathy is exhausted by continually painful situations, resulting in reactions of indifference towards people that need care.

Respect and facilitate autonomy of the residents, while at the same time recognising dependency (which involves compassion and caring).

Encourage participation during occasions (celebrations, holidays, events), where residents may, if they wish, help in the kitchen preparing snacks, desserts, etc.

Study Questions

1. Should the State be involved in promoting professional training and regulating the professional titles of people who work in nursing homes? If so, how could the State do it?
2. How can society recognise–on the economic scale as well—the importance of nursing homes in a welfare society?
3. How can families collaborate with nursing homes so that they are truly an extension of the home?

Chapter Summary

Attention to people in dependence has been one of the main social challenges of developed economies. In recent decades, dependence has changed from being viewed as an exclusively individual or family problem to being perceived as a problem that affects society as a whole.

In this area, one of the centres that deserve special study is the nursing home. From a demographic point of view, we are experiencing—especially in some countries where the age pyramid is being reversed—an "ageing of the ageing" phenomenon: the group of people aged 80 and over doubled in just two decades (from 1970 to 1990), which implies that by 2025 8% of the population—at least in Europe—will be over 80 years of age. This has led to the professionalisation of the centres that house this sector of the population.

The contribution of the present study is the description of a new model of service focused on the person. Hospitality services (menus, treatment of clothing, hygiene) foster communication, personal relationships, education and respect. The environment—the architecture, decoration, design and distribution of spaces—also contribute to the well-being of their residents. For this objective of person-centred care to be achieved, the figure of the Service Coordinator plays a key role.

References

Alvira, R. (2007). *El lugar al que se vuelve. Reflexiones sobre la familia* (Eunsa, Ed.).

Brannon, D., & Smyer, M. A. (1994). Good work and good care in nursing homes. *Generations: Journal of the American Society on Aging, 18*(3), 34–38.

Diaz Veiga, P., & Sancho, M. (2012). *Unidades de convivencia. Alojamientos de personas mayores para 'vivir como en casa'*. Informes Portal Mayores, no. 132 [Publication date: 15/06/2012]. http://www.imsersomayores.csic.es/docume ntos/documentos/diaz-unidades-01.pdf

Evdokimov, P. (1964). *Le età della vita spirituale*.

Gehrke, J. R., & Wattenberg, S. H. (1981). Assessing social services in nursing homes. *Health & Social Work, 6*(2), 14–25.

Jellinek, G. (2019). *The declaration of the rights of man and of citizens*. Good Press.

Kloos, N., Trompetter, H. R., Bohlmeijer, E. T., & Westerhof, G. J. (2019). Longitudinal associations of autonomy, relatedness, and competence with the well-being of nursing home residents. *The Gerontologist, 59*(4), 635–643.

Nightingale, F. (2013). *Notes on nursing; what it is and what it is not*. A & D Books.

Ovidio. (2003). *Metamorfosis*. Alianza Editorial.

Patchner, M. A., & Patchner, L. S. (1991). Social work practice in nursing homes. In *Social work practice with the elderly* (p. 145). Canadian Scholars' Press.

Rejnö, Å., Ternestedt, B. M., Nordenfelt, L., Silfverberg, G., & Godskesen, T. E. (2020). Dignity at stake: Caring for persons with impaired autonomy. *Nursing Ethics, 27*(1), 104–115.

Sacristan, J. A., et al. (2018). *Medicina centrada en el paciente*. Unión Editorial and Fundación Lilly.

Sennett, R. (2004). *Respect in a world of inequality*. W. W. Norton.

Vollset, S. E., Goren, E., Yuan, C. W., Cao, J., Smith, A. E., Hsiao, T., & Murray, C. J. (2020). Fertility, mortality, migration, and population scenarios for 195 countries and territories from 2017 to 2100: A forecasting analysis for the Global Burden of Disease Study. *The Lancet, 396*(10258), 1285–1306.

Watson, S. D. (2009). From Almshouses to nursing homes and community care: Lessons from Medicaid's history. *Georgia State University Law Review, 26*, 937.

Williams, E. I., Savage, S., McDonald, P., & Groom, L. (1992). Residents of private nursing homes and their care. *British Journal of General Practice, 42*(364), 477–481.

Yapijakis, C., Bartsakoulia, M., & Patrinos, G. P. (2013). Hippocrates, the father of clinical medicine and Asclepiades, the father of molecular medicine. *Archives of Hellenic Medicine/Arheia Ellenikes Iatrikes, 30*(1).

10

Exploring Guests Relations, Brand Loyalty, and Repeat Visits in Luxury Hotels of China: A Case of Tianjin

Dijin Wang, Asad Mohsin, and Jorge Lengler

D. Wang (✉)
Tianjin, China
e-mail: wdj624790271@gmail.com

A. Mohsin
Waikato Management School, Hamilton, New Zealand
e-mail: amohsin@waikato.ac.nz

1 Introduction

The development of the global economy and service industry, specifically tourism and hospitality, has generated several opportunities both for the industry and consumers. In 2019, the total contribution of travel and tourism to Gross Domestic Product (GDP) in China was 1581 billion U.S. dollars giving it a second place after USA (Appendix A). This demand has led the Chinese tourism authority to review the star rating system of Chinese hotels to standardize it. The main customers for luxury hotels are domestic and international business travellers and international tourists. Therefore, engaging with different groups of customers has gradually become one of the challenges for luxury hotels. The commercial accommodation industry now comprises several segments, such as bedside hotels, service apartments, boutique resorts, motels, budget accommodations, and Airbnb and its Chinese equivalents. As technology grows, so do online reservations and online payments. Also, each hotel brand can rely on the development of technology to make hotel space a social and event platform. Customers can communicate with each other at any time, which brings a customer's personalized community experience and the hotels accumulate social resources about their clientele.

This chapter uses humanism in the form of guest and customer relations. The perspective of humanism has been adopted in this study to reflect the meaning that ethics and the essentials of society can be grasped in autonomy and moral equality (Özen, 2013).

Customer Relationship Management (CRM) can assist hotels in increasing to increase their existing customer satisfaction and loyalty to attract their customers and achieve long-run profitability with effective management strategies (Kasim & Minai, 2009). The current trends

---

J. Lengler
Durham University Business School, Durham, UK
e-mail: jorge@lengler.org

reflect that CRM is gaining popularity in China as a model of management and sales. However, there are no official statistics about the status of CRM applications in the Chinese hospitality industry. Furthermore, some hotels do not possess systematic guest relationship management, they either lack humanism or lack resources and capabilities to implement CRM, such as the support of top management, financial support, appropriate training, organizational capabilities, and technical capabilities. In addition, some hotels lack information system support. Therefore, tracking and caring for customers becomes difficult (Nguyen et al., 2007). Furthermore, in traditional hotel marketing activities, some hotels only engage new customers and neglect to maintain existing customers. Such actions lead hotel management to concentrate on pre-arrival activities generally.

Tianjin is one of the municipalities of China close to Beijing. During the Coronavirus outbreak, tourism in China and around the world has been hit hard. In terms of Tianjin, most of the hotels closed, except for a few hotels which served their long-staying guests. Long-stay guests usually bring long-term profits to hotels reflecting the significance of the relationship between customers and hotels. So, what impact does CRM have on relationship operations?

The study explores the use of CRM in Tianjin's luxury hotels, the effectiveness of CRM in building brand loyalty and keeping customers satisfied, the influence of customer relations, and WOM (word of mouth) supported by Abdullateef and Salleh (2013), Wahab et al. (2011), and service delivery system on loyalty. Scarce research in the area became the impetus to explore the CRM practices in Tianjin's hospitality industry.

The main objectives of the research in this chapter are to investigate within the context of luxury hotels in Tianjin:

- Impact of guests relations in building brand loyalty.
- Role of WOM and recommendations to build brand loyalty
- Impact of service delivery system on brand loyalty
- Relationship between brand loyalty and repeat visits.

The methodology uses quantitative data accumulation and analysis. It involves the survey administration of a structured questionnaire. The result generates outcomes that have implications for Tianjin's hospitality industry and reflects significant implications for the local industry.

2 Literature Review and Hypotheses Development

2.1 Managing Customer/Guest Relations and Loyalty

Existing studies have indicated that customer loyalty will be positively affected by higher customer satisfaction, which leads to better company performance and brand loyalty (Buttle, 2004; Homburg et al., 2005; Singh, 2006). Satisfied customers will not only repurchase but also share their good experiences with others. Previous research has suggested that effective CRM practices are associated with improving levels of customer satisfaction (Feinberg & Kadam, 2002). In addition, customer satisfaction also has an important influence on interim goals, like customer loyalty and customer retention (Abdullateef & Salleh, 2013). Wahab et al. (2011) affirmed that maximizing customer satisfaction and minimizing complaints are key results of successful CRM performance. Mithas et al. (2005) researched the effectiveness of CRM initiatives, which suggested that companies can deepen the understanding of customers through CRM initiatives, thereby increasing customer satisfaction. Santouridis and Veraki (2017) illustrated that the development and implementation of CRM practices could increase customer satisfaction. For example, personalized services, protecting individual data, providing convenient and flexible payment methods, convenient and efficient customer service, responding to customer needs in time, and affiliate programs can increase customer satisfaction with relationships, enhancing their satisfaction with provided services.

2.2 Hypotheses Development

Concerning CRM, studies have illustrated that CRM has been successfully adopted by the tourism and hotel industry (Chetioui et al., 2017; Gilbert, 1996; Padilla-Meléndez & Garrido-Moreno, 2013; Palmer et al., 2000). However, the definition of customer relationship management (CRM) has not been universally accepted. According to Swift (2001), CRM can be defined as an "enterprise approach to understanding and influencing customer behaviour through meaningful communications to improve customer acquisition, customer retention, customer loyalty, and customer profitability" (p. 12). Kotler et al. (2017) defined CRM as "the overall process of building and maintaining profitable customer relationships by delivering superior customer value and satisfaction" (p. 38). The definition of CRM is "the strategic use of information, process, technology, and people to manage the customer's relationship with your company (Marketing, Sales, Services, and Support) across the whole customer life cycle" (Kincaid, 2003, p. 41). CRM assists corporations in increasing their customer satisfaction, loyalty, and retention and build and manage the long-term relationships with their customers (Bowen & Chen, 2001; Lo et al., 2010). Majid et al. (2016) have conducted research that demonstrated significant and positive impact responsiveness to brand equity. Path coefficient value of their hypothesis indicates that if the response rate to customers increases by 1%, brand equity will increase by 13%. Furthermore, Coker et al. (2013) have revealed that service response plays an intermediary role between the corporate logo and the customer's perception of the brand itself. Consequently, the researchers stated that building relationships with the customer should be a strategic priority for most service companies. Hence authors post the following hypothesis:

H1 Hotels' guests' relationship approach positively influences brand loyalty.

Maintaining a customer is less expensive than creating a new customer, and the engagement of new customers through positive word of mouth leads to loyal customers. Kotler et al. (2017) found that when people have been asked what factor leads them to new restaurants as part of the hospitality industry, 48% of the people answered that friends or relatives took them or recommended them to new restaurants, which occupies the largest proportion (as cited in Kotler et al., 2017). According to Fornell and Wernerfelt (1987), more positive word of mouth and higher customer loyalty gets better resolving the complaints of dissatisfied customers. Addressing customer complaints improve customer loyalty and retention while enhancing customer belongingness towards service providers (Bhat & Darzi, 2016). The research has shown that Word-of-Mouth has significantly influenced the relationship between brand awareness and brand equity (Ansary & Hashim, 2018). Also, Ameri (2015) has affirmed that brand identification requires consumers to distinguish between brands they have seen or heard before. Therefore, brand awareness is important when making purchase decisions and brand loyalty. This helps to raise the following hypothesis.

H2 Word-of-mouth (WOM) recommendations positively influence brand loyalty.

According to Kaushal (2015), there are five dimensions in customer relationship management. The first dimension is technology and automation, which covers managing customer service activities and supplying applications of self-service to allow various types of customers to operate by a single service platform, to seek useful information by filtering data during customer interactions. The second dimension is purchasing behaviour, which is the process of customers determining whether or not to buy merchandise or services. The third dimension is loyalty and retention, including some practices and promotions to engage new customers and maintain the relationship with the existing customers. The fourth dimension is customization, which involves providing products and services consistent with guests' wishes. The last dimension is awareness, spreading the message of the relationship marketing program to every stakeholder, getting feedback, and updating from time to time. In their research, Cox et al. (2007) have mentioned the Lakeland premium brand beef case; the firm has enabled a service delivery system to play a central role in developing and selling brands in the regional foodservice market by improving service levels, product quality, and brand awareness. So, what is the role of the service delivery system as a construct in this study in influencing brand loyalty? It is tested with the help of the following hypothesis:

H3 Service delivery systems positively influence brand loyalty.

Previous research provides dual explanations of customer loyalty (Jacoby & Kyner, 1973). The first is to treat loyalty as an attitude. Various feelings lead customers to become attached to a particular service, product, or hotel (Fornier, 1996). These feelings can be referred to as personal or customer loyalty. The second explanation considers loyalty as a behaviour. Yi (1990) illustrated that behavioural attributes motivate individuals or customers to buy products or services from the same provider. Delighted customers will keep their loyalty and praise the company and its services or products to others. Loyal shoppers are largely the result of the service provider's passion for serving customers. Edelman (2010) states that if customer loyalty is created, customers will "buy," "enjoy," "advocate," and "bond." Therefore, customer loyalty is always pursued in the business world (Han & Hyun, 2012). Six indicators measure the degree of customer loyalty: sharing information, positive speaking, recommending friends, repurchasing, purchasing extra service, and trying new services (Roberts et al., 2003). Rinova and Putri (2020) found in their study that brand loyalty positively affects repeat visits by using multiple linear regression.

Additionally, Wu (2011) has claimed that a positive hospital brand image initially improves the quality of service that patients perceive. Thus, brand image affects satisfaction through quality of service, and quality of service affects loyalty through satisfaction. Hence the following hypothesis is tested:

H4 Brand loyalty positively influences repeat visits.

Consumers consider the price, novelty, accessibility, and other services offered before choosing a given brand. As alternatives grow, consumer loyalty to products and services declines. Hence, the company needs to strive to provide products and services that can fully meet customer expectations and expectations at a lower cost than competitors, thus making customers more loyal (Koçoğlu & Kirmaci, 2012).

3 Research Methodology

3.1 Sample and Data Collection Procedure

The physical location for this research was in Tianjin, China. The survey participants were 400 luxury hotel guests who filled the survey anonymously with the help of the hotel management. Data was collected using the Tencent platform (A popular platform in China for questionnaire administration and data collection). Overall, 400 questionnaires were received, of which 368 questionnaires were valid, and 32 questionnaires were invalid (Appendix B). The response rate of the questionnaire was 92%.

Some informal interviews were held with four directors and six managers from different departments (i.e., Rooms, Sales Marketing, Food, and Beverage) representing six different luxury hotels. Their responses to CRM, service quality and hotel performance were used in the questionnaire development. To keep the anonymity of the person and the hotel, codes "P" representing the person and code "H" representing the hotel are used with a number, e.g. H1P1; H2P2: H3P3, etc. The luxury hotels in the context of the study represent three-star four-star and five-star hotels.

3.2 Development of the Questionnaire

The first section was about the CRM features, divided into four parts: customer acquisition, customer response, customer information system, and customer value evaluation. Each part had several CRM practices; the participants were asked to circle from "1 = Very strongly disagree to 7 = Very strongly agree" based on a 7-point Likert scale. This section reflects the participants' evaluation of hotel CRM practices. The second section was the level of importance of factors linked to choosing a luxury hotel. The respondents were required to circle from "7 = Extremely important to 1 = Extremely unimportant" based on a 7-point Likert scale. This section reflects factors that affect brand loyalty and repeat visits. The third section was the level of importance of factors linked to staying at the hotel again. The participants were asked to circle from "7 = Extremely important to 1 = Extremely unimportant" based on a 7-point Likert scale. This section can reflect what factors can promote the respondents to stay in the hotel again. The last section was for demographics, gender, age, the highest education level, and household income, and the participants were required to tick the respective boxes. The items used in this study were adapted from the work of Tahir and Zulkifli (2011), Kirmaci (2012), Cheng and Yang (2013), and Banga et al. (2013). (Table 1 provides examples of constructs and items used in the current study.)

3.3 Reliability and Validity

An exploratory factor analysis was conducted initially with the nineteen questions that composed the survey questionnaire. Then a confirmatory factor analysis (CFA) led to a structural model using AMOS v26 (see Fig. 1). Content validity is conducted using the tourism management literature to assess the measures used in the questionnaire (Banga et al., 2013; Cheng & Yang, 2013; Kirmaci, 2012; Tahir & Zulkifli, 2011). After those procedures, it can be concluded that the measures included in the questionnaire had content validity.

A confirmatory factor analysis (CFA) is conducted to assess convergent and scale reliability of all measures included in the conceptual model (Anderson & Gerbing, 1988). The results obtained from the CFA reveal that the measurement model has a good fit (chi-square 44,274, degrees of freedom, 137, $p < 0.001$). In addition to the chi-square, four other measures are used to assess the goodness-of-fit of our measurement model: comparative fit index (CFI = 0.920), Tucker-Lewis fit index (TLI = 0.900), Incremental fit index (IFI = 0.921), and root means a square error of approximation (RMSEA = 0.078, see Table 1).

194   D. Wang et al.

Table 1 Constructs measurements summary: confirmatory factor analysis and scales reliability

Constructs and items	Standardized regression weights	t-value
Hotel and Guests Relationship ($CR^a = 0.92$; $AVE^b = 0.58$; $Alpha^c = 0.911$)		
The hotel can tailor its products and services to meet my needs	0.68	Set to 1
The hotel offers various facilities to meet my demands	0.78	13.456
The hotel provides services to meet my specific requirements	0.69	11.902
The hotel provides a variety of service items and information	0.79	13.494
The hotel fulfils its promises on time	0.79	13.809
The hotel staffs are knowledgeable and possess necessary information on the requested service	0.77	13.634
The hotel staffs show sincere interest in solving my problems	0.79	14.138
The hotel uses different measures to meet customers' urgent requirements	0.79	13.61
Service Delivery System ($CR^a = 0.75$; $AVE^b = 0.60$; $Alpha^c = 0.735$)		
The hotel's system can record my information and preferences	0.82	Set to 1
The hotel has systems to record and charge my consumption accurately	0.72	10.262
WOM Recommendations ($CR^a = 0.68$; $AVE^b = 0.54$; $Alpha^c = 0.617$)		
Travel agency recommendation	0.50	Set to 1
Recommendation from others	0.91	6.879
Brand Loyalty ($CR^a = 0.68$; $AVE^b = 0.42$; $Alpha^c = 0.719$)		

(continued)

Table 1 (continued)

Constructs and items	Standardized regression weights	t-value
Brand influence	0.76	Set to 1
Member points	0.63	10.616
Having cooperation with the hotel	0.54	8.987
Repeat Visit (CR^a = 0.85; AVE^b = 0.59; Alpha^c = 0.854)		
Convenient location	0.71	Set to 1
Value for money	0.73	14.917
Excellent hotel customer service	0.86	14.314
Special discount	0.76	12.377

^{a}Composite reliability (CR) (Bagozzi & Yi, 1988)
^{b}Average Variance extracted (AVE) (Fornell & Larcker, 1981)
^{c}Alpha (Cronbach, 1951)

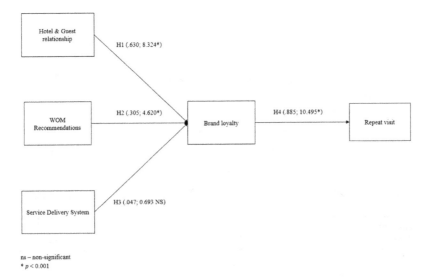

ns — non-significant
* $p < 0.001$

Fig. 1 Final model

The results indicate that the measures employed to measure the constructs are reliable (composite reliability, variance extracted, and internal consistency—Cronbach's Alpha) and valid. The authors assessed convergent validity through the standardized loadings of our variables.

According to Table 1, all variables presented standardized regression loadings above 0.50 ($t > 1.96$; $p < 0.05$). Table 1 also shows that all our constructs have internal consistency as Cronbach's Alpha fell above the cut-off point of 0.6 established by the literature (Cronbach, 1951). Regarding the composite reliability, all our constructs fell above the minimum threshold of 0.60 (Bagozzi & Yi, 1988). In addition, also assessed the average variance extracted. Only one of our constructs (Brand loyalty, AVE $= 0.42$) fell below the minimum threshold defined by the literature of 0.50 (Browne & Cudeck, 1993). Despite the slightly lower average variance extracted value, authors opted to keep this construct in our model as it has a significant theoretical contribution to explaining the phenomenon. Considering the above results, our measurement model was deemed acceptable (Bagozzi & Yi, 1988; Byrne, 2001; Fornell & Larcker, 1981; Hair et al., 2010).

3.4 Hypotheses Testing

The Structured Equation Modelling uses the maximum likelihood method to test the specified hypotheses using AMOS v26. Table 2 shows the results of the model specification and hypotheses testing. The overall chi-square of the model was 438,736 (degrees of freedom $= 138$). We also examined four other goodness-of-fit indices of our structure

Table 2 Coefficients of structural relationships and goodness-of-fit indices of the structural model

Linkages in the model *Hypotheses*	Standardized estimates	*t*-value	Hypothesis result
H1: Hotel and Guests relationship ➔ Brand loyalty	0.630	8.324*	Supported
H2: Word-of-mouth recommendations ➔ Brand loyalty	0.305	4.620*	Supported
H3: Service delivery system ➔ Brand loyalty	0.047	0.693ns	Not supported
H4: Brand loyalty ➔ Repeat visit	0.885	10.495*	Supported
Goodness-of-Fit Indices			
Chi-square 438,736 (138), RMSEA $= 0.077$; CFI $= 0.922$; TLI $= 0.902$; IFI $= 0.922$			

Ns = non-significant
*$p < 0.001$

model: comparative fit index (CFI = 0.922), Tucker-Lewis fit index (TLI = 0.902), incremental fit index (IFI = 0.922), and root means squared error of approximation (RMSEA = 0.077). All fit indices used in this study fell within the recommended thresholds suggested by the literature (RMSEA > 0.04 < 0.08; CFI, IFI, TLI > 0.900 (Byrne, 2001; Hair et al., 2010). Thus, the estimated model was deemed acceptable. The path analysis of the structural model and hypotheses results are presented in Table 2.

The hypothesis testing shows that hotel and guest relationships positively affect brand loyalty as the path coefficient was positive and significant (0.630; $p < 0.001$). As a result, hypothesis 1 is supported.

Supportive results of hypothesis 2 are also obtained. The results shown in Table 2 indicate that word-of-mouth recommendations positively affect brand loyalty (0.305; $p < 0.001$).

The results obtained for H3 indicate that the relationship between the serviced delivery system and brand loyalty was not significant (0.047; $p > 0.10$), failing to support H3.

Hypothesis 4 investigated the effect of brand loyalty on a repeat visit. Our results provide strong support for the notion that brand loyalty positively affects repeat visits (0.885; $p < 0.001$).

In summary, three of our specified hypotheses (H1, H2, and H4) were supported. However, our results fail to provide support for H3. Figure 1 and Table 2 show the hypotheses testing results.

4 Discussion and Conclusions

The main objective of this study was to assess the impacts of guests relations, WOM, and service delivery systems on brand loyalty and repeat visits in luxury hotels in Tianjin, China. The study uses a survey technique. Some views of senior local hotel managers were accumulated through informal interviews.

The first hypothesis tests the relationship between the guests and Tianjin's luxury hotels on brand loyalty. What do hotel guests perceive to be important in building a relationship with the hotels? The concept of relationship marketing was first initiated in the aviation industry in the 1980s when American Airlines established a loyalty program to reward their frequent flyer (Kim et al., 2001; Xiong et al., 2014). The concept of humanism transformed into Customer/Guest Relationship Management in the subsequent studies, which cover various perspectives from technological solutions (Payne & Frow, 2005) to customer-centred (Garrido-Moreno & Padilla-Meléndez, 2011) management principles (Vaeztehrani et al., 2015). In the 1990s, CRM began to grow (Ling & Yen, 2001). The current study determines that relationship with hotel guests through sustained services and products, impact brand loyalty. It is in line with the above-stated studies and senior manager (H01P02) who stated that "Whether hotel can match customers' needs is the premise of establishing customer relationships."

The second hypothesis tested the impact of WOM recommendations to build brand loyalty. Are recommendations from travel agents, friends, and other influential people enough to build brand loyalty? The cost of maintaining a customer is less expensive than creating a new customer (Chetioui et al., 2017; Gustafsson et al., 2005). A positive word of mouth from loyal customers and other sources consequently reduces the marketing cost. Kotler et al. (2017) emphasizes that 48% of people answered that friends or relatives took them or recommended them to new restaurants before they became their regular customers (Kotler et al., 2017). According to Fornell and Wernerfelt (1987), positive word of mouth and higher customer loyalty get better by resolving the complaints of dissatisfied customers. Addressing customer complaints improves customer loyalty and retention while enhancing customer belongingness towards the organizations (Bhat & Darzi, 2016). Hence WOM has a significant impact to build loyalty. Such a view is supported by some senior managers (H01P01, H03P06, H04P07, and H06P10). They stated that 'think about the problem from the guests' perspective, put your feet in guest's shoes so that you can truly understand the customer's feelings. Others (H01P02, H02P04, H03P05, H03P06, H04P08, and H05P09) stated that the positive WOM effects relationship and loyalty. This is also evident in the work of Han and Hyun (2012) that loyalty and word-of-mouth recommendations are very important in the business world. Roberts et al. (2003) state six indicators to measure the degree of customer loyalty: sharing information, positive speaking, recommending friends, repurchasing, purchasing extra service, and trying new services. Hence there is a strong relationship between WOM recommendation and loyalty within luxury hotels in Tianjin, China.

The third hypothesis tested if the service delivery system had any impact on brand loyalty. Kaushal (2015) state that an important dimension in customer relationship management is technology and automation, which covers managing customer service activities by a single service platform. Technology is now frequently used by the hotel industry. Several studies suggest that customer loyalty will be positively affected by higher customer satisfaction (Buttle, 2004; Homburg et al., 2005; Singh, 2006). Santouridis and Veraki (2017) support that a delivery system could increase customer satisfaction. For example, personalized services, protecting individual data, providing convenient and flexible payment methods, convenient and efficient customer service, and responding to customer needs to increase customer satisfaction, relationships, and loyalty. Senior managers (H03P06) believed that in the future, hotels could use advanced technology to help to strengthen the relationship between customers and the hotel so that the hotel can better manage customer relations. However, the findings from the H3 indicate that the relationship between the service delivery system and brand loyalty was not significant (0.047; $p > 0.10$), failing to support H3. Hence, within the context of Tianjin's luxury hotels, the service delivery system does not seem to impact brand loyalty. This is somewhat a surprise as largely literature suggests otherwise.

The last hypothesis tested if brand loyalty influences repeat visits. Earlier research suggests that customer relationship helps improve customer satisfaction (Feinberg & Kadam, 2002), which influences customer loyalty and customer retention and subsequent profitability (Abdullateef & Salleh, 2013). It is further supported by Wahab et al. (2011), stating that maximizing customer satisfaction and minimizing complaints are key results of successful guest relationships and brand loyalty. In addition, some senior managers (H03P05, H02P04) mentioned that if the customer experience is good, the hotel rating will increase, which will make guests feel that the hotel is like a second home. As a result, the guests will be more willing to come to this hotel, take pride, and invite friends to come. The findings from H4 testing provide strong support for the notion that brand loyalty positively affects repeat visits (0.885; $p < 0.001$).

Overall, three hypotheses were supported except for H3 results, which suggest that in the case of luxury hotels in Tianjin, the service delivery system does not influence brand loyalty.

4.1 Implications, Recommendations, and Limitations

An important theoretical implication is that the study has developed a new conceptual model in the context of luxury hotels in Tianjin, China. The model's test findings add a new dimension to the literature by informing that the service delivery system has no significant relationship with brand loyalty. In other areas, a positive relationship is identified between hotel guests and WOM with brand loyalty, as the literature suggests (Abdullateef & Salleh, 2013; Wahab et al., 2011). Brand loyalty leads to repeat visits. It has been supported by our study as well. Interview with senior luxury hotel managers reveals that they agree that guest relationship is crucial for brand loyalty and repeat visits. The study adds to the literature linked with the Chinese hotel industry. Although, as part of practical implications, the luxury hotels in Tianjin lack having an effective guest relationship system in place which also builds humanism in the industry, staff training was identified as a strong recommendation in this area. Our study provides guidelines for hotel managers in several areas. The humanistic perspective of our study sheds light on the individual and their interest. This should be understood by hotel managers who plan and implement hotels' operations.

10 Exploring Guests Relations, Brand Loyalty, and Repeat Visits ...

The study is not without some limitations. One of the limitations is that the sample was restricted to Tianjin, China. Further, there could be subjectivity in responses. Finally, the interview information collected in this study may not be completely reliable because hoteliers are sometimes afraid or unwilling to share the truth. These limitations should be considered when using the findings of the study.

Action Prompts
Build relationships with customers that patronize your brand.
    Use WOM to resolve customer complaints.
    Realize the importance of WOM recommendations.

Study Questions

1. What is the impact of humanism and guest relations in building brand loyalty in hotels? Explain with examples.
2. What is the role of Customer Relationship Management in building a competitive advantage?
3. Discuss and explain the importance of the conceptual model used in this Chapter (Fig. 1).

Chapter Summary
The main objective of this study was to assess the impacts of guests relations, WOM, and service delivery systems on brand loyalty and repeat visits in luxury hotels in Tianjin, China. Some views of senior local hotel managers were accumulated through informal interviews.

The first hypothesis tests the relationship between the guests and Tianjin's luxury hotels on brand loyalty. What do hotel guests perceive to be important in building a relationship with the hotels? The current study determines that relationship with hotel guests through sustained services and products, impact brand loyalty. Can hotel match customers' needs with the premise of establishing customer relationships?

The second hypothesis tested the impact of WOM recommendations to build brand loyalty. Are recommendations from travel agents, friends, and other influential people enough to build brand loyalty? Addressing customer complaints improves customer loyalty and retention while enhancing customer belongingness towards the organizations (Bhat & Darzi, 2016). Hence WOM has a significant impact to build loyalty.

The third hypothesis tested if the service delivery system had any impact on brand loyalty. Kaushal (2015) states that an important dimension in customer relationship management is technology and automation, which covers managing customer service activities by a single service platform. Technology is now frequently used by the hotel industry. Several studies suggest that customer loyalty will be positively affected by higher customer satisfaction. For example, personalized services, protecting individual data, providing convenient and flexible payment methods, convenient and efficient customer service, and responding to customer needs to increase customer satisfaction, relationships, and loyalty.

The last hypothesis tested if brand loyalty influences repeat visits. Earlier research suggests that customer relationship helps improve customer satisfaction (Feinberg & Kadam, 2002), which influences customer loyalty and customer retention and subsequent profitability (Abdullateef & Salleh, 2013). It is further supported by Wahab et al. (2011), stating that maximizing customer satisfaction and minimizing complaints are key results of successful guest relationships and brand loyalty. In addition, some senior managers mentioned that if the customer experience is good, the hotel rating will increase, which will make guests feel that the hotel is like a second home. As a result, the guests will be more willing to come to this hotel, take pride, and invite friends to come.

Overall, three hypotheses were supported except for H3 results, which suggest that in the case of luxury hotels in Tianjin, the service delivery system does not influence brand loyalty.

Appendix A

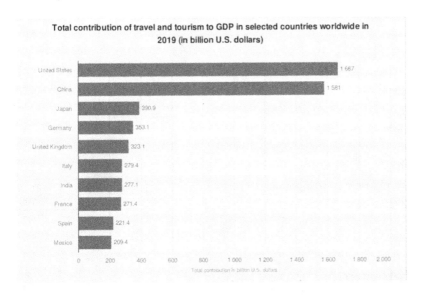

Source Travel and tourism: direct contribution to GDP worldwide 2019, by country Published by Statista Research Department, Feb 4, 2021.

Appendix B

Sample Characteristics

Sample characteristics	Frequency (n)	%
Age		
18–30 years	159	43.2
31–40 years	174	47.3
41–50 years	17	4.6
51–60 years	16	4.3
61—and above	2	0.5
Total	**368**	**100**
Gender		

(continued)

(continued)

Sample characteristics	Frequency (n)	%
Male	199	54.1
Female	169	45.9
Total	**569**	**100**
Income Level		
Below average	39	10.6
Average	115	31.3
Above average	176	47.8
Much Above Average	38	10.3
Total	**368**	**100**
Highest Level of Education		
High school and below	45	12.2
Specialist	87	23.6
Undergraduate	185	50.3
Master's Degree and above	51	13.9
Total	**368**	**100**

References

Abdullateef, A. O., & Salleh, S. M. (2013). Does customer relationship management influence call center quality performance? An empirical industry analysis. *Total Quality Management & Business Excellence, 24*(9–10), 1035–1045.

Ameri, H. S. (2015). The impact of Word of Mouth promotion on brand equity dimensions in sports services. *College of Physical Education and Sport Sciences Urmia University.*

Anderson, J. C., & Gerbing, D. W. (1988). Structural equation modeling in practice: A review and recommended two-step approach. *Psychological Bulletin, 103*(3), 411.

Ansary, A., & Nik Hashim, N. M. H. (2018). Brand image and equity: The mediating role of brand equity drivers and moderating effects of product type and word of mouth. *Review of Managerial Science, 12*(4), 969–1002.

Bagozzi, R. P., & Yi, Y. (1988). On the evaluation of structural equation models. *Journal of the Academy of Marketing Science, 16*(1), 74–94.

Banga, G., Kumar, B., & Goyal, H. (2013). Customer relationship management in the hotel industry. *Pacific Business Review International, 5*(12), 71–81.

Bhat, S. A., & Darzi, M. A. (2016). Customer relationship management. *The International Journal of Bank Marketing, 34*(3), 388–410.

Bowen, J. T., & Chen, S. L. (2001). The relationship between customer loyalty and customer satisfaction. *International Journal of Contemporary Hospitality Management, 1*(2), 213–217.

Browne, M. W., & Cudeck, R. (1993). *Alternative ways of assessing model fit. Testing structural equation models.* KA Bollen and JS Long.

Buttle, F. (2004). *Customer relationship management: Concepts and tools.* Elsevier Butterworth-Heinemann.

Byrne, B. M. (2001). Structural equation modeling with AMOS, EQS, and LISREL: Comparative approaches to testing for the factorial validity of a measuring instrument. *International Journal of Testing, 1*(1), 55–86.

Cheng, L. Y., & Yang, C. W. (2013). Conceptual analysis and implementation of an integrated CRM system for service providers. *Service Business, 7*, 307–328.

Chetioui, Y., Abbar, H., & Benabbou, Z. (2017). The impact of CRM dimensions on customer retention in Hospitality industry: Evidence from the Moroccan hotel sector. *Journal of Research in Marketing, 8*(1), 652–660.

Coker, A., Iyamabo, J., & Otubanjo, O. (2013). Investigating service responsiveness in customer perception of the corporate logo. *International Journal of Business and Management, 8*(11).

Cox, A., Chicksand, D., & Yang, T. (2007). The proactive alignment of sourcing with marketing and branding strategies: A food service case. *Supply Chain Management: An International Journal.*

Cronbach, L. J. (1951). Coefficient alpha and the internal structure of tests. *Psychometrika, 16*(3), 297–334.

Edelman, D. C. (2010). Branding in the digital age: You're spending your money in all the wrong places by David. *Harvard Business Review, 88*(12), 62–69.

Feinberg, R., & Kadam, R. (2002). E-CRM web service attributes as determinants of customer satisfaction with retail websites. *International Journal of Service Industry Management, 13*(5), 432–451.

Fornell, C., & Larcker, D. F. (1981). Evaluating structural equation models with unobservable variables and measurement error. *Journal of Marketing Research, 18*(1), 39–50.

Fornell, C., & Wernerfelt, B. (1987). Defensive marketing strategy by customer complaint management: A theoretical analysis. *Journal of Marketing Research, 24*(4), 337–346.

Fornier, S. (1996). *A consumer-based relationship framework for strategic brand management* (published PhD dissertation, University of Florida).

Garrido-Moreno, A., & Padilla-Meléndez, A. (2011). Analyzing the impact of knowledge management on CRM success: The mediating effects of organizational factors. *International Journal of Information Management, 31*(5), 437–444.

Gilbert, D. C. (1996). Relationship marketing and airline loyalty schemes. *Tourism Management, 17*(8), 575–582.

Gustafsson, A., Johnson, M. D., & Roos, I. (2005). The effects of customer satisfaction, relationship commitment dimensions, and triggers on customer retention. *Journal of Marketing, 69*(4), 210–218.

Hair Jr, J. F., Babin, B. J., & Anderson, R. E. (2010). *A global p-erspect-ivie*. Kennesaw: Kennesaw State University.

Han, H., & Hyun, S. S. (2012). An extension of the four-stage loyalty model: The critical role of positive switching barriers. *Journal of Travel & Tourism Marketing, 29*(1), 40–56.

Homburg, C., Koschate, N., & Hoyer, W. D. (2005). Do satisfied customers really pay more? A study of the relationship between customer satisfaction and willingness to pay. *Journal of Marketing, 69*, 84–96.

Jacoby, J., & Kyner, D. B. (1973). Brand loyalty versus repeat purchase behavior. *Journal of Marketing Research, 10*(1), 1–9.

Kasim, A., & Minai, B. (2009). Linking CRM strategy, customer performance measures, and performance in the hotel industry. *International Journal of Economics and Management, 3*(2), 297–316.

Kaushal, A. (2015). Customer relationship management practices adopted by the hospitality industry in selected states of North India. *Journal of Hospitality Application & Research, 10*(1), 1–14.

Kim, W. G., Han, J. S., & Lee, E. (2001). Effects of relationship marketing on repeat purchase and word of mouth. *Journal of Hospitality & Tourism Research, 25*(3), 272–288.

Kincaid, J. W. (2003). *Customer relationship management: Getting it right!* Prentice Hall Professional.

Kirmaci, S. (2012). Customer relationship management and customer loyalty: A survey in the sector of banking. *International Journal of Business and Social Science, 3*(3), 282–291.

Koçoğlu, D., & Kirmaci, S. (2012). Customer relationship management and customer loyalty: A survey in the sector of banking. *International Journal of Business and Social Science, 3*(3), 282–291.

Kotler, P., Bowen, T., Makens, J. C., & Baloglu, S. (2017). *Marketing for hospitality and tourism* (7th ed.). Pearson.

Ling, R., & Yen, D. C. (2001). Customer relationship management: An analysis framework and implementation strategies. *Journal of Computer Information Systems, 41*(3), 82–97.

Lo, A. S., Stalcup, L. D., & Lee, A. (2010). Customer relationship management for hotels in Hong Kong. *International Journal of Contemporary Hospitality Management, 22*(2), 139–159.

Majid, M. A. A., Alias, M. A. M., Samsudin, A., & Chik, C. T. (2016). Assessing customer-based brand equity ratings in family restaurant. *Procedia Economics and Finance, 37,* 183–189.

Mithas, S., Krishnan, M. S., & Fornell, C. (2005). Why do customer relationship management applications affect customer satisfaction? *Journal of Marketing, 69*(4), 201–208.

Nguyen, T., Sherif, J., & Newby, M. (2007). Strategies for successful CRM implementation. *Information Management & Computer Security, 15*(2), 102–115.

Özen, U. (2013). Contemporary humanism: Sartre's existentialist humanism and Heideggerean humanism. *Mediterranean Journal of Social Sciences, 4*(6), 665–665.

Padilla-Meléndez, A., & Garrido-Moreno, A. (2013). Customer relationship management in hotels: Examining critical success factors. *Current Issues in Tourism, 17*(5), 387–396.

Palmer, A., McMahon-Beattie, U., & Beggs, R. (2000). A structural analysis of hotel sector loyalty programs. *International Journal of Contemporary Hospitality Management, 12*(1), 54–60.

Payne, A., & Frow, P. (2005). A strategic framework for customer relationship management. *Journal of Marketing, 69*(4), 167–176.

Rinova, R., & Putri, N. M. D. R. (2020). The effect of digital marketing and brand awareness of intention to visit millennials generation to Tanjung Lesung. *HUMANIS (Humanities, Management and Science Proceedings), 1*(1).

Roberts, K., Varki, S., & Brodie, R. (2003). Measuring the quality of relationships in consumer services: An empirical study. *European Journal of Marketing, 37*(1/2), 169–196.

Santouridis, I., & Veraki, A. (2017). Customer relationship management and customer satisfaction: The mediating role of relationship quality. *Total Quality Management and Business Excellence, 28*(9–10), 1122–1133.

Singh, H. (2006). The importance of customer satisfaction in relation to customer loyalty and retention. *Journal of the Academy of Marketing Science, 60*(193–225), 46.

Swift, R. S. (2001). *Accelerating customer relationships using CRM and relationship technologies.* Ringgold Inc.

Tahir, I. M., & Zulkifli, Z. (2011). A preliminary analysis of CRM practices among banks from the customers' perspectives. *Journal of Public Administration and Governance, 1*(1), 274–285.

Vaeztehrani, A., Modarres, M., & Aref, S. (2015). Developing an integrated revenue management and customer relationship management approach in the hotel industry. *Journal of Revenue and Pricing Management, 14*(2), 97–119.

Wahab, S., Othman, A. K., & Rahman, B. A. (2011). The evolution of relationship marketing (RM) towards customer relationship management (CRM): A step towards customer service excellence. In *The 2nd International Research Symposium in Service Management Yogyakarta, Indonesia* (pp. 327–335).

Wu, C. C. (2011). The impact of hospital brand image on service quality, patient satisfaction and loyalty. *African Journal of Business Management, 5*(12), 4873–4882.

Xiong, L., King, C., & Hu, C. (2014). Where is the love? Investigating multiple memberships and hotel customer loyalty. *International Journal of Contemporary Hospitality Management, 26*(4), 572–592.

Yi, Y. (1990). *A critical review of consumer satisfaction.* American Marketing Association.

Part III
Societal Impact Perspectives

This last part brings in a "social impact" theme. Topics such as vulnerability, sustainability, and corporate social responsibility inform the discussion. Also very relevant, in the light of the impact of global health crises on the industry and its humanistic core, is the discussion on the pandemic; the contributors offer recommendations towards recovery.

11

Hospitality, Tourism and Vulnerability

Vivian Isichei

V. Isichei (✉)
Wavecrest College of Hospitality, Lagos, Nigeria
e-mail: isichei.vivian@gmail.com

1 Introduction

Vulnerability is an openness to attack or hurt, either physically or in other ways and the persons susceptible to this in the context of this book are mostly those who are involved actively in organizations offering and or receiving hospitality and tourism services, the elderly and persons with disability and special needs. This chapter presents humanistic perspectives as regards vulnerability in the hospitality and tourism industries in general (of employers, of employees and of guests); as regards persons with special needs (persons with disability and the elderly) and as regards safety in terms of work-life balance and physical and psychological safety.

We human beings are vulnerable to many kinds of affliction and most of us are at some time afflicted by serious ills. How we cope is only in small part up to us. It is most often to others that we owe our survival and, more than that, our flourishing, as we encounter bodily illness and injury, nutritional deficiencies, mental defectiveness and disturbance or human aggression and neglect. This dependence on others for protection and sustenance is most obvious in early childhood and in old age. But the years between these first and last stages our lives are marked by longer or shorter periods of injury, illness or other disablement, while some among us are disabled for their entire lives (MacIntyre, 1999).

The hospitality and tourism industries are in themselves also vulnerable to various situations such as: climate change, fraud, misconceptions, unfavorable government policies, global crises (terrorism and natural disasters), restrictions and threats posed by illnesses like the coronavirus and prejudices. In this chapter, vulnerability is taken to be the degree to which a system is susceptible to and unable to cope with a shock or stressor. It is a product of the interaction between exposure, sensitivity and adaptive capacity (Fyall & Alvarez, 2020). While hospitality and tourism contribute a great deal to a country's gross domestic product and economy in general, they can also be negatively exploited to give room for abuses such as legal and illegal sex tourism in some places. Some countries restrict themselves to niche tourism (such as religious pilgrimages) for fear of abuses to their culture while others take the risk of embracing tourism with all its consequences good and bad. Also, in some places, hotels still grapple with the misconception of being thought to be brothels. Many countries in Europe are facing over-tourism (where large groups of tourists travel all at the same time to the same destination).

In a study conducted by Wen et al. (2020) on sex trafficking, it was discovered that vulnerabilities that human traffickers can exploit are identifiable in the hotel sector, as many use hotels as conduits for human trafficking (see also Paraskevas & Brookes, 2018b). Even worse, hotel employees and managers may unknowingly serve as "guardians" of human traffickers and victims due to a lack of awareness around this criminal activity within tourism and hospitality businesses, largely due to an absence of training or of authority to act (Paraskevas & Brookes, 2018a). The two major issues this chapter discusses are: how employees, employers and guests in the hospitality and tourism industry are vulnerable and how the hospitality and tourism industry treats persons who are vulnerable.

To aid the discussion, the chapter offers an in-depth explanation and practical application of the concentric circles, notable characteristics of the human person; the *actus essendi*; and the "throw away"[1] culture as these insights are invaluable in dealing vulnerabilities and related problematic issues.

2 Vulnerability in the Hospitality and Tourism Industries in General

Employers are vulnerable to policies that hinder their activities, such as multiple taxation and unfavorable labor laws. They are also susceptible to employees who engage in upward bullying (Wallace et al., 2010) and to troublesome guests who, in order to take advantage, create situations in which the employer is compelled to compensate them. Employees are vulnerable in the areas of over-utilization and burnout, low pay with a minuscule or no welfare package, emotional and psychological abuse from toxic work environments, unjust accusations from guests and colleagues, etc. Guests are vulnerable to being taken advantage of through "tipping", bad quality service, deceptive marketing, etc.

---

[1] Disposal of anything that is not seen as useful or is considered a burden at any point in time.

The very definition of hospitality opposes vulnerability as can be seen in its Latin root—*hospitalitat, hospitalitas*—meaning "entertainment of guests". The Merriam-Webster dictionary defines hospitality as the hospitable treatment, reception or disposition of guests and also as the activity or business of providing services to guests in hotels, restaurants, bars, etc. It is also defined as the provision of food, drink and accommodation to guests and the provision of a home away from home. Tourism, according to the United Nations World Tourism Organization, is defined as "activities of persons traveling to and staying in different places for not more than a consecutive year for leisure, business or traveling purpose" —which makes even more acute the need for a "home away from home" for those brief periods.

Vulnerability shows the weak side of humans that ought to be protected by other humans. Whether or not this protection is given depends on the deep understanding of the bedrock ideas on which the hospitality and tourism industry is built—the notions of care, safety and trust evoked by the above concepts of providing hospitable treatment, providing a home away from home. Through safeguarding the concentric circles, protection can be established and strengthened within the industry.

3 The Concentric Circles

The concentric circles can be used to explain the total well-being of a human person which the hospitality and tourism industries are committed to achieving in the delivery of their services. The nucleus of the concentric circles is the human person. The circles begin from the innermost circle to the outermost circle; thus, we have the basic benefits, higher benefits, social benefits and the transcendental benefits. The first circle, the basic benefits, refers to the basic corporeal needs of the person. If these are not taken care of in a balanced way, then there is a disorder produced in the person and this ultimately will affect society. Through the body, i.e., corporeality, the whole person is reached body and soul. The basic benefits are food (nutrition), housing, clothing and order.

11 Hospitality, Tourism and Vulnerability 215

3.1 The Basic Benefits

- Food (Nutrition): is for corporeal, mental and psychic health. Eating is more than a social function; it is also a protective factor: scientific studies show that some disorders such as obesity, bulimia and anorexia are caused by a lack of proper nutrition. Food nourishes the body and the soul.
- Housing: Hygiene, decoration, beauty and feeling at home are ways to aid the integral development of the person. It is good to declutter occasionally, both externally and internally. The cleanliness and neatness of the place of accommodation reflect the dignity of the persons who live in it.
- Clothing: This mirrors the dignity of a person. We dress to cover our interiority from others' gaze, to respect others, as a sign of identity, as a protective measure from harsh weather conditions, and as a social means of communicating ideals, customs, values, etc.
- Order: Material orderliness transmits serenity to everyone around and helps maintain an interior orderliness within the person.

3.2 The Higher Benefits

This circle solidifies personal identity and self-esteem and makes them grow because the person feels taken care of by another. Interdependence plays a big role in our maturity because we realize that we are not self-sufficient. No man is an island; our limitations and opportunities lead us to relate and learn from others. Indeed, to be a person entails being a being in relation. It is in this second circle that the notion of protecting the vulnerable is embedded.

3.3 The Social Benefits

- Gratuitousness: This is the realization that things are given to one as gifts, and it leads to respect for creation and created beings.

- Spirit of service: This is about sharing our interior richness, realizing that others care for one should move one to care for them and to serve them in return.
- Resilience: This is being able to bear problems because one possesses interior strength.
- Ecology: This leads one to take care of Mother Earth by avoiding the "throw away" mentality, taking care of things so they last longer, and avoiding consumerism[2] and materialism.[3]
- Social responsibility: This is considering things not as one's only, but as things held for the common good. It involves taking care of the vulnerable and sharing what one has with others.
- Interpersonal relationships: In the home and workplace, one learns to relate with others. It is here that one is understood and cared for. One is loved for being oneself and not for what one can do or possess.
- Humanization of work: The nucleus for work in the home is to work for the persons as persons, i.e., serving others not because of what one will gain, not because of money nor of becoming successful but because one cares for them as persons, and this should be applied in every form of hospitality.

3.4　The Transcendental Benefits

This is the joy of self-giving by the actor or the persons who serve. The slogan for the service industry ought to be "We take care of you so that you can take care of others". It involves care of anyone in need, especially the aged, children, the sick, those chronically ill, the handicapped, and anyone who is vulnerable at any point in time. According to Bertolaso and Rocchi (2020), caring bestows dignity and value on both the carer and the person cared for.

---

[2] Consumerism is the idea that increasing the consumption of goods and services purchased in the market is always a desirable goal and that a person's well-being and happiness depend fundamentally on obtaining consumer goods and material possessions.

[3] The theory that physical matter is the only reality and that everything, including thought, feeling, mind, and will, can be explained in terms of matter and physical phenomena; the theory or attitude that physical well-being and worldly possessions constitute the greatest good and highest value in life.

In the provision of food, drink and accommodation, the basic benefits are fulfilled. In providing a healthy work environment, the higher, social and transcendental benefits are met. It is precisely in the fulfillment of the concentric circles that protection from vulnerability is achieved. In practice, this takes as many varied forms as there are ways of caring for people in the hospitality and tourism industry.

4 Persons with Disability and Care of the Elderly

The scope of the hospitality and tourism industries encompasses hotels, restaurants, service apartments, tour agencies, restaurants, theme parks, resorts, out-door catering, the welfare sector, etc. The welfare sector consists of hospices, orphanages, old people's homes, etc., and it is widely known as a sector that is not-for-profit and that is focused on care for the elderly and for persons with disability and special needs.

Realist philosophy defines a person as *suppositum*, that is, an individual substance whole and entire which is not part of nor assumed by another being. From this comes this classic definition[4] of a person as an individual substance of a rational nature (Martí Andrés, 2017). The *actus essendi* of a person is *"being a person"*, not the totality/rationality/incommunicability which are properties of the person. With this in mind, we can say that disability of any kind does not hamper the dignity of the human person. The elderly and those with disability and special needs may be limited in their psychomotor and intellectual abilities but nonetheless, as persons, they should be treated in accordance with the dignity they possess.

The tendency to despise, avoid and or "dispose of" persons with disability and special needs and the elderly is high nowadays because of a widespread inclination towards utilitarianism,[5] materialism and consumerism, hence the adoption of the "throw away" culture. In fact,

---

[4] Formulated by Boethius, a philosopher.
[5] A moral doctrine that highlights utility (use) as the moral principle of things above any other characteristic or quality.

the absence of a human faculty is only a *negation* (an absence of something that naturally should be present) and cannot lead to "discarding" the whole person in any way.

The hospitality and tourism industries being service industries play a huge role in recognizing the dignity of the human person in persons with disabilities and the elderly. They do this by providing fit-for-purpose facilities such as ramps in vehicles, wheelchairs, accessible restrooms and sturdy flat floors for ease of movement around resorts, hotels, parks, restaurants and accessible hotel rooms with technology aiding the utility of the facility in terms of access to power, water, the bedroom and security locks. In addition, the creation of tour packages that involve fit-for-purpose vehicles for ease of movement around destination sites and the search for ways to integrate them in the industries as guests and staff in an attractive way is other ways of respecting their dignity. Special job positions in the "back-of-the-house[6]" can be reserved for persons with disability and or special needs. The relevant unit in the organization can also dedicate a large chunk of its corporate social responsibility to the elderly and persons with disability.

Four notable characteristics of a human person—intimacy, dialogue, giving and freedom (von Balthasar, 2000)—play a big role in the care for the elderly and persons with disability and special needs and also in ensuring personal safety.

4.1 Notable Characteristics of a Person

Intimacy is that which the person alone knows, and the person alone can manifest this intimacy to the others through dialogue. At the same time, the person is the master of his or her own acts and principle of all his or her actions expressed through his or her freedom. The person can also give—presupposing the capacity to receive or accept—through that same freedom. These characteristics stand out in the context of hospitality and tourism because they constitute a backdrop—of understanding the

---

[6] The functional areas of the hotel in which employees have little or no guest contact, such as the kitchen, the business offices, the laundry, housekeeping departments, etc., also known as BOH.

person and personal boundaries—against which these industries deliver goods and services and protect the persons they serve. For example, hospitality respects the privacy of customers by protecting their personal data and personal belongings, and tourists are provided a tour guide to dialogue with all through their tour, etc.

4.2 Intimacy

This refers to the acknowledgment that each human being has something interior which the person alone knows, and which is hidden from the others. Intimacy is the maximum grade of immanence, not only because the person alone knows but because it is from within it that inventions and ideas come. Intimacy can grow. It also has a creative aspect, for example, creating various food plating designs, finding a way to achieve service recovery, deliberately choosing to practice a virtue, etc.

Intimacy is the interior ambient or ambience as proper or personal, as opposed to the exterior—that place where the person alone can enter and only he or she is master. This is the *interior world* or *human sanctuary*. Part of the intimacy is in its being unique and dynamic. No intimacy is equal to another because each one is unrepeatable or incommunicable. Each person is unique because this is not someone nor a "what" but a "*Who*". Thus, the person is closely associated with a name by which society recognizes the person. Hence, the person answers the question—"Who are you?" which implies a name which is proper, personal and non-transferable. Persons are not interchangeable, unlike chickens. Intimacy is that which no one else may take over.

4.3 Dialogue

One form of manifesting intimacy is by speaking. The human being needs to dialogue; he or she is a dialoguing being. We need to express ourselves; we need to speak with an other person—to a someone rather than to an object. We need to encounter the "you", otherwise we address ourselves to nature, animals, etc. Lack of communication is often the cause of discordance both at the interpersonal and at a wider level. This then emphasizes the idea that there is no "I" without a "you". The knowledge of oneself or one's proper identity is arrived at only by inter-subjectivity, i.e., an encounter with others. This process is the formation of the human personality, which molds the character. It is a never-ending process, an educational dialogue.

4.4 To Give

Human beings have a capacity to give that is actuated when, as a person, they extract something from their intimacy and give it to another as "something of value". This action involves the use of the will and can also be described as effusion, which entails going out of oneself and is what is most proper to a person. Thus, intimacy is constituted and enriched by what others give, with what we receive as gifts. This also happens with the formation of the human personality, whereby the richness of intimacy is proportional to the number of giving and receiving interchanges.

4.5 Freedom

A person is free because he or she is the master of his or her own actions and the principle of those actions. It does not refer to the act of being but rather, to the principle of the person's actions. Aristotle defines freedom as "*causa sui*" (cause of oneself) when one determines oneself with the choices that one makes.

Many important reflections can be made around these characteristics and the industry. For example, the type of policies translated to standard operating procedures[7] is important to protect vulnerable persons since if this is not done, their intimacy, their freedom, dialogue and or their giving capacity can be overtly or covertly taken away from them.

---

[7] A document that specifies a certain method for the accomplishment of a task.

5 Safety: Work-Life Balance, Physical and Psychological Safety

To be safe is knowing and feeling secure interiorly and exteriorly. Safety has its roots in the concentric circles, especially the basic and higher benefits. Guests will not patronize any hospitality or tourism outfit that is not secure. Unfortunately, organizations tend to give priority to external safety such as the prevention of accidents, thefts, fraud, data breaches, etc., while neglecting internal workplace safety for staff such as upward and downward bullying, emotional and bodily exploitation, sexual harassment, physical and psychological burnout from working long hours in addition to not being compensated, denial of breaks, off days, sick leaves, annual leaves, lack of dignified staff meals, lack of proper work equipment and agents, lack of basic amenities for staff, lack of proper welfare packages as regards health care and even a lack of provision of staff uniforms. Figuratively speaking, the list is endless but one major point for emphasis stems from recognizing the substantial unity of body and soul. If the body is not taken care of then it affects the soul and vice versa, thereby destabilizing the person and also hindering productivity.

One subtle area for checking that there is psychological safety is in the creation of a work environment that is not characterized by "fear". If fear rules, employees will not have the enabling environment to be creative, to be a part of the decision-making process, or to express themselves and their concerns as regards the business. The workplace would be rigid, hostile and full of threats of queries, outright dismissals or even physical abuse inflicted on persons from their supervisors. This is a cause for worry especially for the hospitality and tourism industry which is very competitive and demands creativity as new trends emerge daily.

A lot of scholarly articles have been written on work-life balance and work-life integration: Bharithi and Rajapushpam (2017) on work-life balance of food and beverage service employees; Derry and Jago (2009) on a framework for work-life balance practices; Blomme et al. (2013) on the relationship between organizational culture and negative work-home interference, but our focus here will be on its relationship with the "telos". A human person has a "telos"—a Greek word which means "end". By end, we mean purpose which is the perfection proper to the nature of a thing. Other beings tend to their end spontaneously while humans tend to their end consciously. They do have a natural tendency to reach towards their end though; this is embedded in the dynamism of the soul and extends to its powers. The importance of work-life balance and integration lies in that humans cannot reach the "telos" without happiness, and human happiness comes from a transcendental fulfillment that does not result from just the workplace but from a balance of every aspect of being including family and social relations.

Humans are not solitary beings; they live together with others. They build up relationships with others which gives rise to societies. Sociability is a natural tendency for human beings because they tend to join one another in order to achieve their goals. Sociability is also a response to the natural inclination of human beings to communicate their own good to others. Practical implications of this include the need for hospitality and tourism organizations to create work shifts that support work-life balance and work-life integration. An example in the hotel industry is running eight hours shifts with one-hour break, giving each employee two days off weekly and an annual leave including sick leaves and casual leaves for emergencies. These, just to mention a few, are ways of achieving a certain level of work-life balance.

Ways to minimize vulnerability include justice-oriented organizational features such as creating an open-door policy for grievances to be poured out through the right channel, having a fair and transparent policy on promotions, rewards and punishments; allowing all levels of staff to contribute to decision-making; boosting staff professionalism with training programs; paying a just wage; establishing a just policy on tips given by guests and paying compensation for overtime work. One practical idea that perhaps speaks more directly to the issue of vulnerability is that of creating protective structures for staff vulnerable to abuse, such as room attendants, air hostesses, kitchen staff, waiters, waitresses and those staff in the frontlines. Examples of these protective structures could be policies that ensure that no staff is left alone with guests; providing a decent dress code for staff; empowerment for them to call for security when they sense danger and tactful policies to place guests who have been unruly to staff on a blacklist.

6 Initiatives Working to Protect the Vulnerable in the Hospitality and Tourism Industry

ECPAT[8]-USA is a nonprofit organization that advocates for policies to protect sexually exploited children. ECPAT-USA announced that Real Hospitality Group (RHG) has become the first hotel management company in the United States to enter the fight against the commercial sexual exploitation of children by signing the Tourism Child-Protection Code of Conduct (Hohnholz, 2012). This was done in July 2012 and the Code focuses on the protection of children from sexual exploitation in the travel and tourism industries. As a subscriber to the Code, RHG will develop and implement policies that condemn child trafficking and provide training to help their employees identify and report trafficking activities. The company will also help raise awareness among customers and business partners about the issue and about the Code of Conduct. In the United States, the Code has been signed by 7 companies to date: Carlson Companies, Delta Airlines, Global Exchange, Nix Conference and Meeting Management, Hilton Worldwide, Millennium Hotel St. Louis and Wyndham.

Palms Australia is an organization that started in Sydney in 1954 to help develop local and international community projects. Palms Australia recruits, prepares, sends and supports program participants to mentor counterparts with the aim to sustainably reduce poverty. These programs occur in a number of countries, including Australia, and operate in collaboration with local partner organizations. Palms Australian Child and Vulnerable Adults Protection Policy and Code of Conduct was reviewed, amended and approved by the Palms Australia Board of Directors on 8 April 2020 to cover various issues such as types of abuses, confidentiality, handling particularly vulnerable people, risk management and training of staff to mention a few.

In conclusion, it is a duty of each human person to look after human dignity for oneself and for others, regardless of the challenges. In this

---

[8] End Child Prostitution, Child Pornography and the Trafficking of Children for Sexual Purposes.

V. Isichei

vein, the hospitality and tourism industry and its owners, investors and professionals are called to embrace the fulfillment of the concentric circles, the notable characteristics of the human person, the actus essendi and the telos in actively protecting the vulnerable and protecting itself from vulnerability.

Action Prompts
(for employers)

Establish policies that promote work-family integration for employees such as 8–10 hours per shift, stipulated off days, sick leaves, annual leaves, casual leaves and study leaves. Also, establish an all-inclusive welfare package and incentives for employees including win–win policies for tips received from guests and service charges.

Do what you can to influence the creation of suitable job roles for persons with disabilities. Establish a special standard operating procedure on handling guests with disabilities.

(for employees)

Put in quality hours of work, give due notice before resignation, make up any hours of work lost due to absenteeism or lateness.

Treat persons with disabilities with dignity by addressing them by their names; aid them with whatever they need in the organization and go the extra mile to make them feel comfortable.

(for government, NGOs, CSOs, investors and owners)

Prepare policies and codes of conduct to prevent abuses of any kind to employers, employees and guests/clients. Ensure that these policies are implemented and enforced.

Study Questions

1. State three ways in which the people in the hospitality and tourism industry are vulnerable and, with your study of more humanistic perspectives, give concrete points to deal with these vulnerabilities in the light of any of the following:

a. Man's substantial unity of body and soul.
b. The notable characteristics of the human person.
c. The concentric circles.

2. Explain the importance of work-life balance in relation to "the telos". Give concrete ideas in creating protective structures and "safety nets" to persons susceptible to vulnerabilities in the hospitality and tourism industries.

3. A person is an individual substance of a rational nature and the *actus essendi* of a person is not the totality/rationality/incommunicability of that person but rather the *actus essendi* is "being a person". Discuss this using a relevant example in the hospitality and tourism industry regarding care for the elderly and persons with disabilities or special needs.

Chapter Summary

This chapter attempted to answer the questions; how are employees, employers and guests in the hospitality and tourism industry vulnerable? And how does the hospitality and tourism industry treat persons who are vulnerable? Vulnerability stems from a lack of protection for those susceptible to various harm and it is the right and duty of every human person to defend and protect the dignity of the human person. Vulnerability in the context of hospitality and tourism is very important because it provides goods and services that protect man and creates a home which can easily be exploited to harm man. In past and recent times, the hospitality and tourism industries have been vulnerable to government policies, natural disasters, pandemics, epidemics, multiple taxation, exploitation by criminals, terrorism, a misconception as brothels, a breeding ground for various abuses, etc. Workers in turn have experienced low salaries and enormous work hours/load, a lack of prestige among peers to mention a few. Employers have also been exploited by guests and their employees. Persons with disability seeking drink/food/accommodation or employment have suffered rejection. All these necessitates a call to action for adequate policies to be in place

> to protect the vulnerable because persons with disability and the elderly suffer a negation, i.e., an absence in one or more faculty but this does not in any way reduce or take away their dignity as persons. Safety, on other hand, has its roots in the concentric circles and is necessary for the success of any industry beginning with those employed there. Work-life balance and integration contribute greatly to the human person achieving his telos through unifying work with family and social relations. It is important that readers connect the various concepts described in this chapter to the reality, translated not in lofty words or ideas but in concrete deeds seen, felt and lived by everyone.

References

Bertolaso, M., & Rocchi, M. (2020). Specifically human: Human work and care in the age of machines. *Business Ethics: A European Review*, 1–11. https://doi.org/10.1111/beer.12281

Bharithi, S., & Rajapushpam, R. (2017). A study on work life balance of food and beverage service employees at hotels in Salem city. *International Journal of Research in Social Sciences, 7*(9), 427–439. ISSN 2249–2496.

Blomme, R. J., Sok, J., & Tromp, D. M. (2013). The influence of organizational culture on negative work-home interference among highly educated employees in the hospitality industry. *Journal of Quality Assurance in Hospitality and Tourism, 14*(1), 1–23. https://doi.org/10.1080/1528008X.2013.749384

Derry, M., & Jago, L. (2009). A framework for work life balance practices: Addressing the needs of the tourism industry. *Tourism and Hospitality Research, 9*(2), 97–108.

Fyall, A., & Alvarez, S. (2020). *Tourism vulnerability, sustainability and resilience.* Retrieved November 5, 2021, from https://hospitality.ucf.edu/wp-content/uploads/sites/2/2021/02/Fyall-Alvarez-updated-Colloquium-February-12.pdf

Hohnholz, J. (2012). *Real Hospitality Group signs code of conduct to protect children from sexual exploitation.* Retrieved November 6, 2021, from https://

www.bing.com/newtabredir?url=https%3A%2F%2Feturbonews.com% 2F58790%2Freal-hospitality-group-signs-code-conduct-protect-children-sexua%2F

MacIntyre, A. C. (1999). *Dependent rational animals*. Carus Publishing Company.

Martí Andrés, G. (2017). Individual substance of a rational nature—The personifying principle and the nature of the separated soul. *Metaphysics and Person* (1). https://doi.org/10.24310/Metyper.2009.v0i1.2849

Palms Australian Child & Vulnerable Adults Protection Policy & Code of Conduct. (2020). Retrieved November 7, 2021, from https://palms.org.au/wp-content/uploads/2020/12/Safeguarding-Vulnerable-People-Policy-Code-of-Conduct-1.pdf

Paraskevas, A., & Brookes, M. (2018a). Nodes, guardians and signs: Raising barriers to human trafficking in the tourism industry. *Tourism Management, 67*, 147–156.

Paraskevas, A., & Brookes, M. (2018b). Human trafficking in hotels: An 'invisible' threat for a vulnerable industry. *International Journal of Contemporary Hospitality Management, 3*(3), 1996–2014.

von Balthasar, H. U. (2000). *Theo-logic: Theological logical theory I: Truth of the world* (A. J. Walker, Trans.). Ignatius Press

Wallace, B., Johnston, L., & Trenberth, L. (2010). Bullying the boss: The prevalence of upward bullying behaviours. *The Australian and New Zealand Journal of Organisational Psychology, 3*, 66–71. https://doi.org/10.1375/ajop.3.1.66

Wen, J., Goh, E., Klarin, A., & Aston, J. (2020). A systematic review of the sex trafficking-related literature: Lessons for tourism and hospitality research. *Journal of Hospitality and Tourism Management*. https://doi.org/10.1016/j.jhtm.2020.06.001

12

Sustainability Dimensions of Hospitality and Tourism: Care for Our Common Home

Omowumi Ogunyemi and Andrew Onwudinjo

O. Ogunyemi (✉) · A. Onwudinjo
Institute of Humanities, Pan-Atlantic University, Lagos, Nigeria
e-mail: oogunyemi@pau.edu.ng

A. Onwudinjo
e-mail: aonwudinjo@pau.edu.ng

© The Author(s), under exclusive license to Springer Nature Switzerland AG 2022
K. Ogunyemi et al. (eds.), *Humanistic Perspectives in Hospitality and Tourism, Volume II*, Humanism in Business Series,
https://doi.org/10.1007/978-3-030-95585-4_12

1   Introduction

The environment is threatened by natural phenomena. With global warming, melting glaciers are causing a rise in sea levels and various water bodies to overflow their shores and banks causing floods around the world. The rise in ambient temperatures also causes drought, wildfires and difficulties in crop production. Earthquakes, tsunamis, landslides and droughts occur naturally, however, other ecological disasters such as desert encroachments, some floods, chemical spillages, environmental pollution etc. are caused or worsened by unchecked human activity. The ecological concern raised by the effect of some human activity on the environment causing its degradation is a contemporary issue addressed by scholars in many fields (Francis, 2015). Our activity that is largely within our control is often poorly regulated with regard to their effects on the availability and good use of natural resources in a way that will make them last enough to be available for use by many future generations. Various human activities cause the aforementioned damages to different degrees and professionals in different industries can make an effort to avoid the harm caused by their activity. For example, increased vulnerability to health hazards and other negative effects of sustainability issues like climate change, can be traced to the effects of gases released from domestic and industrial productions.

Many activists, firms and individuals have started making conscious efforts to raise awareness of the need for responsible management of ecological resources, encouraging everyone to do their part in maintaining the sustainability of the planet. Like other industries, tourism and hospitality practices can contribute to global warming and it is therefore unsurprising that we need to discuss the role of the professionals in the field for protecting our common home. When faced with choices of processes, it is important for professionals to know the advantages and the impact of implementing sustainability friendly options. As Pope Francis says, 'Everything is connected. Concern for the environment thus needs to be joined to a sincere love for our fellow human beings and an unwavering commitment to resolving the problems of society' (Francis, 2015). This chapter discusses the role of hospitality and tourism in sustainability. It then highlights some opportunities for sustainability practices within the fields and proposes ways of attaining them.

2 Understanding Hospitality and Tourism

People often need to make trips to places away from the location of their usual residence or work. Such trips may be formal (for instance, a business trip or an academic conference) or informal (for example, visiting a friend or relative or vacations). The sojourner often hopes that the basic needs of human comfort will be met by the host whether it be a formal institution, as with hotels and resorts, or informal as with friends and families.

Here, we explore the impact of hospitality and tourism on sustainability, with a view to propose ways of ensuring that such activities use natural resources responsibly thereby helping to sustain the environment. As a prelude to the exploration proper, it is necessary to present the concepts of hospitality and tourism.

Hospitality and tourism are related but distinct concepts which are sometimes used interchangeably. According to Walker and Walker (2014), hospitality as a concept is as old as civilization. Its development from the ancient custom of breaking bread with a passing stranger to the operations of today's multifaceted hospitality conglomerates makes fascinating reading, and interesting comparisons can be made with today's hospitality management. Being hospitable is an attitude that is expected in social relationships at all times. Hospitality is essential to tourism studies and practices, even though as a general concept its meaning is broader than tourism. Kunwar (2017) explains that most professionals in hospitality sectors refer to hospitality as the friendly and welcoming behaviour towards guests. The relationship between guests and hosts is however reciprocal and attaining the goals of each institution requires the collaboration of both hosts and guests. The relationship between the service providers and the client in the context of services offered is complex and generates sustained debates within the hospitality discourse. Other chapters in this book discuss the relationships of service and reciprocity between the hosts and guests. We will only limit ourselves to giving general information on hospitality and tourism to the extent that the information helps us to understand their impact on and role in fostering sustainability.

There are four basic characteristics of hospitality. First, hospitality indicates the behaviour of a host towards a person, often a guest, who is away from home. The second characteristic focusses on the dimension of interrelations, i.e. hospitality is interactive in nature and involves personal contact between the provider and receiver. Thirdly, hospitality comprises of a blend of tangible and intangible factors. The practice involves the use of materials which are quantifiable, but it also entails inputs from the hosts which are not directly quantifiable, for example, an eye for details in making the services provided suited for the client's needs in a more or less personalized way. Finally, the host provides for the guest's security, psychological and physiological comfort (Kunwar, 2017). The characteristics can be enriched by Lashley's (2015) submission that hospitality can be seen as a fundamental and ubiquitous feature of human life, and hospitableness indicates the willingness to be hospitable for its own sake, without any expectation of recompense or reciprocity.

Camilleri (2018) explains that individuals become tourists when they voluntarily leave their normal surroundings, where they reside, to visit another environment where they engage in various activities. Such activities are called tourism. Tourism has grown very fast in recent times with notable impact in economics, on cultural diversity and on the environment. The United Nations World Tourism Organisation (UNWTO) sees tourism as a social, cultural and economic phenomenon that entails the movement of people to countries or places outside their usual environment for personal or business/professional purposes. These people, called visitors may be tourists, excursionists or short-term residents. Their activity contributes to tourism expenditure (Skripak & Ron, 2020) and generates revenue for their hosts. One expects that the revenue generated will include the host's expenses on managing the environment in a way that makes it more attractive to other clients.

Arrangements for tourism and occasions for hospitality can be in both formal and informal settings and both can include sustainability practices. For example, the accommodation subsector of the tourism industry includes formal accommodation such as hotels and guest houses, etc., camping sites, rooms in private houses and bed and breakfast type arrangements (Lickorish & Jenkins, 1997). These options for accommodation will have to manage waste and energy use and could make arrangements that comply with high standards that promote sustainability. Travel agents and tour operators are a key part of another distinct subsector, in addition to the transport sector including airlines, shipping, rail and car hire, cars and coaches. The optimal use of carbon fuels by such transportation can be a source of concern for environmental pollution. There are countries where shopping and production of handmade crafts are associated with tourism and are thus tourism products. Other forms of tourism include urban (or city) tourism, seaside tourism, rural tourism, ecotourism, wine tourism, culinary tourism, health tourism, medical tourism, religious tourism, cultural (or heritage) tourism, sports tourism, educational tourism, business tourism (including meetings, incentives, conferences and events), etc. (Camilleri, 2018).

3 Some Current Issues

A presentation of some aspects of sustainability that are connected to hospitality and tourism is necessary if one is to reflect on the role of hospitality professionals in advancing it. Tourism plays an important role in society. In addition to its economic importance, tourism has recreational and cultural relevance. The challenging effects of tourism on the environment include the management of waste generated and human physical activities that have a direct impact on the environment. For instance, when visitors or tourists do not dispose of plastics and other wastes properly, there can be stagnation and contamination of rivers, pollution of lakes etc. Human excursions into natural parks may also disturb the serenity of wildlife, fauna and landscape of some natural habitats.

Specifically, some aspects to consider when planning sustainability practices in hospitality and tourism include judicious water use, waste reduction and waste management, the use of eco-friendly equipment and chemicals such as green cleaning agents, judicious use of energy and appropriate irrigation of surroundings and management of the environment. While making advertisements, it is possible to engage in green marketing and branding in order to promote environmental sustainability. All these aspects above should constitute important reference points for evaluating the acceptability of practices in hotels and tourist centres. The massive expansion of tourism in the 1950s and 1960s has had a significant impact on the environmental, social and cultural milieu of the tourist sites, the contamination of natural sites, air and water pollution, economic changes, competition with other economic sectors for the use of lands, alterations in the ecosystems, etc. The above examples are some areas in which hospitality professionals can study ways of ensuring judicious use of resources in a way that fosters sustainable development. Implementation of ideas from such studies would go a long way to prevent or mitigate the negative effects that could arise from tourist activities. At the base of the professional care of other humans is the need to recognise their dignity. An interest in fostering sustainability within the practice of hospitality with a view to protect the conserve natural resources and protect the habitat could be understood as a part of the conversations on the concern for humanity. In the case of sustainable practices, one is concerned about the needs of the future generations of humans. Important topics in the sustainability discourse include environmental sustainability and climate change.

4 Environmental Sustainability

Environmental sustainability is one of the challenges of contemporary society. The need to relate with the environment in ways that ensure that future generations will derive maximum benefits from the environment is at the heart of the sustainability discourse. This section presents some issues surrounding environmental sustainability and human activities that could endanger the environment. It looks at how the hospitality and tourism industries have impacted the environment.

Our general existence takes place on this planet which has the specific features that are apt for human inhabitants and it is then our collective responsibility to see to its care and maintain these features that make it possible for us to live and flourish on earth. In line with conversations on sustainable development, scholars affirm that a general approach to understanding environmental stability is seeing it as 'meeting the resource and services needs of current and future generations without compromising the health of the ecosystems that provide them,' ('our common future'). More specifically, Morelli defines environmental sustainability as:

> ... a condition of balance, resilience, and interconnectedness that allows human society to satisfy its needs while neither exceeding the capacity of its supporting ecosystems to continue to regenerate the services necessary to meet those needs nor by our actions diminishing biological diversity. (Morelli, 2011, p. 5)

Touristic activities affect the environment in ways that can modify our 'common future.' An attractive environment, whether natural or manmade, appeals to tourists, and the development of tourism in a locality often depends on maintenance of the areas around such recreational venues (Zaei & Zaei, 2013). Negative impacts from tourism often occur when the level of visitor use exceeds the environment's ability to cope with the use such that the consequent changes exceed acceptable limits (Sunlu, 2003). Some of the negative environmental impacts of tourism: increase in water and energy consumption; increase in pollution (air, water, noise, etc.); destruction of flora and fauna, deforestation; increase in solid waste; disruption of wildlife behaviour and feeding and breeding patterns; crowding and congestion; impact on aesthetic appeal of destination and disturbing ecosystems (Zahedi, 2008).

The popularity of tourist centres is often enhanced by a healthy clean environment and some characteristics of the local culture (Mashika et al., 2020), the activities of tourists in many places can become a threat to this beauty of nature. Marine settings which are popular for tourists are an example. Throughout history, beaches have been by far the most popular, and in particular, beaches that are located near urban centres. Other important locations are the islands, which also include beaches and resorts, hotels and restaurants. Such large-scale recreational centres have contributed to economic development for people and businesses in proximity to them (Orams, 2003).

Sadly, harmful tourist behaviours are today threats to marine life. The attractive blueness of several oceans has been lost because of poor waste disposal and dumping of non-biodegradable waste into the oceans.

These waste deposits, in addition to destroying the beauty of the water and aesthetics of the surrounding areas, threaten the survival of various species of life in the oceans. Plastic debris litter the ocean to the extent that some beaches need to be sealed off and abandoned after several years of exposure to misuse. Of all the activities that take place in coastal zones and the near-shore coastal ocean, none is increasing in both volume and diversity more than coastal tourism (Hall, 2001). Litter from holidaymakers form part of the estimated weight of rubbish dumped into the world's ocean annually. These wastes are said to be three times the number of fish caught (Tsagbey et al., 2009). The above findings reflect areas in which professionals who manage such venues could set targets to collaborate with government bodies working to ensure sustainability.

5 Climate Change

The consequence of climate change has brought about a dilemma in the tourism and hospitality industries. On the one hand, it is difficult and nearly impossible to stop individuals from travelling for leisure, knowledge or business. On the other hand, it is difficult and nearly impossible to stop destinations from hosting guests. Regrettably, the threats of climate change are real, and their menace necessitates a re-appraisal of the hospitality industries and their role in protecting the environment. Oladokun et al. (2015) capture this scenario when they put it aptly that due to the climate-sensitive nature of tourism an attempt to separate the union between tourism and a good weather portends danger. As a primary resource for tourism, some authors may contend that climate co-determines the suitability of locations for a wide range of tourist activities, it is a principal driver of global seasonality in tourism demand, and has an important influence on operating costs, such as heating–cooling, snowmaking, irrigation, food and water supply and insurance costs.

It is worthy of note that there is a reciprocal contributory relationship between climate on the one hand and the tourism and hospitality industry on the other hand (OECD/United Nations Environmental Programme, 2011). To put it in the words of Jones and Phillips (2011) 'the relationship between climate and tourism growth has thus been one of the driving forces in the phenomena of emerging global tourism markets.' The attractiveness of sites and other outdoor recreational activities which characterise tourism make it a delight for leisure seekers (Hall & Higham, 2005). These experiences derived from the aesthetic aspects of climate make tourists enjoy their visitation. When the climate becomes harsh, it makes the visitor uncomfortable, takes away any fun and may even portend danger. Thus a beautiful environment is fascinating for visitation in the right climatic condition.

But in the absence of proper regulations, there are threats to the climate that derive from the activities of guests (either as tourists, delegates, business visitors, participants at a workshop or conference, relatives or any other individual who fall under these categorisations). Thus, when visitors to an island or other natural habitats leave behind waste (especially plastics as will be discussed later in this paper) there is a threat to the environment. There is also the challenge of too many people visiting particular places (termed as hotspots). Such massive physical visit may negatively affect the site. Becken and Hay (2007), for instance, cite the depletion of freshwater owing to the increasing number of people who visit islands and consume freshwater. Furthermore, the amount of fuel burnt during the transportation of visitors by air, sea or land, the amount of energy consumed at hotels and guest houses all contribute to environmental challenges.

The contributions of tourism and hospitality industries to climate change and their consequent impact on the environment calls for an exercise of caution by practitioners within both industries. The damage that some 'hotspot' destinations undergo sometimes requires that they be removed from tourist sites. In such cases, there may be a 'last chance' phenomenon, where tourists are given the opportunity of visiting such site for the last time. The extent of the devastation has not yet been fully documented. There are warnings that there is a dearth of studies to truly give an understanding of the impact in a few decades' time. Scott (2021) notes that growing evidence indicates that the magnitude of projected impacts on tourism is highly dependent on the magnitude of climate change and that sector harm will be much greater under higher emission-temperature increases. This calls on both the tourist and hospitality industries to join in the drive towards using the environment in a sustainable manner.

6 The Future of the Environment

The earth is our common home but human activities have to a large extent endangered it for all. Our activities now have adverse effects on nature to the extent that natural events now occur at extreme limits. There is extreme drought on the one hand while there is massive flooding on the other. Extreme temperatures now bring about heat waves that lead to deaths and wildfires that destroy expanse of land, properties and in some instances individuals. Ironically, the roles of hospitality and tourism cannot be underestimated in our lives. Truly we need to relax, we need to recreate, we need to travel for business and conference, we need to enjoy the waves of the oceans and islands, we need to build befitting hotels, restaurants and shopping malls, we need the roads that lead to these facilities and we need other infrastructures to make them functioning effectively and to make us as comfortable as possible … But then we must remember that we need all these just as those coming after us need them, hence the need to be more responsible and act in a sustainable manner.

Humans are reliant on the environment for our survival. We live in it, we feed from it, we need its comforting landscapes for leisure and relaxation, the beaches, and so much more that nature gives us. Thus, since the environment cares for us, we need to care for it so that we can continue to receive its care and ensure that future generations are not denied of same care. When we stop caring as we ought to, then we have set the stage for severe consequences. The need to care is the thought behind environmental sustainability and the care for our common home. These are reflected in submissions of agencies, groups, individuals and governments who are all focussed on ensuring safety now and in the future.

While presenting the report of the World Commission on Environment and Development, the Chairman Gro Harlem Brundtland aptly stated that 'Our Common Future' is not a prediction of ever-increasing environmental decay, poverty and hardship in an ever more polluted world among ever-decreasing resources. We see instead the possibility for a new era of economic growth, one that must be based on policies that sustain and expand the environmental resource base. This call to action emphasizes the need to act collectively to ensure that the hospitality and tourism industry joins the train towards enjoying our needs today without compromising the needs of the future. Environmental sustainability, as Mashika et al., (2020) point out, ensures development compatibility with the maintenance of basic environmental processes, biological diversity and biological resources. The hospitality and tourism industry need to be dedicated partners in the drive towards a sustainable environment.

A possible approach to caring for our common home is to operate with the ambit of sustainable tourism and ecotourism which gives credence to the environment. The essence of the concept of sustainability is to re-orientate individuals, groups, institutions, corporations and other fields of human endeavour to think of the 'other' and act in ways that considers the interest of this 'other.' Acting in such interests is essential for the immediate and distant future. Acting responsibly involves a symbiotic relationship between the one (in this instance hospitality and tourism industry) and the environment. Păvăluc et al. capture the essence for such reciprocity in their argument that:

> ...the symbiotic relationship between tourism and environmental conservation aims for both components to obtain a certain advantage. Tourism promotion and development has the purpose to obtain a financial benefit, and people's concern for environmental preservation and protection tends to contribute to the preservation of natural resources in their primary state and/or to the improvement of the environmental quality. (Păvăluc et al., 2020, p. 4)

Responsible tourism implies a proactive approach by the tourism sector through the promotion of balanced and sustainable tourism. Such an approach has to be underpinned by decisions based on the precautionary principles which are responsible for sustainable environmental practices (Muhanna, 2006). Responsible choices and actions in hospitality can build practices which enable us to enjoy the resources we have now while ensuring that the future generations will also have enough resources. Interestingly, the future of tourism and hospitality can be greatly influenced by the attention we pay to sustainable practices and our promotion of care for the environment.

7 Sustainability Practices Within the Hospitality Industry

We now discuss ways in which the industry can promote sustainability. The main issues discussed above are management of waste and energy, care of the environment and a concern for climate change and global warming. Each centre for hospitality and tourism can adopt a clearly defined strategy to meet the needs of the environment. The processes for work and services should include options that encourage responsible use of resources in a way that enables us to maximize the benefits from their use while ensuring that they are not depleted or that they will still be available for use for many generations to come.

The World Tourism Organisation (WTO) in collaboration with the United Nations (2005) noted there is a need to make optimal use of environmental resources. These resources are often indispensable for tourism development and their maintenance as well as the conservation and protection of ecological resources is essential to sustainability in tourism. All guests should respect the socio-cultural uniqueness of their host communities and protect their cultural heritage while engaging in inter-cultural dialogue that can facilitate a mutual enrichment between the host and their guests. In addition, professionals should adopt processes that are viable for long-term economic operations, such that the socioeconomic benefits to relevant stakeholders are attained. The professionals should be well remunerated as the industry provides jobs and can thus contribute to alleviating poverty.

Some features of sustainable tourism include quality, continuity and balance. With regard to quality, sustainable tourism aims to provide excellent services creating a memorable experience for visitors, while it simultaneously improves the quality of life of the host community and protects the environment. Sustainable tourism ensures the continued availability of the natural resources upon which it is based and the continuity of the culture of the host community which contribute to the satisfying experiences of visitors. Balancing the needs of the tourism industry, supporters of the environment and the local community is the third necessary feature. There is a need for cooperation among visitors, the host community in the care of their destinations by working towards sustainable mutual goals (Yazdi, 2012).

Other scholars have suggested that adhering to the principles of sustainable development in hotel business might provide benefits for guests, who will be satisfied with a preserved environment, as well as with the service quality. The return and sharing positive experiences to other potential users could provide benefits for hotels. Such favourable reviews may lead to improved motivation of employees to better perform the business tasks including decreased operating costs and other sustainability practices. Furthermore, savings from such sustainable practices, e.g. through decreased operating costs, could be invested in the maintenance and preservation of a tourist site's environment and in development projects for the local community (Mijatov et al., 2018).

Policy instruments such as environmental certification can help to regulate hospitality sites operating with a business model. Regulatory bodies can evaluate compliance of tourist facilities and hospitality centres with standard processes that contribute to sustainability. Examples of such processes include the use of green energy, recycling of water and of other waste, giving the guests options of reusing towels in order to preserve water and reduce waste, availability of separate waste collection bins to sort them for recycling, green marketing and branding etc.

It is however important to highlight that the onus of good practices for sustainability is not solely the task of hospitality professionals. Consumer behaviour is important for attaining the sustainability goals. The joint project involves regulating the activity of the guests even though the care provider needs to have sustainable options for their guests. For example, a resort that has bins in attractive fashions, clean with hygienic options for disposal of waste such as foot pedals for opening the bins, would facilitate their use by guests. Similarly, when the waste bins are clearly labelled with the type of waste to be deposited in them, they could foster a recycling culture thereby conserving resources. It is also true that the hosts may provide incentives for the guest to make choices of services which favour sustainable developments, e.g. loyalty points which add up to small discounts or gifts. At the base of it all is the need to educate both hospitality professionals and their clients about their role in protecting our common home.

Simple adjustments in the processes can have a significant impact on the contribution of the industries to sustainability. For example, fostering a culture of recycling by providing appropriate containers for waste differentiation, using sources of energy that cause less pollution, offering incentives to guests who protect the environment by not printing on paper unless absolutely needed etc. All these changes would require study and strategic planning in order to have viable plans within one's context. One cannot however overemphasize the importance of beginning the plan in each location of hospitality practice and tourism sites.

8 Conclusions

The earth is our common home but human activities have to a large extent endangered it for all present here and for future generations. Among the fields of human endeavour that can make a positive impact, the hospitality sector is one that can help create awareness for responsible use of resources for sustainability. The roles of hospitality and tourism cannot be underestimated in our lives. The processes involved in caregiving and hosting people can contribute to human flourishing and our sense of well-being. There is a need for joint effort of both the hosts and guests in order to have the much-needed balance between the demands on resources for hospitality uses and a respect for sustainable development. Hospitality practitioners, professionals working in the field of tourism, consumer of all the services provided and other stakeholders should see themselves as protagonists for a new narrative for sustainability in the fields. Such professionals and end-users can and should adopt processes that align with the sustainability goals promoted by other fields of human activity. Government regulation properly monitored and community awareness of the duty to protect natural resources can contribute to the quest for sustainability.

Action Prompts

Think of the future generation as you use and manage resources.

Contribute to the attainment of the sustainability goals by consuming responsibly.

Dispose of refuse correctly; avoid littering the environment.

Study Questions

1. What is the connection between sustainability, tourism and hospitality industries?
2. In what ways can the different stakeholders in the fields contribute to sustainability?
3. How can stakeholders halt the negative effects of climate change and contribute to environmental sustainability?

Chapter Summary

Hospitality and tourism are important industries for human flourishing. The industries and the issues they address play vital roles in the life of individuals and states and their role has evolved over the years. They serve as sources of revenue for their stakeholders and they are avenues for human flourishing. Sustainability is key to caring for the earth in order to ensure that resources are sufficient not only for those who currently live in the world but also for future generations. The contributions of these industries (hospitality and tourism) to sustainability in contemporary times largely depends on the appropriate use of the resources available such that they can satisfy their clients' needs and make profits. The consideration of one's responsibility and interest in defending human dignity by ensuring that the future generations have a good home, should influence the attitude to the professionals and motivate them to try to improve the sustainability indices of their activities. Since sustainability practices involve the care of others they require a humanistic approach. Sustainability can be profitable. Environmental concern and other aspects of sustainable development demands that our natural resources, including those used in and for hospitality and tourism purposes, ought to be managed in such a way that though we depend on it for our sustenance, we must care for it so that it can sustain us. Tourists their hosts and regulatory bodies for the hospitality profession need to be aware of the importance of environmental sustainability and the role can they play in promoting it. They can contribute to attaining some of the targets of sustainability.

References

Becken, S., & Hay, J. E. (2007). *Tourism and climate change: Risks and opportunities*. Channel View Publications.

Camilleri, M. A. (2018). *Travel marketing, tourism economics and the airline product*. Springer Nature.

Francis, P. (2015). *Laudato Si: On care for our common home*. Our Sunday Visitor.

Hall, C. M. (2001). Trends in ocean and coastal tourism: The end of the last frontier? *Ocean and Coastal Management*.

Hall, C. M., & Higham, J. (2005). Introduction: Tourism, recreation and climate change. In C. M. Hall & J. Higham (Eds.), *Tourism, recreation and climate change* (pp. 3–28). Channel View Publications.

Jones, A., & Phillips, M. (2011). Introduction: Disappearing destinations: Climate change and future challenges for coastal tourism. In A. Jones & M. Phillips (Eds.), *Disappearing destinations: Climate change and future challenges for coastal tourism* (pp. 1–9).

Kunwar, R. R. (2017). What is hospitality? *The Gaze: Journal of Tourism and Hospitality, 8,* 55–115.

Lashley, C. (2015). Hospitality and hospitableness. *Research in Hospitality Management, 5*(1), 1–7.

Lickorish, L. J., & Jenkins, C. L. (1997). *An introduction to tourism.* Butterworth-Heinemann.

Mijatov, M., Pantelic, M., Dragin, A., Peric, M., & Markovic, S. (2018). Application of sustainable development principles in hotel business. *Journal of the Geographical Institute Jovan Cvijic SASA, 68*(1), 101–117.

Mashika, H., Davydenko, I., Olshanska, O., Sydorov, Y., Komarnitskyi, I., & Lypnytska, Y. (2020). Modelling of development of ecological tourism. *International Journal of Scientific & Technology Research, 9*(4), 683–688.

Morelli, J. (2011). Environmental sustainability: A definition for environmental professionals. *Journal of Environmental Sustainability, 1*(1), 1–9.

Muhanna, E. (2006). Sustainable tourism development and environmental management for developing countries. *Problems and Perspectives in Management, 4*(2), 14–30.

Oladokun, O. J., Adedara, T. M., & Adedadamola, J. O. (2015). Tourism and climate change: Combating climate change effects on tourism participation in Nigeria. *Journal of Tourism, Hospitality and Sports, 5,* 1–5.

Orams, M. B. (2003). Sandy beaches as a tourism attraction: A management challenge for the 21st century. *Journal of Coastal Research* (Special Issue No. 35).

Organisation for Economic Cooperation & Development/ United Nations Environmental Programme. (2011). *Climate change and tourism policy in OECD countries.* OECD.

Păvăluc, C., Anichiti, A., Niţă, V., & Butnaru, G. I. (2020). Analysing the relationship between tourism development and sustainability by looking at the impact on the environment: A study on the European Union countries. *CES Working Papers, 12*(1).

Scott, D. (2021). Sustainable tourism and the grand challenge of climate change. *Sustainability, 13,* 1–16.

Skripak, S. J., & Ron, P. (2020). *Fundamentals of business* (3rd ed.). VT Publishing.

Sunlu, U. (2003). Environmental impacts of tourism. In D. Camarda & L. Grassini (Eds.), *Local resources and global trades: Environments and agriculture in the Mediterranean region* (pp. 263–270). CIHEAM

Tsagbey, S. A., Mensah, A. M., & Nunoo, F. K. E. (2009). Influence of tourist pressure on beach litter and microbial quality—Case study of two beach resorts in Ghana. *West African Journal of Applied Ecology, 5*(1).

United Nations Environmental Programme & World Tourism Organisation. (2005). *Making tourism more sustainable: A guide for policy makers.* United Nations Environmental Programme and World Tourism Organisation.

Walker, J. R., & Walker, J. T. (2014). *Introduction to hospitality management.* Pearson Education Limited.

Yazdi, S. (2012). Sustainable tourism. *American International Journal of Social Science, 1*(1), 50–56.

Zaei, M. E., & Zaei, M. E. (2013). The impacts of tourism industry on host community. *European Journal of Tourism Hospitality and Research, 1*(2), 12–21.

Zahedi, S. (2008). Tourism impact on coastal environment. *WIT Transactions on the Built Environment, 99,* 45–57.

is no one clear product. It includes a broad category of businesses that provide specialized facilities for comfort and leisure for guests (travelers, visitors, and tourists' etcetera) and includes hotels, restaurants, transportation, and other related services. We will adopt here a broad but relevant description of hospitality. We take hospitality to mean the act of arranging means in view of providing customers a personalized and fulfilling experience of a product or service. Going by this description, we will apply the term in two different but consistent ways. First as a process and, then as an end. As a process, it underlines deliberate and systematic sets of actions that go beyond the value due to the customer as a fair exchange and in furtherance of the customer's positive experience of the product or service. As an end, it points to that positive emotional response of fulfillment elicited in the customer and sustained while a product or service is being delivered.

To go deeper into the subject matter, we will follow three steps: First, we will explore Archie Carroll's CSR pyramid. This popular CSR model provides a four-part framework for thinking about the different obligations of business to society. Second, within the context of the model, we will then look at some challenges of implementing CSR in hospitality practice, especially from a developing country perspective. Finally, the work concludes by drawing on the limitations of Carroll's CSR framework to make a case for a humanistic CSR practice. By humanistic CSR, we refer to any CSR model that goes beyond wealth creation and contributes to the well-being of society by recognizing and prioritizing the dignity and humanity of all business actors in the course of defining and carrying out business activities.

2 Carroll's CSR Model

This section explores one of the most influential CSR models and arguably the most inclusive CSR framework. Carroll (1979) put forward a four-aspect CSR definition which he represented graphically in a pyramid (Visser, 2006). Carroll had explained that the different aspects of social responsibility of business involve society's expectations about business in the economic, legal, ethical, and philanthropic aspects at

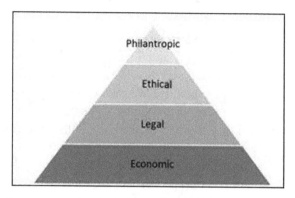

Fig. 1 Carroll's social responsibility framework (1979)

some point in time. These four categories delineate the four responsibilities of business to society and are arranged in their relative order of importance. As we discuss Carroll's pyramid, one thing to remember is that it is not necessarily a model you apply in making decisions about CSR, but a framework for thinking about CSR. In what will follow, we will explore each of the four categories of Carroll's Pyramid, starting from the base of the pyramid or, if you like, what he had considered the most fundamental requirement of business to the least in that specific order (Fig. 1).

2.1 Economic Responsibility

As the diagram illustrates, Carroll placed economic responsibility at the base of his CSR pyramid and assigned precedence over other responsibilities. In fact, he refers to economic responsibilities as the foundation of the responsibility of business. Carroll goes on to explain that businesses do have a responsibility to sustain themselves. This means that a business must be profitable first before undertaking other responsibilities such as philanthropic and ethical responsibilities. He shows that profit is important because it serves as an incentive and compensation to investors and business owners who have borne the ultimate risk to ensure business continuity. Profit maximization makes it possible for business investors to reinvest and grow the business to stay competitively strong.

13 Corporate Social Responsibility in Hospitality Industry ... 253

This profit-oriented approach has encouraged the understanding of CSR mainly in terms of how it adds or subtracts from profit. Hence, CSR has been interpreted to mean any or all of the following: *cost, profit-sacrificing, public relations tool*, and *investment for more profit*. These interpretations raise some concerns. By implying that profit comes before legal and ethical responsibilities, a good business decision is as good as that decision that makes the most profit first before committing to other responsibilities. This is an odd conclusion. To fully appreciate the implications of this profit-oriented approach, consider these hypothetical situations:

(a) A restaurant owner has to decide whether or not to invest in replacing kitchen equipment following several employees saying that they suffer cramped hand muscles because of the design of the equipment. He contacts an expert and was informed that procuring better-designed equipment would significantly reduce the discomfort experienced by his employees, but the cost of getting new equipment is quite significant, and output would not be affected by the change to a new equipment.

(b) If a hotel manager puts out a notice for rooms at a cheaper rate, offering a 30% discount off the original price of its executive rooms to customers willing to spend more than a night in the facility but lowered the standard of the rooms by using inferior supplies. For example, using poor quality toiletries, substituting the specialty sheets and pillows, and using the cheapest sheets and pillows they can find, or instead of cleaning the sheets, they simply tuck them back in between for customers to use as long as the sheets still look clean. This lets the hotel charge customers a little less for rooms, while misleading guests to believe they are getting same value as those who paid prediscount rates.

The restaurant owner and hotel manager above can be said to have satisfied the profit responsibility, but we can observe that there is something

254   O. Ikejimba

odd in these situations. To take a profit-oriented decision in the situations above will be for the business to ignore its social responsibility and to disrespect the humanity of both the employees and the customer who deserves to be treated with dignity. We shall draw other implications of this profit-oriented approach later in this work. In the meantime, let us consider legal responsibility.

2.2   Legal Responsibility

Carroll places legal responsibility as the most basic responsibility of business after economic responsibility. This hierarchy has been contested by some scholars (Nalband & Al Kelabi, 2014) who argue that legal and not economic responsibility is the primary responsibility of business. For businesses to start, they must first comply with the law of the country. The law must be able to address and redress the neglect or social irresponsibility of businesses so as to make society a better place. Carroll points out that business must fulfill the responsibility to obey the law. This includes a wide range of laws and regulations that businesses need to comply with. These laws govern business practices such as health and safety, competition, employment and contract, procurement and consumer rights, etc.

Although laws help regulate business, we can find examples that suggest that this is barely enough (see scenarios a and b above). There are always gaps in these laws or regulations to be exploited by businesses, even in the more developed societies with strong institutions. Moreover, the ever-changing nature and scope of business operations driven by technology and globalization have made many laws inadequate. This is due to the twin challenge of weak law enforcement and judicial systems, especially in developing nations. To appreciate this point, consider this hypothetical situation:

A hotel agreed to an offer of 100 million nairas from a major political party as rent to use the hotel's facility for their upcoming national convention. The hotel manager is excited that the deal would give the business an after-tax profit of about 35 million nairas. In his report to executive management, the manager points out that the major challenge

13 Corporate Social Responsibility in Hospitality Industry ... 255

in organizing the event is the parking space for guests. The hotel's car park can only accommodate 40% of delegates expected at the event. Since the hotel is located along a major motorway, the foreseeable consequence is that the event will exponentially increase traffic on the road. The overflow of parked vehicles from the hotel into adjoining streets would significantly harm other road users and neighbors. To minimize harm to other road users, management approved that a car park proximate to the hotel be rented at 12% of the expected profit from the deal.

The above scenario shows that the business does not breach the law if it decides not to take any ameliorative action to avert harm to other road users. However, there is a responsibility to avoid harm by introducing some ameliorative interventions in its planning. This type of responsibility is categorized as an ethical responsibility. Many argue that there are no compelling incentives to take this kind of action that can cut back on profit (in the case above, about 12%). To highlight this, also imagine an alternative scenario where it is proven that there is an actual legal infraction. Let us say, for example, that the business and not the individual car owners who park on the streets are at risk of being charged for a traffic offense. The slow grind of judicial processes and the vulnerability of law enforcement institutions to corruption, especially in developing countries, often serve as a disincentive to comply with the law. Business commitments to ethical responsibility can be especially helpful in this circumstance. The more individuals and businesses act because they recognize that it is the right thing to do and not just for mere legal compliance, the better the common good is promoted.

2.3 Ethical Responsibility

After arguing for the economic and legal responsibilities, Carroll introduces the ethical responsibility of business. Here, Carroll talks about the responsibility of businesses to do the right thing, to act morally. This goes beyond the narrow limits or minimum of what the law often requires from businesses and moves to demand more in terms of specific actions. For example, how a business treats its employees and the working conditions the business offers or how it relates to consumers, suppliers, etc.

Carroll had assumed that profit and compliance to laws are the only true basic business requirements while ethical and philanthropic responsibilities are mere society's expectations from businesses. Since philanthropy involves voluntary and charitable disposition towards others, it may amount to a genuine expectation. Carroll's description is valid, but there seems to be a far more than a semantic problem. An expectation does not equate to a responsibility. Responsibility is more obligatory and can be demanded or need to be accounted for. Ethics is not a mere social expectation but a responsibility and, importantly, a basic business requirement.

It has been argued that ethics and business are inseparable. Evidence shows that ethical irresponsibility in business is more likely to lead to unpleasant results for the business and society, such as disregard for human dignity and fulfillment, consumer boycotts, and even loss of profitability. The need for ethics in business becomes clearer when profit-oriented decisions start negatively impacting society and the environment. The argument that ethics have no business with business (Friedman, 1970) is increasingly unpopular. To think that businesses have no ethical responsibility beyond obeying the law is unreasonable considering the far-reaching implications of business decisions on humanity. Businesses should not be thought of strictly as separate from society nor should business actors be considered separate from humanity. It is an exercise in contradiction if one is willing to agree that the decisions and actions of individual citizens are subject to ethical consideration while the decisions and activities of businesses should not.

2.4 Philanthropic Responsibility

Carroll believes that after the economic, legal, and ethical responsibilities, the next layer of responsibility is what he calls philanthropic. This is where business goes beyond acting legally or ethically to start giving back to society. For example, business owners fund community or charitable projects such as sponsorship of scholarships or local sports teams, giving staff time off work to support community initiatives, etc. As already argued, philanthropy is a social expectation and as such should come

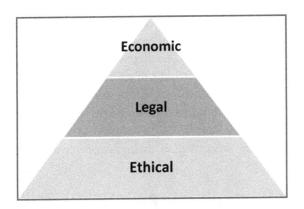

Fig. 2 Humanistic CSR model

after a business must have satisfied its responsibilities; ethical, legal, and economic responsibilities in that specific order (Fig. 2).

One very clear idea that stands out in Carroll (1979) is the fact that CSR involves more than one aspect. This idea set Carroll apart from CSR studies before him. However, like those before him, Carroll insists that economic responsibility is the primary responsibility of business. This attempt to ground CSR ultimately in economic terms has influenced CSR scholarship to a relationship between corporate social responsibility and corporate financial performance, almost a cause-and-effect relationship (Arnaud & Wasieleski, 2014). To rethink Carroll's framework will be to reorder the social responsibility priority to reflect a more humanistic CSR framework. This framework considers the following priorities in their relative order of importance: Ethical requirements, legal requirements, and economic requirements.

We acknowledge that businesses are required to be profitable and self-sustaining. It also follows that a business can best fulfill its responsibility when it is profitable. However, businesses do not also exist in isolation or in a vacuum. Businesses are not separate from the community. A business is like any other citizen with rights and duties. Communities are founded to promote the common good. Hence, businesses cannot pursue their objective of profit maximization without considering the well-being of others. To ensure that the profit objective of businesses does not harm the community, social responsibility needs to be grounded in ethics. It is not enough to have laws, and it often only covers the minimum. As stated earlier, the judicial system in many parts of the world is less than efficient considering the delays and financial requirements to prosecute a case. Even in societies with efficient judicial and law enforcement systems, the recompense often awarded for social irresponsibility is usually incommensurate to the harm inflicted on society. Another point to note is that some laws are quite unjust and objectionable and socially irresponsible businesses easily take advantage of such situation.

3 CSR in Hospitality Practice

We can infer from our foregoing discussions on Carroll's four-part framework that businesses have a responsibility to take care of their shareholders, customers, employees, the larger society, and the environment. This recognizes the three main bottom-line of business-care for people, the physical environment, and profit. To begin with, we recognize that businesses in the hospitality space have contributed significantly to society in areas such as job creation, development of new facilities for leisure, travel and connectivity, and the appreciation of local industry and craft.

However, the activities of some of these businesses also create some unpleasant experiences and cause intentional and unintentional harm such as polluting the surroundings, processing food in an unhealthy and unsafe environment, or exploiting employees with low wages and long work hours. Studies have shown that some businesses have taken up initiatives to minimize the negative impacts of business activities on people and the physical environment.

These initiatives often include social initiatives such as ensuring safe and dignified work conditions, fair and timely payment of wages, encouraging workforce diversity, and other progressive work conditions. As a result, customers are becoming more interested in the social performance of the businesses. They like to patronize a business that commits to basic ethical principles regarding their relationship with their employees and society. Even in situations where customers do not particularly care about how the business treats its employees, they surely care about meeting cheerful and motivated rather than fatigued and long-faced employees. This shows that when businesses simply treat employees as cost and fail to recognize their humanity, they significantly harm their fulfillment as persons. Unfortunately, the customer often also bears the brunt of that indifference.

Employees are neither tools nor assets of the business. Unlike tools and assets, which serve as a means to an end and whose worth is defined by its relative utility, employees are radically different because they are ends in themselves. In outlining his categorical imperative, Immanuel Kant speaks to this basic character of humanity as an end in itself. Humans are required never to treat others merely as a means to an end but always as ends in themselves (1785). That is, as valuable business partners whose relationship with the business is that of cooperation for mutual benefits. The main point here is that there is a relationship between getting employees happy and fulfilled and getting customers who come to the business happy and fulfilled.

There are also some attempts to minimize the negative impacts of business activities on the environment through practices such as the reduction of water and food waste in restaurants, commitment to clean energy and energy conservation in hotels, increase in fuel efficiency in airlines, and elimination of noise pollution from loud music in open pubs. Contrary to widely held claims which suggest that the more a business invests in environment management and sustainability systems, the greater the cost. It has been argued that over time, businesses that invest in such systems improve operational efficiency by reducing waste production and water usage, increasing energy efficiency, recycling, and so on. These are specific means businesses can reduce its cost. The point here is that the well-being of man depends directly or indirectly on the protection of the environment. This places on businesses the moral responsibility to protect the environment. The foundation of this responsibility is strictly in the interest of man. Therefore, in trying to assess environmental responsibility and how it impacts interest pulling at the other end, such as profit, the ultimate standard is the well-being of the human person, directly or indirectly; affected now or in the future.

Some businesses have also focused more on philanthropic initiatives such as donations to schools and hospitals and funding scholarship and feeding programs for the poor, just to mention a few. Although these philanthropic initiatives are voluntary, studies have identified some countries implementing mandatory CSR for businesses (Cheruvalath, 2017). Mandatory philanthropy is no longer philanthropy because it moves from social expectation to a business requirement. This effectively collapses philanthropy into a legal responsibility. However, there is strong evidence to show that there are benefits for businesses that take philanthropic initiatives seriously. For example, the involvement of the Nigerian airline business, Air Peace, in the free evacuation of Nigerians back to Nigeria from South Africa during the infamous xenophobic killings by indigenous South Africans in 2019.

This effort gained not only favorable media attention but it also led to a positive brand image and awareness. For instance, the CEO of the business, Mr. Allen Onyema, received both local and international commendation for the decision of Air Peace Airline to prioritize humanity over economic considerations. Consequently, many Nigerians, including senior government officials and Federal Lawmakers, vowed to give the first priority to Air Peace when flying to any part of the country (Adepegba, 2019).

Hilton Hotels & Resorts provides another relevant example. On 6th April 2020, Hilton Hotels & Resorts announced a donation of one million free hotel room nights for health care workers fighting against the coronavirus pandemic in the United States of America. Many frontline workers at that time were advised not to return to their homes due to the risk of exposing their loved ones to the virus. The clear alternative was for health workers on duty to sleep in office spaces, benches and make-shift tents after several hours of attending to health emergencies. It is important to note that Hilton Hotels & Resort's decision came at a time when hotel businesses were experiencing precipitous declines in occupancy and loss of profit (Hilton ESG Report, 2020). This human-centric business decision contributed significantly to sustain the fight against Covid-19 and also demonstrates the priority of the well-being of the healthcare workers and the common good.

Soon after Hilton Hotels & Resorts made its announcement, Marriot International announced on 9th of April 2020 that it would support frontline healthcare workers with accommodations, essential protective equipment, food, and other essential resources. The reputational capital derivable from such social initiatives as discussed above is significant and often translates to public goodwill. Customers are, in turn, more willing to identify with and even pay premium prices patronizing such businesses. The point here is that philanthropic initiatives are meaningful when a business has first satisfied its basic responsibility to its employees, customers, shareholders, suppliers, the environment, and other relevant stakeholders. For example, it would be unreasonable for a restaurant that offers its waiters undignified wages and an unsafe and unhealthy environment to initiate and fund a school feeding program.

CSR practices can also encourage customer loyalty due to a positive perception of service, and this goes a long way to improve the brand. This is particularly true in the hospitality industry, where products are non-material, and customers typically directly experience the products and not through a third party. A highly competitive industry that provides substitutable services like hotel rooms creates product differentiation and can be a significant competitive advantage. Also, studies have shown those social and environmentally conscious consumers and their (consumers) emerging appetites that need to be satisfied have created a unique demand, especially in the travel, restaurant, and hotel space. Many green environment-complaint hotels take advantage of the demand for green hotels, an emerging market that considers sustainability when making hotel decision choices. Finally, evidence suggests that businesses that prioritize social responsibility have better employee satisfaction and motivation records. This shows that employees stake pride in and want to work for a business with a reputation for doing what is good. This will typically lead to reduced employee turnover, which is a long-standing problem in hospitality business.

In practice, public good is often taken to imply philanthropy. This usually includes the support businesses provide for social initiatives like donations for building hospitals, a public library, funding scholarships, and other social welfare initiatives we have pointed out in the preceding discussion. While it is true that support for a social project is a worthy cause, it is not all there is to CSR. For example, there is the moral responsibility of business not to cause intentional harm, to be just, and so on. In fact, there are conditions under which donations by businesses in support of social initiatives are controversial and arguably will not be considered as CSR. Take the following two as an example: (1) Support for social initiative primarily with marketing or reputational objective and (2) support for social initiative to make up for intentional harm caused by the activities of the business (Elegido, 2009).

For example, given the growing number of social and environmentally conscious consumers and their (consumers) emerging appetites that need to be satisfied, some businesses have collapsed CSR into a marketing strategy to meet their economic objectives. Although some scholars have emphasized the relationship between CSR and Corporate financial performance, it is important to keep in mind the need to maintain balance. That is, to de-emphasize the idea that economic objective is the ultimate end of the business. The clear implication of undertaking CSR as one more marketing tool is that it becomes a means to an end—profit maximization. The assumption here is that there is a chance that this approach will lead to a win–win situation. That is, serve the interest of both the business and the society.

The problem here is that CSR collapsed into a marketing portfolio, forms one more line item in the budget. The budget for marketing promotions typically hits the cost center and is built into the product's price, which the customer will ultimately bear. This then invalidates the assumption that CSR involves some form of profit-sacrificing or hinders profit maximization. The second challenge with this approach is that it is often taken for granted that CSR is about choosing social or environmental initiatives to pursue. Often CSR can be a dilemma. That is, trying to resolve tensions between competing responsibilities. Recall the example of the restaurant owner who has to decide whether to invest in replacing kitchen equipment following employees' complaints. This illustrates the point made earlier, a situation where the interest of shareholders and the interest of society are pulling in two different directions. The third but associated problem with this approach is the fact that it erodes sustainable CSR initiatives. This is because businesses with this approach in mind will tend only to support community initiatives that are good for the business and not what the community needs. Again, support for the social initiative in order to make up for the harm caused by the activity of the business will not pass as CSR no matter how generous it is. It is true that business ultimately involves different levels of risks which often may result in unintended harm. This is significantly different from harm caused due to neglect or indifference to humanity and the common good.

4 Why Humanistic CSR

CSR has evolved in the last two to three decades from just being an expectation to a requirement for remaining in business. Some decades ago, it was fine for a business to publish financial reports detailing margins of profit increase or cost-saving and showing that it could run efficiently. Today, the market is more social responsibility-conscious and wants to know more; that is, the business is not making decisions or acting in such a way that does not harm the need and objectives of other stakeholders. As a result, businesses now create CSR reports as well as financial reports. Just as financial reports show how a business has performed over a specific period of time, many businesses also now publish CSR reports showing how it has operated within a given period in terms of meeting its social responsibility obligations. This suggests that while a business aims to attain its economic objectives, people also want businesses to create greater value than just financial value, which is to better humanity.

This shift of social accountability from economic to ethics emphasizes the new social expectation of stakeholders. One outstanding approach that businesses have come to adopt in order to create value that will better humanity is the humanistic management approach. The humanistic approach is rooted in the principle of the common good and involves cooperation to promote those conditions in business that allow for human flourishing. Notice that we speak of the following: (1) cooperation and not a strict war-like competition; (2) the good of all and not self-interest and (3) human fulfillment and not maximizing economic gain. Humanistic CSR, therefore, refers to any CSR model that goes beyond wealth creation and contributes to the well-being of society by recognizing and prioritizing the dignity and humanity of all business actors in the course of defining and carrying out business activities.

Humanistic corporate responsibility also involves creating opportunities for people to work in environments where the purpose and ways of doing things are not only efficient but just. This is because not everything that is efficient is desirable. It is possible to have a socially irresponsible business and yet structured and run efficiently. In addition to the capacity of a business to sustain itself, it must be just or if you like, ethical. This includes the recognition and respect for the dignity, freedom and self-realization of all human actors involved in a business activity. In the context of freedom, individuals should be able to decide and choose freely, actions that contribute to their personal development and ultimate fulfillment. To achieve this, it is important that the foundation of the business is right from conception. What does the business want to achieve? In other words, what is the mission of the business? The mission statement should be concrete, feasible, and just. By justice, we mean that the businesses need not be reduced to the achievement of individual gain but designed to align to the promotion of common good. When the mission statement is reduced to individual gains, it takes away the possibility of cooperation and entrenches conflict (of interest). It is also common knowledge that business structures, systems, policies (including CSR), processes, and culture are all influenced by the mission of the business. Therefore, a healthy humanistic CSR begins with the mission statement.

5 Conclusion

This work has examined Carroll's four-part hierarchy of business responsibilities and notes that there is the need to reorder and prioritize ethics as the foundation of CSR in hospitality. Through this lens, we have seen that although philanthropy promotes public good, it is only a social expectation, and businesses need not prioritize it over its social responsibilities. Although ethical, legal, and economic responsibilities have different requirements, they are interconnected and should ultimately have as an end, the good of man. CSR can be used as a means

13 Corporate Social Responsibility in Hospitality Industry ...

to increase profit, provided that the business fulfills all its responsibilities to those who work in and for the organization, to the community, and to the environment. To fulfill these responsibilities, stakeholders in the hospitality business have to understand that social responsibility is human-centric and not simply profit-oriented. It is also not about philanthropic activities as most businesses see it today. Businesses' decisions will better serve the business when it promotes not just the self-interest of its owners but the good of all humanity as the means, circumstances, and opportunities afford it.

Action Prompts

Take decisions that promote the good of humanity.

Prioritize ethics as the foundation of CSR.

Understand that corporate responsibility should be human-centric and not profit-focused.

Study Questions

1. Is the future chosen correctly for the business? Is the mission statement of the business concrete, feasible and does it support the development of the human person?
2. Does the business structure, policies, and culture create opportunities for employees and customers to make decisions and cooperate freely towards promoting the common good?
3. Does the business recognize the well-being of the human person, directly or indirectly, affected now or in the future as the standard of deciding its actions and responsibilities?

266   O. Ikejimba

Chapter Summary

Over the last two decades, businesses in the Nigerian hospitality industry have felt the need to rethink their commitment to Corporate Social Responsibility (CSR) due to the growing number of social and environmentally conscious consumers and their (consumers) emerging appetites that need to be satisfied. Stakeholders in the industry find it problematic reconciling emerging consumer appetites with the responsibility to stay competitively strong in the market as well as maximize profit. In other words, they seem to think that their corporate responsibility to society and their business sustainability are separate ventures. While it is clear that the responsibility of businesses goes beyond making-profit to include responsibilities to others such as: host communities, employees, and the environment within which they carry out their business activities, it is a worthwhile task to clarify which approach to CSR best creates a sustainable corporate responsibility practice that offers value, not only to the emerging market of social and environmentally conscious consumers; but also to all stakeholders in the business. Archie Carroll (1977) had proposed a four-part CSR framework that has, over time, shaped the understanding, strategy, and level of commitment of many businesses within the hospitality industry. Carroll's CSR model offers important benefits over competing models of CSR. His quadrant of economic, legal, ethical, and charity dimensions to CSR are useful in thinking about the social responsibility of businesses in the industry. However, this work argues that Carroll's idea of placing economic and legal responsibility at the heart of his CSR model is problematic when considered from a developing country perspective where enforcement of legal and regulatory frameworks are weak or almost non-existent. A strict implementation of Carroll's model can create a poor foundation for legitimate business growth. It is the position of this work that ethical responsibility is the foundation of the social responsibility of businesses and not just a social expectation. Thus, Carroll's CSR model needs to be reordered to take into account the significant role of ethics in promoting the conditions for human flourishing through a humanistic approach to CSR. This research adopts a qualitative analysis approach which involves critical analysis and conceptualization of Carroll's CSR framework to examine their adequacy to match the unique demands of the hospitality industry and human flourishing.

References

Adepegba, A. (2019, September 19). Evacuation: Reps ask Buhari to honor Air Peace boss. *The Punch Newspaper*. https://punchng.com/evacuation-reps-ask-buhari-to-honour-air-peace-boss/

Arnaud, S., & Wasieleski, D. (2014). Corporate humanistic responsibility: Social performance through managerial discretion of the HRM. *Journal of Business Ethics, 120*(3), 313–334. Retrieved July 31, 2021, from http://www.jstor.org/stable/42921340

Bowen, H. R. (1953). *Social responsibilities of the businessman*. University of Iowa Press.

Carroll, A. B. (Ed.). (1977). *Managing corporate social responsibility*. Boston: Little, Brown and Company

Carroll, A. B. (1979). A three-dimensional conceptual model of corporate social performance. *Academy of Management Review, 4*(4), 497–505.

Carroll, A. B. (2008). A history of corporate social responsibility: Concepts and practices. In A. M. Andrew Crane, D. Matten, J. Moon, & D. Siegel (Eds.), *The Oxford handbook of corporate social responsibility* (pp. 19–46). Oxford University Press.

Cheruvalath, R. (2017). Need for a shift from a philanthropic to a humanistic approach to corporate social responsibility. *Annals of Public and Cooperative Economics, 88*(1), 121–136.

Elegido, J. M. (2009). *Fundamentals of business ethics: A developing country perspective*. Criterion Publishers.

Friedman, M. (1970). The social responsibility of business is to increase its profits. *The New York Times Magazine*.

Hilton. (2020). *Hilton 2020 environmental, social and governance (ESG) report*. https://cr.hilton.com/wp-content/uploads/2021/04/Hilton-2020-ESG-Report.pdf

Kant, I. (1785). *Groundwork of the metaphysic of morals* (J. W. Ellington, Trans., 3rd ed.). Hackett.

Latapí, M. A., Jóhannsdóttir, L., & Davídsdóttir, B. A. (2019). A literature review of the history and evolution of corporate social responsibility. *International Journal of Corporate Social Responsibility, 4*, 1. https://doi.org/10.1186/s40991-018-0039-y

Marrewijk, M. (2003). Concepts and definitions of CSR and corporate sustainability: Between agency and communion. *Journal of Business Ethics, 44*(2), 95–105.

Nalband, A., & Al Kelabi, S. (2014). Redesigning Carroll's CSR pyramid model. *Journal of Advanced Management Science, 2*(3), 236–239. https://doi.org/10.12720/joams.2.3.236-239

Reinhardt, F. L., Robert, N. S., & Richard, H. V. (2008). Corporate social responsibility through an economic lens. *Review of Environmental Economics and Policy, 2*, 219–239.

Smith, A. (1759). *The theory of moral sentiments.* Printed for A. Millar, and A. Kincaid and J. Bell.

Visser, W. (2006). Revisiting Carroll's CSR pyramid: An African perspective. In M. Huniche & E. P. Rahbek (Eds.), *Corporate citizenship in developing countries—New partnership perspectives* (pp. 29–56). Copenhagen Business School Press.

14

COVID-19, Its Effects on the Hospitality and Tourism Sector in Kenya and Recommendations Towards Recovery

Jane Wathuta, MaryJoy Karanja, and Clara Kariuki

J. Wathuta (✉) · M. Karanja · C. Kariuki
Strathmore University, Nairobi, Kenya
e-mail: jwathuta@strathmore.edu

M. Karanja
e-mail: maryjoy.karanja@strathmore.edu

© The Author(s), under exclusive license to Springer Nature
Switzerland AG 2022
K. Ogunyemi et al. (eds.), *Humanistic Perspectives in Hospitality and Tourism, Volume II*, Humanism in Business Series,
https://doi.org/10.1007/978-3-030-95585-4_14

1   Introduction

One of the ways we define ourselves distinctively as individuals and as the human race is through human work. There are various specializations, and various needs to meet on a daily basis. Human work is not only supposed to fill a gap but also to uplift and positively edify the quality of life of any human. This presupposes that fundamental elements of the human person have to be embedded in human work. These elements are such as human dignity, human rights, respect, and independence. Over the years, we have witnessed these foundations challenged through child labor, human trafficking, and poor working conditions, among other ways. COVID-19 has uniquely exposed some of these cracks, while also creating new ones. Whereas the lack of jobs has been a huge problem in Kenya, the pandemic only underscored this fact. Many people lost their livelihoods, and the worst-hit sector was the Tourism and Hospitality Sector. This chapter will explore the background of the tourism industry in Kenya, how it has been affected, the various ways key factors such as managers can help in revitalizing the industry and recommendations on the way forward.

2   Background

In 2020, Kenya was ranked as the third-largest tourism economy in Sub-Saharan Africa (Mboya, 2020). Furthermore, in 2018, the tourism sector in Kenya contributed about 8.8% to the country's Gross Domestic Product (GDP) (Nyasuguta, 2019). The industry has created many employment opportunities ranging from chefs to drivers and tour guides. Local and international tourism is the bread and butter for these people. COVID-19 became a major hindrance to both employers and employees

---

C. Kariuki
e-mail: kariuki.clara@strathmore.edu

in this sector and thus hugely affected people's source of income as well as the acquisition of profits.

The first case of COVID-19 in Kenya was reported on 13th of March 2020 (Kenya National Emergency Response Committee, 2020a). Like other countries in the world, this provoked mass hysteria regarding the virus. The government was working with the little information available to ensure that all its citizens were protected from the virus. Among other measures, the government partially shut down hotels and restaurants by only allowing them to sell take-away food and limited drinks. International borders were also shut down and people were advised to work from home (Kenya National Emergency Response Committee, 2020b).

3 Impact of COVID-19 on the Tourism and Hospitality Sector

As expected, this sudden turn of events caused a huge shock to the economy and to individual actors in the tourism and hospitality industry. Initially, the immediate impact was the cancelation of already booked trips by tourists. There was also a temporary shift in how people would report for work, which in turn reduced transport-related incomes (Ministry of Tourism, 2020). Fewer employees were allowed to be on-site while others were laid off. With the regulations set in place, less people would eat in restaurants and thus the flow of customers greatly decreased and affected sales.

Prior to COVID-19, the hospitality industry was a key contributor to the strong performance of services in the Kenyan economy. The industry formally employed over 82,900 people and, together with trade services in 2019, engaged over 9 million people. The industry was the worst hit by the pandemic, contracting by 83.3% in the second quarter of 2020 compared to an expansion of 12.1% in the second quarter of 2019. This contraction was attributed to the measures implemented by the government to contain the spread of COVID-19 (Central Bank of Kenya, 2021).

Figure 1 is from the Central Bank of Kenya (CBK) report, showing

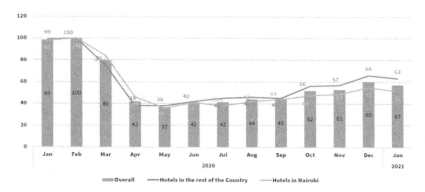

Fig. 1 Employment

employment, which in this case, is shown as the percentage of the number of employees in February 2020.

Tied to the hospitality industry and a growing sector in Kenya is the Meetings, Incentives, Conferences and Exhibitions (MICE) sector which took a huge blow when COVID-19 hit the country. Kenya is becoming a central destination for international meetings to be held. The people who attend these meetings are bound to stay in a hotel, some may even go exploring. Nationally, the country boasts of a beautiful array of scenery in places where meetings with Non-Governmental Organizations (NGOs) and even conferences can be held. International events lasting 2–5 days have a per capita direct spending of about $3591 while domestic ones come to about $655.80 (Ministry of Tourism, 2020). With the closure of borders and social distancing measures, this sector suffered massive losses. Most of these meetings and conferences were held online. The entire world had to undergo a major shift in how they conduct meetings and tech companies facilitating such services, such as Zoom and Google, stole the limelight during the pandemic.

Furthermore, the pandemic affected the suppliers involved in the industry more so suppliers of perishables like food and flowers. Small, Micro, and Medium Enterprises (SMMEs) have largely been affected by this. Food global supply chains were affected in one way or another by the pandemic. This led to an increase in food prices due to a ripple effect caused by a gigantic disruption in the global economy. Food suppliers have thus had to reduce the quantity they supply. Hotels and restaurants suffered major losses at first because they had to dispose of food as less people were allowed in hotels and restaurants. Food suppliers furthermore, had to reduce their staff because they could not keep up with paying them. They also had to increase their inputs so as to ensure that they can still get food to supply. The above factors led to a decrease in volume of production since the beginning of the pandemic (Global Alliance for Improved Nutrition, 2020).

The harsh economic times brought about by the loss of jobs and a fall in remittances pushed approximately two million Kenyans into poverty (The World Bank, 2020). The government of Kenya thus came up with a stimulus package that entailed sending low-income families a weekly stipend. The distribution was however riddled with irregularities, such that struggling families did not receive any money. Yet, as of 2019, about 36.1% of the total population of Kenya was already living below the poverty line (Human Rights Watch, 2021). Kenya is therefore slipping when it comes to fulfilling the goals of Sustainable Development Goal (SDG) number 1: Zero Poverty.

Poverty affects various dimensions of people's lives. It is not only material but also social and psychological. When people cannot provide basic needs for themselves and their children, it affects them mentally and physically too. Poverty affects people's capability to enhance themselves. It is a limitation. It is precisely because of this that Amartya Sen (2001) affirms that development should be a conscious effort to increase individuals' capabilities to enrich their lives. It entails a freedom to choose from a variety of paths in order for one to become the best version of themselves. SDG 8 (Decent Work and Economic Growth) was also affected by the pandemic. Fundamental elements of the human person have to be embedded in human work. These elements are such as human dignity, human rights, respect, and independence. This is expressed in the workplace through favorable working conditions, availability of sick leave, and access to medical insurance among other factors. However, this has not been the case in Kenya. Case in point is that currently, four out of five Kenyans have no access to medical insurance (UNDP, 2020).

The pandemic forced people to remain in their homes, triggering a loneliness epidemic, especially among those who live alone. People were filled with fear, stress, and a constant worry that they or their loved ones might catch the virus. The loneliness epidemic, which began short of a century ago with the onset of urbanization, has only gotten worse with the pandemic (Sweet, 2021). Loneliness is 'grief, distended' (Lepore, 2020). The pandemic came with resolutions such as social distancing and staying home. With reduced social interaction, many people experienced loneliness. We then have to evaluate the invisible role that the tourism and hospitality industry plays, that is, the fact that it creates avenues for people to meet, establish connections, build bonds, and strengthen them. Hotels and restaurants provide spaces for people to meet up with their friends, loved ones, and offer an opportunity for strangers to become acquaintances through activities such as team building. In this way, people get to actively participate in the happiness of their loved ones.

Aristotle, in his *Nichomachean Ethics* (Ross & Brown, 2009), states that we achieve happiness by participating in the happiness of others. What we search for the most cannot be found in ourselves solely but in the other. Thus, having meaningful relationships with those around us is not only beneficial but also vital in ensuring that we live a life of quality. The role of the hospitality industry thus cannot be downplayed as it is one of the many ways we can participate in the happiness of another. This is particularly important in maintaining good mental health (Ybaraa et al., 2008).

4 Implications for Leadership and or Managing People in Hospitality and Tourism

Relying on secondary data, largely articles published by researchers in the hospitality field, this section explores how the economic and psychosocial effects of a crisis, particularly the COVID-19 pandemic and the loneliness epidemic, can be mitigated through ingenious action grounded in a humanistic approach.

During times of crises, a unique approach to human resource management (HRM) is necessary, as operations are more delicate than they have ever been. In a time where there are more layoffs of workers and more changes to the structure and running of the restaurant or hotel, employee well-being remains as paramount to the success of the industry in the long run as much as customer satisfaction is. Employee well-being in hotels is significantly more important than that in other sectors because the positive experience of customers depends on the positive state of hotel employees (Karatepe, 2013).

Due to COVID-19, HRM professionals are under significant pressure to reskill their workforce rapidly. There is pressure on hotels to strategically design HRM systems and processes to meet the pressing market demands caused by the pandemic (Carnevale & Hatak, 2020). With all the impacts of crises noted earlier, a study done in India on employee well-being highlighted that employees of the hospitality industry have been feeling an overwhelming sense of job insecurity because of the high levels of staff layoffs (Agarwal, 2021). Non-managerial employees and manual workers reported that they are in financial distress because of pay cuts, those who managed to retain their jobs reported burnout as they had to fill in the gaps the layoffs had formed, hotel staff reported that being constantly alert due to interaction with potential carriers of COVID-19 had taken a physical toll on them. Constant exposure to such an environment had led to fear and anxiety about catching the coronavirus. This is despite the fact that hotels were following all procedures and necessary precautions—working for guests during COVID-19 instilled a sense of fear. Furthermore, those working from home reported a lack of organizational support for those who had no internet access (Agarwal, 2021). These concerns are not limited to India alone as there have been various media reports in Kenya, highlighting the same, or similar concerns. To reduce the stress and pressure in the workplace, managers should be able to assess the situation and act accordingly in order to ensure a smooth-running workplace.

Action Prompts *(for managers regarding employee well-being during a crisis)*

Communicate consistently and transparently with the employees, thus, reducing uncertainties and anxieties due to a lack of clarity on what changes are taking place. Employees are bound to appreciate honesty from the start, rather than experience sudden shocking news that had been in the planning stages awaiting execution.

Foster an open and positive working environment where employees are encouraged to air any grievances and they are assured of a follow-up on the same. Also, taking care of employees beyond the working hours is important for forming a community in the hotel or restaurant, meaning that, when a crisis does come around, the close-knit community is there for support. So, have regular team building activities.

Have trainings geared towards the situation being faced, for example, with COVID-19, having safety-based trainings is incredibly beneficial for a smooth transition into the full reopening of the hospitality industry and curbing any employee fears.

Provide mental health support for employees by having a resident counsellor with an open-door policy and an approachable personality, encouraging good mental well-being.

Have provisions for those who cannot access the virtual meetings or work.

In terms of customer concerns, these are mainly centered around contracting the virus. Preliminary findings of a longitudinal study conducted by the editorial team of the *Journal of Hospitality Marketing & Management* suggest that customers would only be comfortable enough to go to a dine-in restaurant or destination stay when their community is effectively able to test, trace and isolate COVID-19 cases (Dogan Gursoy, 2020). This is not the case in Kenya as there is a lack of such infrastructure and customers make calculated decisions independently of the factors mentioned above. For example, in December 2020, a report by the Central Bank of Kenya showed that there was an increase in hotel room bookings as it was the festive season and people decided to book destination stays in places like the Kenyan coast, despite the lack of proper COVID-19 tracking infrastructure (Central Bank of Kenya, 2021).

More findings suggested that customers would feel more confident eating out and booking stays in hotels when the COVID-19 vaccine became available. These findings have been supported by the opening of events in bars and restaurants concurrent with the vaccine rollout, which does provide a slight sense of security despite the slow uptake of the vaccine (Central Bank of Kenya, 2021).

So far, the return of guests to the hospitality industry has been largely dependent on macro factors, beyond the industry's control, but Dogan Gursoy (2020) went deeper and found that around one-third of restaurant customers and around 40% of the hotel customers are willing to pay more for increased safety precautions because customers expect hospitality businesses to implement more rigorous safety and cleaning procedures. A portion of customers is willing to pay for those added safety measures.

Due to this, the industry has had to adapt to a more automated approach to service, one with minimal human contact. Various methods have been employed; one major one is the use of digital payments. Digital payment mainly via M-pesa was already widespread in Kenya before the pandemic, but since the onset of the pandemic, it has been highly emphasized as restaurants have adopted a no-cash policy and only accept card or M-pesa, which is a mobile money transfer application. This can be seen in other countries as well, using various mobile money applications.

Many restaurants have adopted a cloud kitchen model where no dine-ins are allowed and food is ordered online for delivery, which is helping with cutting down costs, and potentially opening up restaurants to a wider client base. For those restaurants allowing dine-ins, a 'contactless experience' (Vig & Agarwal, 2021) is prioritized where guests can scan a code for the menu or pre-order online to minimize waiting time; there are also temperature checks at the door and small group or individual sitting options only. There has also been the rise of drive-through and home food deliveries, putting riders in high demand.

COVID-19 has led to a revolution in menu engineering at restaurants. The restaurants are trying to develop new food options such as immunity-boosting menu items because customer preferences have changed amid the pandemic (Vig & Agarwal, 2021). Consumers are more health-conscious now and a multitude of healthy food fads have resurfaced.

In terms of booking stays, a popular app has made its way under the hospitality wing, guests are opting to stay at Airbnb's more as one can book the whole space for themselves or their family, reducing the risk of contracting COVID-19. Airbnb has also made it possible for Airbnb owners to stay afloat on the platform by introducing a host fund of $250 million to help the hosts experiencing increased cancelations (Airbnb, 2020). Airbnb stays have a personal touch and interactions with the host, making them more attractive to guests looking for genuine human dealings, which is why, 'super hosts' on Airbnb are those providing great services and amenities along with human companionship, which cannot necessarily be said for hotels.

5 Industry Recovery and Challenges Experienced

As the Kenyan economy has opened up slowly, there has been a slight increase in hotel bookings, as per the Central Bank report. Most guests are locals, which goes against the previous trend of having more foreigners booking hotels than locals. Restaurant flow has increased over the past few months (August–December 2020) in and out of Nairobi. The pace of going back to work has been interfered with by fear of resurgence of the virus. However, on average, 58% of hotels have indicated that they expect to resume normal operations by the end of 2021 (Central Bank of Kenya, 2020). A few challenges experienced by actors in the industry in terms of reopening are the length of time it takes to acquire necessary documentation for operating in the middle of a pandemic and the problems with accessibility of a vaccine (Central Bank of Kenya, 2020).

The government is trying to ensure that businesses in the hospitality industry get back on their feet. For instance, the Cabinet Secretary of Tourism, Hon. Najib Balala, promised to set aside $3 million that will be injected into the recovery of the industry post-COVID-19 (Ministry of Tourism, 2020). In addition, the President of Kenya established a few parameters that would enable the hospitality industry to fully recover. Some of these parameters include but are not limited to: a total of $18,481,144.00 to be set aside to aid in restructuring businesses involved in the industry and the provision of soft loans to business owners so that they can be able to uplift their businesses post-COVID-19 (The Presidency, 2020).

Globally, the rise of 'staycations' (a vacation spent in one's local vicinity/ country) has been attributed to the pandemic and is enabling less frequented areas to put themselves on the global tourism map. Restaurants and hotels have largely increased their social media presence, staying in touch with their customers and sending offers to promote their 'bounce back'.

These changes have been widely embraced, in areas such as Nairobi, Kenya, and other cosmopolitan cities, but they have also posed some challenges. With the rise in demand for riders and home deliveries, Uber promised their riders that they would provide financial assistance if they needed to take sick leave, but they backtracked on their word (Sonnemaker, 2020), clearly taking advantage of the increased dependency on delivery workers and their lack of official employee rights. Additionally, with the rise in contactless service delivery, there is a lack of human warmth to it, promoting more screen time on phones and electronics like when ordering online, rather than promoting genuine human connection.

A study on the effects of COVID-19 on Israel, Sweden and the United States showed that the rebuilding of the hospitality industry is heavily influenced by the social systems of the area (Shapoval et al., 2021), and the type of culture represented ther. So, for example, with a more uncertainty-avoidant culture, the hospitality industry may suffer an even greater loss, because, there is lack of flexibility in adopting strategies to move past the crisis, it is the opposite with cultures with low uncertainty avoidance, those willing to take risks. Therefore, as mentioned earlier, it is always important for a manager to contextualize their situation and forge a way forward based on that.

> **Action Prompts**
>
> Essentially, managers should aim to ensure that:
>
> - All government protocols are set in place, promoting customer confidence and comfort.
> - They know and contextualize all the best practices adopted in other areas (Vij et al., 2021). By keeping themselves aware of the situation and the emerging trends.
> - There is a constant stream of engagement with all relevant stakeholders.
> - The aspect of human interaction is not lost, despite the circumstances.

6 Recommendations

All in all, *the hospitality industry needs to be flexible enough* to adapt to the future of the industry post-COVID. The same mentality can be applied in various crisis situations, where the managers in the industry need to consider working on both the subjective (personal) and the psychological employee well-being, which will translate into customer satisfaction. They also need to consider how to ensure customer safety with a human touch. The approach to navigating extraordinary circumstances needs to be innovative and multifaceted, without omitting the fundamentals of employee and customer well-being. The resilience of the industry is in its people.

There needs to be *efficiency in distribution of government allocated funds.* Corruption is a big issue in Kenya. According to Transparency International through the Corruption Perception Index (CPI), Kenya has a rank of 124/180 when it comes to corruption (Transparency International, 2020). The organization does its evaluation through asking people about their corruption-related experiences. By introducing better accountability and transparency systems, the government will be able to deliver what is meant for its people. About 30 health-associated non-Governmental Organizations (NGOs) based in Kenya have come together and asked for an audit for the usage of funds allocated to mitigating the virus (Imende, 2020). They also suggested that the President should add anti-corruption agencies and civil societies to the National Emergency Response Committee (NERC), but this was not done. Participatory development is important as it enables people to own the project. When kept out of it, as it is in this case, the ones responsible should be able to give concrete answers to those whom the project directly affects.

The above point is tied to the idea of *responsible leadership*. As much as each man is free to do as he pleases, leaders should lead by example. Leaders evoke strong emotions among their followers and thus the followers tend to do what they do. Since we are approaching an election period in Kenya, leaders have begun campaigns even before the designated campaign period (Thiong'o, 2021). This has made people gather in big groups, sometimes without masks. This calls for more responsible leaders. This time, people's lives are at stake. Holding frequent political rallies takes the whole essence of leadership away since leaders are expected to secure the welfare of the people.

7   Conclusion

Every society has various capacities and vulnerabilities. This time round, the pandemic, a major source of vulnerability, united the world's various societies into one unit experiencing a shared ordeal. How people get back up is dependent on our various capacities as nations and the level of responsibility each government bears to its people. Kenya has shown its capability in fighting the pandemic. However, it needs to improve in some areas to ensure that less people are affected. This also applies to the Hospitality Industry. Various measures such as training of workers in digital media should be done so as to protect the industry from another shock situation. It is also important to invest in the physical, mental, and social well-being of employees in the industry to ensure that they not only produce the best results but also find purpose in work. As Kenya enters the fourth wave of the pandemic in August 2021, it can only be hoped that individual responsibility paired with government initiative will see the country through this prolonged and unique tribulation.

Study Questions

1. What has been the impact of COVID-19 on the value of human work and connection?
2. Does human work have any relation to the psychological wellness of employees?
3. What structures have been put in place to protect workers in the Tourism and Hospitality Sector from future shocks?

Chapter Summary

The effects of COVID-19 were largely unprecedented. The pandemic has taught the world to be more vigilant and has forced governments to re-assess their preparedness when it comes to shock events. All the same, the human soul, which refuses to settle, is once again proving that it has various capacities to adjust, adapt and overcome. This has not only been the case in Kenya but in the rest of the world as well. As COVID-19 vaccines are being dealt out to populations around the world, various things are getting back to normal. As different world processes unfold, the tourism and hospitality industry is tightening its sails in order to ensure its recovery as a major contributor to Kenya's revenue.

References

Agarwal, P. (2021). Shattered but smiling: Human resource management and the wellbeing of hotel employees during COVID-19. *International Journal of Hospitality Management, 93*, 102765.

Airbnb. (2020, March 30). *Airbnb Resource Center*. Retrieved from airbnb.com: https://www.airbnb.com/resources/hosting-homes/a/250m-to-support-hosts-impacted-by-cancellations-165

Carnevale, J., & Hatak, I. (2020). Employee adjustment and well-being in the era of COVID-19: Implications for human resource management. *Journal of Business Research, 116*, 183–187.

Central Bank of Kenya. (2020). *Report of the survey of hotels*. Central Bank of Kenya.

Central Bank of Kenya. (2021). *Monetary Policy Committee hotels survey*.

Dogan Gursoy, C. C. (2020). Effects of COVID-19 pandemic on hospitality industry: Review of the current situations and a research agenda. *Journal of Hospitality Marketing and Management, 29*(5), 527–529.

Global Alliance for Improved Nutrition. (2020). *Impact of COVID-19 on food systems: A situation report*. Retrieved from gainhealth.org: https://www.gainhealth.org/resources/reports-and-publications/impact-covid-19-food-systems-situation-report-i

Human Rights Watch. (2021, July 20). *We are all vulnerable here*. Retrieved from hrw.org: https://www.hrw.org/report/2021/07/20/we-are-all-vulnerable-here/kenyas-pandemic-cash-transfer-program-riddled

Imende, B. (2020, August 24). *The Star*. Retrieved from the-star.co.ke: https://www.the-star.co.ke/news/2020-08-24-civil-societies-call-for-audit-of-covid-19-expenditure/

Karatepe, O. (2013). High-performance work practices, work social support and their effects on job embeddedness and turnover intentions. *International Journal of Contemporary Hospitality Management, 25*(6), 903–921.

Kenya National Emergency Response Committee. (2020a, March 13). *Ministry of Health-Press Releases*. Retrieved from Ministry of Health-Press Releases: https://www.health.go.ke/wp-content/uploads/2020a/03/Statement-on-Confirmed-COVID-19-Case-13-March-2020-final.pdf

Kenya National Emergency Response Committee. (2020b, March 22). *Ministry of Health-Press Releases*. Retrieved from Ministry of Health-Press Releases: https://www.health.go.ke/wp-content/uploads/2020b/03/CORONA-PRESS-STATEMENT-MARCH-22.pdf

Lepore, J. (2020, March 30). The history of loneliness. *The New Yorker*. https://www.newyorker.com/magazine/2020/04/06/the-history-of-loneliness

Mboya, E. (2020, June 5). Kenya overtakes Angola as third-largest economy in Sub-Saharan Africa. *Business Daily*. https://www.businessdailyafrica.com/bd/economy/kenya-overtakes-angola-as-third-largest-economy-in-sub-sahara-africa-2291948

Ministry of Tourism. (2020, June). *Impact of COVID-19 on tourism in Kenya, the measures taken and the recovery pathways.* Retrieved from tourism.go.ke: https://www.tourism.go.ke/wp-content/uploads/2020/07/COVID-19-and-Travel-and-Tourism-Final-1.pdf

Nyasuguta, F. (2019, April 16). Kenya ranked third largest tourism economy in Sub-Saharan Africa. *The Star Kenya.* https://www.the-star.co.ke/business/kenya/2019-04-16-kenya-ranked-third-largest-tourism-economy-in-sub-saharan-africa/

Ross, W. D., & Brown, L. (2009). *The Nicomachean ethics.* Oxford University Press.

Sen, A. (2001). *Development as freedom.* Knopf.

Shapoval, V., Hägglund, P., Pizam, A., Abraham, V., Carlbäck, M., Nygren, T., & Smith, R. M. (2021). The COVID-19 pandemic effects on the hospitality industry using social systems theory: A multi-country comparison. *International Journal of Hospitality Management, 94,* 102813.

Sonnemaker, T. (2020, April). Uber promised to pay drivers who couldn't work because of the coronavirus: But drivers say Uber has been closing their accounts after they seek sick pay, and then ignoring or rejecting their claims. *Business Insider Australia.*

Sweet, J. (2021, January). The loneliness pandemic. *Harvard Magazine.* Harvard Magazine Inc.

The Presidency. (2020, May 23). *The seventh presidential address on the coronavirus pandemic: The eight point economic stimulus programme stimulus.* Retrieved from president.go.ke: https://www.president.go.ke/2020/05/23/the-seventh-presidential-address-on-the-coronavirus-pandemic-the-8-point-economic-stimulus-programme-saturday-23rd-may-2020/

The World Bank. (2020, November 25). *Worldbank.org.* Retrieved from worldbank.org: https://www.worldbank.org/en/country/kenya/publication/kenya-economic-update-covid-19-erodes-progress-in-poverty-reduction-in-kenya-increases-number-of-poor-citizens

Thiong'o, J. (2021, July 6). Untouchables: Kenyan politicians at it again breaking Covid-19 protocols. *The Standard.* https://www.standardmedia.co.ke/politics/article/2001417586/untouchables-kenyan-politicians-at-it-again-breaking-covid-19-protocols

Transparency International. (2020). *Corruption Perception Index.* Retrieved from transparency.org: https://www.transparency.org/en/cpi/2020/index/ken

UNDP. (2020). *Articulating the pathways of the socio-economic impact of COVID-19 pandemic on the Kenyan economy.* United Nations Development Programme.

Vig, S., & Agarwal, R. (2021). *Repercussions of COVID-19 on small restaurant entrepreneurs: The Indian context.* Wiley Online Library.

Vij, M., Upadhya, A., & Abidi, N. (2021). Sentiments and recovery of the hospitality sector from Covid-19—A managerial perspective through phenomenology. *Tourism Recreation Research, 46*(2), 212–227.

Ybaraa, O., Burnstein, E., Winkielman, P., Keller, M., Manis, M., Chan, E., & Rodriguez, J. (2008). Mental exercising through simple socializing: Social interaction promotes general cognitive functioning. *Personality and Social Psychology Bulleting, 34*(2), 248–259.

15

Corporate Social Responsibility as Person-Centred Care

Kemi Ogunyemi

If you take care of your employees, they will take care of your customers and your business will take care of itself. *("10 Quotes on Small Business Success by JW Marriott—Logo Maker", founder of the Marriott Corporation)*

K. Ogunyemi (✉)
Lagos Business School, Institute of Humanities,
Pan-Atlantic University, Lagos, Nigeria
e-mail: kogunyemi@lbs.edu.ng

© The Author(s), under exclusive license to Springer Nature Switzerland AG 2022
K. Ogunyemi et al. (eds.), *Humanistic Perspectives in Hospitality and Tourism, Volume II*, Humanism in Business Series,
https://doi.org/10.1007/978-3-030-95585-4_15

1 Introduction

It is difficult to find a universally accepted definition of corporate social responsibility (CSR), as its definition varies depending on the context in which scholars attempt to address the concept (Kristoffersen et al., 2005). CSR generally implies the way an organisation achieves a balance among its economic, social and legal responsibilities in its operations so as to address shareholder and other stakeholder expectations (Carroll, 1979). Organisations may practice CSR for various reasons, for example, to enhance organisational reputation or to forestall government intervention or sanctions. Even when such instrumental reasons prompt it, the notion of CSR is an improvement on the traditional profit-making model of the firm (Kristoffersen et al., 2005) which focussed primarily on the shareholders, since CSR brings a social dimension to the profit focus.

The concept of corporate social responsibility itself is largely a product of the debate between business and the society (Jenkins, 2005). The debate attempts to define the role of business in the society and its responsibilities thereto, determine whether these responsibilities go beyond profitmaking (Carroll & Shabana, 2010); agree on what contributions businesses should make to the society, and ascertain whether these contributions are morally and or legally binding. A theoretical review of CSR reflects the lack of consensus as to unified answers to these questions. Efforts made by numerous authors in this regard have come up short. Yet, according to Dahlsrud (2006), CSR definitions can be categorised into five dimensions: the ethical, social, economic, voluntary and stakeholder dimensions. Using frequency counts to determine these dimensions, this author determined that although CSR definitions are at variance in terms of context, they are consistent. Following Dahlsrud, this paper assumes that CSR definitions are, despite their divergence, consistent and finds, in literature over the years, lenses affirming the ethical (economic, environment and social perspectives) and the emerging governance dimension to CSR. These set the stage for considering whether the place CSR in the hospitality and tourism industry can be viewed as being rooted in person-centred care as ethical behaviour towards the persons in the industry, especially the employees who make up the workforce.

In defining CSR, some scholars like Friedman (1962) have taken the position that CSR for an organisation entails the increase in its profits in accordance with laid down laws and that, by doing this, organisations are already playing their role in the society. According to Friedman, the social responsibility of a business is to use resources and engage in activities aimed at increasing the company's profits while competing openly and freely and avoiding deception or fraud. Going by this definition, a business might not need to care about other stakeholders except those who have an obvious claim on its profits—its shareholders. Provided it has not deceived its employees or suppliers, it would have no need to care about their well-being or to be concerned about the environment or the society. Over time, other scholars such as Sacconi (2007) have taken a wider view and somewhat opposite stance and define CSR as an improved model of corporate governance, arising as a result of the incomplete nature and abuse of authority that occurs with the older model. This view adopted in this paper is in line with Sacconi's[1]: CSR as responsible behaviour rooted in an understanding of corporate organisations that holds that business should be done responsibly and with regard to all stakeholders, including employees, because this is the right way for business to operate. Thus, one could say that the need to practice CSR and, specifically, workplace CSR, is rooted in ethical considerations that include the concern for internal and external stakeholders. This is no less true in an industry like that of hospitality and tourism, where the primacy of people comes with the terrain. In this final chapter of the second volume of *Humantistic Perspectives in Hospitality and Tourism* which is subtitled CSR and Person-Centred Care, we follow up this introduction to the topic with a depiction of CSR as ethical behaviour towards all stakeholders, a focus on CSR towards the workforce and a discussion of how the chapters illustrate this; a brief discourse on points

---

[1] Who in turn was following Freeman and a number of others who held views opposed to Friedman.

derived from applying the responsibility essentials from Chapter 2 to the other chapters, and finally, a few concluding reflections for hospitality and tourism enterprises.

2 CSR as Ethical Behaviour

The ethical lens for viewing CSR is at best represented by the definition of the World Business Council for Sustainable Development (WBCSD) (Ijaiya, 2014). The WBCSD broadly defines CSR as, "the ethical behaviour of a company towards society" (WBCSD, 2000, p. 6) and then explains it as "the continuing commitment by business to behave ethically and contribute to economic development while improving the quality of economic life of the workforce and their families as well as the local community and society at large". This definition combines corporate financial responsibility with corporate environmental responsibility and corporate social responsibility (WBCSD, 2000). The Council advocates values in CSR such as human rights, employee rights, environmental protection, community involvement, supplier relations, monitoring and stakeholder rights (WBCSD, 2000). This position aligns with that of Hopkins (1998) who saw CSR as a dedicated treatment of the stakeholders within and outside the firm ethically or in a socially responsible manner. Thus, the stakeholder dimensions to CSR are embodied within the ethical perspective: envisaging an autonomous corporation free to decide how to utilise its resources while aware that these decisions should hold up to ethical scrutiny. If the corporation is a very powerful one, it could make a great positive or negative impact in developing countries where there are weak regulatory environments and where governments are in some cases found wanting with regard to protecting customers, employees, society and the environment (Ijaiya, 2014; Margolis & Walsh, 2003; Matten & Crane, 2005). When it is a socially responsible corporation, its substantial organisational, technological and financial resources (Holmes, 1976; Moir, 2001) would, to be used ethically, be directed towards positive impacts (Levy & Kaplan, 2007).

3 Workforce CSR Within the Wider Governance View

Again, in line with this, while not deemphasising the economic dimension to CSR, the WBCSD's (2000) description already referred to above is very useful—viewing CSR as the "continuing commitment by business to behave ethically and contribute to economic development while improving the quality of economic life of the workforce and their families as well as the local community and society at large. WBCSD identified the following "core values" as integral to CSR: human rights, employee rights, environmental protection, community development, supplier relations, monitoring and stakeholder rights. Earlier on, Hopkins (1998), had already defined corporate social responsibility as focussed on handling the stakeholders of the firm ethically or in a socially responsible manner. Everyone knows that stakeholders exist both within and outside the firm. Consequently, a company behaving socially responsibly will increase the human development of stakeholders both within and outside the corporation. The company remains free to decide how to use its resources but does this within the context of responsible behaviour, having regard to the common good. Examples of ways to do this with regard to internal stakeholders include paying fair wages promptly, eliminating workplace bullying, having a fair complaints process, ensuring safety protocols are adhered to and having a code of ethics and ethics training—all these contribute to make the workplace an environment conducive for human flourishing.

In agreement with the foregoing, Helg (2007, p. 7) says that "corporate social responsibility is the continuing commitment by business to behave ethically and contribute to economic development while improving the quality of life of the workforce and their families as well as of the local community and society at large". It has also been said that corporate social responsibility is akin to promotion of fundamental human rights, e.g., right to property, dignity of labour and good livelihood, and thus ethically necessary, morally obligatory and within the sphere of compulsory regulation (Amao, 2008; Utting, 2005; Wettstien, 2009). This would mean that companies have a moral obligation to promote a peaceful atmosphere within the company itself and within the society in the course of carrying out their lawful operations. Within the company, the spotlight falls on employees and the responsibility of the company to them.

Recent studies of organisational effectiveness reveal that employers historically misused their right to hire and fire at will and that human resource management, employee rights, benefits, training and re-training, etc. were traditionally given secondary priority in an organisation's business. Nowadays, things have changed: in many companies, plans have been redesigned and strategies aligned to ensure greater attention to employment issues and the human resource advantages of the organisation.

According to Elegido (1996), the ethical management of employees includes the following humanistic philosophical principles:

- Acknowledging the value and dignity of human beings; meaning that employees should be treated with respect and concern.
- Discharging the obligations freely undertaken in contracts with employees.
- Treating employees as valued members of the company, who co-create value rather than as strangers contracted to supply labour.

Incidentally, fulfilling these moral obligations helps organisations perform better. When an organisation incorporates CSR into its human resources strategy by respecting employees' human rights, providing good working conditions, promoting respect for dignity and diversity and enabling all employees to perform at their full potential, they in turn do their best for the organisation and this leads to enhanced commitment and productivity. Therefore, as companies now operate in the digital era and global village where CSR increasingly is an important element for analysing corporate governance practices, it becomes critical for companies to have clear CSR policies in general and with respect to their employees in particular. Even if one takes Friedman's point of view, considering that a company is expected to have executed its primary responsibility to employees before declaring profits, one could surmise that there is an unspoken expectation that the company would find a way to ensure that its responsibilities to its employees are fulfilled. That being said, in the space of workforce CSR, there is a wide variety of levels of compliance. Companies often do it as a response to the need to motivate employees, create economic value and promote good business practices. While most local hospitality businesses would use a combination of the domestic legislation and informal regulations, most multinationals (larger hotels, airlines, etc.) tend to follow the Global Reporting Initiative (GRI) and the International Organisation for Standardisation (ISO) guidelines and to bring in some of the practices that are adopted in their global branches.

3.1 Sustainability Reporting: ISO 26000 and GRI

From an international perspective the Global Reporting Initiative (GRI) and the International Organisation for Standardisation (ISO) have helped provide guidance to corporate entities in achieving social responsibility. These guidelines encourage corporate entities to be socially responsible towards employees and other stakeholders. The GRI and ISO have provided "Sustainable Reporting" and "ISO 26000" guidelines, respectively (ISO Official Website, 2022; Sustainable Reporting Guidelines, 2021). The Global Reporting Initiative (GRI) produces the world's de facto standard in sustainability reporting guidelines. Sustainability reporting is the practice where an organisation publicly communicates their economic, environmental and social activities. This reporting by all organisations should be done routinely and should be comparable to its financial reporting. With regard to CSR towards employees, GRI's sustainability reporting requires organisations to provide disclosure on Management's Approach to employment; labour and management relations; occupational health and safety; training and education; diversity and equal opportunity and equal remuneration for women and men.

ISO 26000, created in 2010, is a standard on social responsibility that provides guidance that organisations can voluntarily adopt. ISO 26000 describes CSR as the responsibility of an organisation for the impacts of its decision and activities on society and the environment, through transparent and ethical behaviour that contributes to sustainable development, accounts for stakeholders' expectations, is compliant with applicable laws and international norms and integrates throughout the organisation. The standard serves as a guide for organisations to be socially responsible, envisaging that stakeholders are people or groups affected by the actions of the business. It enumerates seven core areas for reporting among which are organisational governance; human rights (treating all human beings with fairness while paying special attention to vulnerable people); labour practices (provision of a safe working environment) and community involvement and development.

3.2 Workforce and Workplace CSR in Hospitality and Tourism

The preceding chapters explore several interesting aspects of CSR—concern for employees, service to external customers, caution regarding environmental and social impact of the business and sensitivity to elderly and vulnerable people as well as to the effects of COVID-19 on the industry. In this way, they provide a deeper understanding of employee-related or workplace CSR as well as of external-facing CSR. These are base-level expectations from businesses striving to be humanistic. Apart from following the laws (on labour, pension, health insurance, etc.) to ensure that employees are treated well, and their rights are protected, humanistic workplaces sensible of their responsibility to society would go beyond justice to demonstrate care for their employees in their efforts to establish an environment conducive to human flourishing at work.

Many details contribute to establishing such an environment and influence the quality of the relationship between an employer and its employees—respect for human rights, healthy working conditions, payment of minimum wage, giving written contracts, etc. At times companies have a handbook for staff, not only to drive efficiency but also to promote harmony in the employer/employee relationship by providing a humane response to realities in the workplace that fall beyond the scope of the law. Thus, for example, companies could allow for more leave days than stipulated by law and allow for casual or compassionate leave, study and exam leaves, work-hour flexibility, etc.

It is also part of the company's responsibility to ensure that the environment in which employees conduct their daily activities is healthy, safe and conducive. The chapter speaking about the impact of COVID-19 (Wathuta et al., Chapter 14) is a timely reminder about the criticality of providing safety gear for employees when needed—for example, gloves to protect the hands of those cleaning from the chemicals with which they work, protective clothing when required and the right appliances to work with.

In addition, there should be active effort to reduce accidents at work, policies and plan for controlling exposure to diseases, training and development to build staff competence for their roles and for career growth (Eloka, Chapter 7), opportunities for physically challenged persons and protection for vulnerable persons within the industry (Isichei, Chapter 11); checks to avoid discriminatory practices and policies to promote employment and gender equity. These having been taken care of, the business should also be alert to the environmental impact of its operations (Ogunyemi and Onwudinjo, Chapter 12) and should invest in improving society to the extent that it is able to (Ikejimba, Chapter 13). Four categories of employee CSR stand out clearly here: fair reward systems, occupational health and safety, gender and diversity equity and vulnerability and disability protection. These often have some legal backing, but humanistic organisations would attend to them without waiting for regulation and so, in the case of multinationals, would extend the same standards to less regulated environments. Society stands to benefit as well as the staff involved since, when the humanistic workplace constitutes a venue for human flourishing for its workforce, it also enables the external customer to flourish either within homes or in the industry.

Companies that practice workplace CSR enjoy a good corporate reputation and image, improved customer engagement, better recruitment and staff retention indices and increased growth and innovation, due to having more satisfied and more committed employees. Conversely, a company with poor workforce CSR risks higher costs (low productivity, absenteeism, presenteeism, turnover, etc.), threats to business sustainability, backlash from pressure groups and greater vulnerability to competition. Companies with high levels of workplace CSR tend to engender corresponding high levels of commitment and sense of ownership among their employees. Apart from these economic benefits, however, the numerous formal and informal standards that exist for regulating CSR to employees are a way for companies to hold themselves to high governance standards locally and globally. It therefore is good for hospitality and tourism business owners and human resource professionals to commit themselves to these from an ethical and not merely a utilitarian perspective in order to create a sustainable relationship with employees—one of the most important, yet often overlooked, group of stakeholders in the business.

4 The CSR of Business to Customers and Potential Customers; Saul's Essentials

While attention to employees is not often prioritised, especially when there is a strong concern for cutting costs, it is usually easy for businesses to see their responsibility to treat their customers well. The case study from China supports this by showing how it leads to loyalty and enhances the brand (Wang et al., Chapter 10). However, organisations that take their corporate social responsibility standards seriously would not do this only because it promises more profits but rather because they had already decided to hold the values that make for responsibility and live by them. Such are probably the type of conscientious companies that would understand hospitality as gift-giving and a way to lead others, as suggested by Okoye (Chapter 6). This is not a new way of acting. In unveiling the essence of hospitality extracted from the Odyssey of Homer and proposing it as relevant for hospitality professionals today, Saul (Chapter 2) makes it clear that the people who showed hospitality to Odysseus were not doing it in order to receive it back but simply because they understood the gift of gift-giving and the fulfilment it brought to them as hosts. In essence, recovering this spirit behind hospitality would be a matter of going back to our roots in many cases (see

15 Corporate Social Responsibility as Person-Centred Care

also Ukagwu, Chapter 3). Chapter 2 distils four essentials of responsible hospitality from Odysseus's experiences as he travelled for ten years, highlights their occurrence at four of his major stops: binarity, space, limited stay duration, nourishment and service. It shows how hosts that lack the basic knowledge of hospitality end up treating their guests wrongly and making their stay uncomfortable. We now discuss the social responsibility of hospitality corporates along these four essentials.

4.1 Binarity

The development of interpersonal relations is important in hospitality. Chapter 3 points out the strength of language when it comes to welcoming our guests. According to Ukagwu, language is culture and culture and hospitality build on each other, and thus hospitality develops society. Although the author focusses on Nigerian cultural rules of hospitality, the main idea is valid for many other cultures globally. Continuous interaction as social beings means that value is constantly exchangeable by both parties if the mutuality of the relationship is respected. A win–win approach to the relationship is important for effectively discharging one's responsibilities. Binarity is facilitated by good interpersonal relations and this in turn enhances the stay experience, as is seen between Odysseus and his various hosts.

The binarity extends beyond the duration of the actual interaction: when there has been a good experience, the guest/tourist retains an impression and memory that leads to repeat business and recommendations. In Chapter 10, we see how important guest relations, word of mouth recommendations and service delivery is to brand loyalty and repeat visits to luxury hotels in Tianjin, China. The goal is to see what works and the extent to which they all depend on one another so that staffs, hoteliers and managers alike can put that into consideration as they improve their Customer Relationship Management (CRM). This chapter tested a few hypotheses to understand how CRM methods contribute to brand loyalty and repeat visits in luxury hotels in Tianjin, China. Through the use of questionnaire and targeted interviews, they were able to find out what was right and wrong about the hypotheses and it is upon that that recommendations were made for improvement of CRM. The main contribution of this chapter to humanism in hospitality and tourism is its emphasis on the importance of treating guests not as mere customers but as co-protagonists in the success of the hotel industry. Hence, the chapter emphasises the guest/customer relation, which may at times be overlooked by practitioners, using the Tianjin case as a living example of the realistic and practical application of humanism in the industry.

4.2   Space

Chapter 3 hints at the importance of the spiritual aspect of man in creating an ideal hospitable ambience. This is a reasonable supposition, given that the industry caters to the full human being and not just to his body, as was highlighted in several chapters of Volume 1. Of course, guest and tourist relations are like any other human relations, but these take place in a specific venue—the hospitality industry—that is charged with providing care and warmth for persons. If they are to find themselves in a good space, guests and tourists should be treated like visitors to a home—for example, the hotel in Chapter 10—and as human persons to whom we owe the utmost respect. On a broader scale, the space used for hospitality and tourism is a small portion of our society and our planet, hence all industry professionals must remember to preserve the sanity of that bigger space by promoting social equity and caring for the planet as our common home.

4.3   Duration

The length of hospitality varies, and the care provided needs to be configured to last the time necessary. This may require careful planning to attend to the guest or tourist's comfort in a consistent manner over the time of the stay. A reluctance to end a stay is a good sign, where hospitality and tourism are concerned. Yet the traveller must go on and the external place of hospitality cannot replace the destination—home—of the guest or tourist. This is clearly seen in the way Odysseus continues

15 Corporate Social Responsibility as Person-Centred Care 299

his journey home despite the efforts of some hosts to hold him back (Chapter 2). When the length of hospitality is necessarily extended or indefinite, then even more responsibility devolves on the host to make the guest feel no longer a guest; person-centred care helps to achieve this in nursing homes (Bértiz Colomer, Chapter 9).

4.4 Nourishment and Service

As already mentioned, the historical practice of hospitality in form of traditions regarding welcoming strangers in some indigenous cultures is shared in both Saul's and Ukagwu's chapters one drawing from Greece (Europe) and the other drawing from Nigeria (Africa). The idea is supported by Okoye (Chapter 6) who looks into the humanistic philosophy behind serving. The concepts of gift and care are discussed, and they resonate solidly with the societal cultural tones already put forward. The same societal sense of service and nourishing relationships is what is recreated in enterprises in the hospitality and tourism sector, now commercialised and sold for profit.

Serving and nourishing take on a multiplicity of forms. Eldercare is one of these. As populations age globally, a broader debate about the services provided by governments and society gains importance. The contributions of Bértiz Colomer (Chapter 9) and Isichei (Chapter 11) about eldercare for residents in nursing homes and sensitivity towards vulnerable members of society are therefore relevant and timely. A truly humanistic industry must be ready to care for those who are in greater danger of being neglected or abused and constantly study how to address their needs.

In terms of recency, the issues that have touched on humanism in the industry include rapid digitisation and the pandemic. Nnamani (Chapter 5) deals with the use of technology to enhance service in hospitality and tourism. It has potential for good or for harm, for example, there are privacy and security concerns. When it comes to the harnessing of technology, ethics must be inputted at every stage of innovation (ideation, design, production, marketing and selling) technology so that we do not all become unsuspectingly vulnerable to digital predators. The

COVID-19 pandemic has affected the industry. Using Kenya as a case in point, Wathuta et al. (Chapter 14) point out the humanistic dimension of the situation—even in extraordinary circumstances (war, epidemics, pandemics and natural disasters) hospitality must strive to stay human and humane under the pressure.

5 Some Additional Reflections

5.1 Finding Motivations for Humanistic Management and Person-Centred Care

It is possible to derive intrinsic satisfaction from taking care of others. Based on a worldview in which one is interested in the good of the other, some organisations tend to be humane and fair whenever they must take decisions that affect employees or customer. This in turn spurs employees to consider the organisation when taking personal decisions that may affect their work, and customers to consider the company as a cordial partner in a series of value exchanges. In short, it inspires loyalty. For example, certain organisations hold it as a matter of policy to ensure work-life balance for staff. This removes the risk of exploiting them just because they have a lower bargaining power than the organisation and therefore do not complain when treated badly. Similarly, as an expectant mother gets close to term, colleagues and service personnel may be more understanding of the hormonal, behavioural and attitudinal changes she may experience. Supervisors tend to become more patient with their subordinates and sellers more understanding with their buyers.

5.2 Giving and Following Good Example

It is common to see a company adopting workforce CSR practices that they see in other companies operating in the same industry. At times they do this in order to have a better reputation and to attract talented professionals from competition. Such practices range from minor ones such as celebrating employees' birthdays, to bigger ticket items like providing

15 Corporate Social Responsibility as Person-Centred Care 301

crèche facilities for nursing mothers, gym facilities, discounted food services and providing staff buses among others.

5.3 Having Ears to the Ground and Whistleblowers

To ensure that its efforts to practice CSR and act as a humanistic enterprise are not in vain, organisation should have a process in place for lack of compliance to be reported so that it could be corrected. For example, if someone observes bullying, incivility or sexual harassment in the workplace, there should be a known system to make it known. It could be as simple as an open-door policy that allows employees to easily voice their concerns, or it could be an ombudsman internal or external to the company. In some moments, the person reporting would be in effect acting as a whistleblower and would therefore need some protection from the possibility of retaliation. Other possible ways to make the workplace more humane for staff include providing meals (especially where it is a restaurant or a tour), facilitating health and wellness training; listening and addressing concerns and allowing a voice in decision-making to employees likely to be affected by the outcomes; providing learning and career development openings; design and redesign jobs to make them more humane; establishing mentoring programmes; recognising and celebrating outstanding staff; sharing value co-created by staff with them; loans at below market rate; having bonus schemes, etc.

6 Conclusions

Corporate social responsibility includes ethical and humanistic behaviour towards all stakeholders—employees, customers and the society. As a result, it is often used by companies to heighten their competitive advantage and as a strategy to attract the best talents as well as conscious consumers who are concerned about the vulnerable in society and the planet. A number of benefits are enjoyed by companies who engage in such a CSR approach. Companies that go beyond the statutory requirements for employee welfare are able to motivate their employees better and create a sense of belonging and ownership in the company. Consequently, such companies tend to have high employee retention rates. Another advantage that accrues to employers who take care of their employees in the ways discussed above is that the expenses for training programmes, medical bills and other employee welfare related activities may be termed as tax-deductible expenses in their accounting books.

Bigger brands have a special responsibility to the society, since smaller and local entities look to the bigger ones for an example that they can copy. From the evidence gathered by Wang, Mohsin, and Lengler (Chapter 10), it appears that the Tianjin hotel has done a good job. These bigger actors also have a voice in professional associations and can influence CSR and humanism in the industry through these networks.

One challenge would be the lack of a good grasp of the wider concept of CSR among the industry actors. Many people see CSR as a few good projects rather than as the overall strategy of the responsible, ethical and humanistic company. A re-education in this direction would enhance their ability to act in favour of all stakeholders, and therefore ultimately in favour of the company. The chapters of this book are useful for this purpose, as resources for teaching hotel and tourism management courses, consultancy services and policy advocacy.

In the first volume of Humanistic Perspectives in Hospitality and Tourism, we had looked at the foundational pillars for flourishing through a humanistic lens and at the hospitality professional's self-developmental path to flourishing. This second volume has turned our lens to focus on the interactions of hospitality professionals, in the course of their work, with their colleagues and their customers or clients. We achieved our objectives by exploring the role of service for and the professional's contribution to the development of their colleagues (internal customers) and the people they serve (external customers and society). The outcome is a good number of robust theoretical and practical implications for professionalism and leadership in hospitality. This chapter assumes all such implications into the concept of CSR as the way to be humanistic, ethical and responsible in society and discusses them from this angle before ending with a few recommendations for professionals

15 Corporate Social Responsibility as Person-Centred Care 303

and organisations in the industry. Overall, Volume 2's message is that it is advisable for all the industry actors to increase their CSR levels towards their employees and customers and to manage their impact on society and the environment better.

Action Prompts

Draw up a chart showing how the consequences of treating employees well at a hotel or tourist agency can reach customers, other people in society and the environment.

Suggest three innovative ways in which a hospitality or tourism company you know can show its staff more person-centred care.

Explain the difference between CSR as an extra project and CSR as being socially responsible.

Study Questions

1. What kind of actions do you expect to see in a company that is striving to be socially responsible?
2. What can a hospitality or tourism company do to help the workforce to practice a healthy and helpful concern towards one another as well as towards customers?
3. Why should a hospitality or tourism organisation pay its employees a fair wage if others in the industry are not doing so and the employees have not complained?

Chapter Summary

Defining hospitality in terms of the four essentials (Saul, Chapter 2), we could say that it involves the development of interpersonal relations within a space and a time with a purpose of providing nourishment and service. In the process, the hospitality and or tourism organisation, like all others, needs to live up to its responsibilities to be ethical, humanistic, responsible and sustainable. It also needs to give and follow a good example to others in the industry, be ready to care for those who are vulnerable or have special needs and be alert to the dangers of technology to avert harm to others. An organisation carrying out all these is being socially responsible, i.e., it is carrying out its corporate social responsibilities—CSR.

It is true that many people see CSR as a few social projects rather than as the overall strategy of the responsible, ethical and sustainable company. We prefer the other perspective on offer: whereby corporate social responsibility includes ethical and humanistic behaviour towards all stakeholders—employees, customers and the society. Incidentally, several benefits are enjoyed by companies who engage in such a CSR approach. A re-education to recognise this could enhance hospitality and tourism organisations' ability to treat all stakeholders well.

The first volume of *Humanistic Perspectives in Hospitality and Tourism* dealt with the foundational pillars for flourishing through a humanistic lens and at the hospitality professional's self-developmental path to flourishing. This chapter in this volume has focussed on the interactions of hospitality professionals, in the course of their work, with colleagues, customers, society and the environment. Two main ideas are (1) that workforce CSR translated into person-centred care motivates employees better and can lead happy employees to make customers happy and (2) that responsibilities to customers can be practised in terms of the four essentials of binarity, space, duration and nourishment. This chapter assumes the responsibilities to stakeholders into the concept of CSR and discusses them in the light of the two main ideas mentioned above before ending with a few reflections for the industry.

References

Amao, O. (2008). Corporate social responsibility, multinational corporations and the law in Nigeria: Controlling multinationals in host states. *Journal of*

15 Corporate Social Responsibility as Person-Centred Care   305

African Law, 52(1), 89–113. School of Oriental and African Studies. United Kingdom.

Carroll, A. B. (1979). A three-dimensional conceptual model of corporate social performance. *Academy of Management Review, 4*(4), 497–505.

Carroll, A. B., & Shabana, K. M. (2010). The business case for corporate social responsibility: A review of concepts, research and practice. *International Journal of Management Review, 12*(1), 85–105.

Dahlsrud, A. (2006). How corporate social responsibility is defined: An analysis of 37 definitions. *Corporate Social Responsibility and Environmental Management.* https://doi.org/10.1002/csr.132

Elegido, J. (1996). *Fundamentals of business ethics.* Spectrum.

Friedman, M. (1962). *Capitalism and freedom.* The University of Chicago Press.

Helg, A. (2007). *Corporate social responsibility from a Nigerian perspective.* Retrieved February 2010, from https://gupea.ub.gu.se/bitstream/2077/4713/1/07-23.pdf—Similar.

Holmes, S. L. (1976). Executive perceptions of corporate social responsibility. *Business Horizons, 19*, 34–40.

Hopkins, M. (1998). *The planetary bargain: Corporate social responsibility comes of age.* Macmillan.

Ijaiya, H. (2014). Challenges of corporate social responsibility in the Niger delta region of Nigeria. *Journal of Sustainable Development Law and Policy, 3*(1), 60–71. Afe Babalola University.

ISO Official Website. (2022). http://www.iso.org/iso/home/standards/iso26000.htm

Jenkins, R. (2005). Globalization, corporate social responsibility and poverty. *Journal of International Affairs, 81*(3), 525–540.

Kristoffersen, I., et al. (2005). *The corporate social responsibility and the theory of the firm* (School of Accounting, Finance and Economics & FIRMAC Working paper series).

Levy, D., & Kaplan, R. (2007). *CSR and theories of global governance: Strategic contestation in global issue arenas.* Oxford University Press.

Margolis, J., & Walsh, J. (2003). Misery loves companies: Rethinking social initiatives by business. *Administrative Science Quarterly, 48*(2), 268–305.

Matten, D., & Crane, A. (2005). *Corporate citizenship: Towards an extended theoretical conceptualization.* International Centre for Corporate Social Responsibility. ISSN 14795124.

Moir, L. (2001). What do we mean by corporate social responsibility? *Corporate Governance, 1*(2), 16–22.

Sacconi, L. (2007). Social contract account for CSR as an extended model of corporate governance (II): Compliance, reputation and reciprocity. *Journal of Business Ethics, 75*(1), 77–96.

Sustainable Reporting Guidelines. (2021). https://www.globalreporting.org/resourcelibrary/G3.1-Guidelines-Incl-Technical-Protocol.pdf

Utting, P. (2005). Rethinking business regulation: From self-regulation to social control technology. *Business and Society Programme* paper number 15.

Wettstien, F. (2009). Beyond voluntariness, beyond CSR: Making a case for human rights and justice. *Business and Society Review, 114*(1), 125–152.

World Business Council for Sustainable Development. (2000). *Corporate social responsibility: Making good business sense.* World Business Council for Sustainable Development.

Index

A

Actus essendi 213, 217, 224
Artificial intelligence (AI) 11, 80, 81, 84, 85, 88, 91–96
Assurance 118
Authenticity 65, 72, 74
Authority and responsibility 140
Autonomy 171, 178, 180, 186

B

Back-of-the-house 218
Benin culture 52
Binarity 27, 28, 31, 297
Brand awareness 190, 191
Brand loyalty 187, 188, 190, 191, 193, 194, 196–200, 297
Building 9, 12, 65, 71, 84, 92, 129, 173, 179, 187, 189, 198, 261, 274

C

Care 2, 3, 6, 9, 43, 47, 94, 106–108, 115, 119, 133, 137, 155, 168, 170–176, 179–181, 214–218, 221, 234, 238, 240–242, 258, 260, 289, 294, 295, 298–300, 302
Carroll's CSR framework 251
Causa sui (cause of himself) 220
Celebration 10, 11, 48, 53, 60–66, 68, 69, 71–74, 176, 179
Chatbox 11, 89, 90
Chinese hospitality industry 187
Classic Literature 34
Climate change 13, 212, 230, 234, 236, 237, 240
Compassion 3, 108, 110, 150, 171, 181
Concentric circles 213, 214, 217, 221, 224

© The Editor(s) (if applicable) and The Author(s), under exclusive
license to Springer Nature Switzerland AG 2022
K. Ogunyemi et al. (eds.), *Humanistic Perspectives in Hospitality and Tourism,
Volume II*, Humanism in Business Series,
https://doi.org/10.1007/978-3-030-95585-4

Index

Consumerism 216, 217
Consumer satisfaction 128
Corporate social responsibility
  (CSR) 4, 9, 10, 218, 248,
  249, 251–253, 257, 260–264,
  288–296, 301–303
COVID-19 11, 12, 93, 178, 250,
  260, 270–272, 274–279, 300
Critical thinking 114, 116, 152
Cross-functional coordination 129,
  130
CSR pyramid 251, 252
Culture 2, 5, 8, 23, 26, 43–47, 51,
  54, 60–62, 65–67, 69–74, 80,
  126, 127, 132, 138, 140,
  150–152, 170, 212, 235, 241,
  242, 264, 279, 297
Customer relationship 7, 11, 128,
  199
Customer/Guest relationship
  management (CRM) 10, 84,
  186–190, 192, 193, 198, 199,
  297, 298
Customer satisfaction 10, 126–128,
  138, 140, 186, 188, 189, 199,
  200, 275, 280

D

Data 11, 54, 84, 88–90, 92, 129,
  131, 133, 149, 154, 170, 172,
  188, 190, 192, 199, 219, 221,
  274
Deduction 116, 117
Dependency 171, 279
Dialogue 4, 136, 218–220, 240
Digital kiosks 87
Dignity 4, 6, 7, 33, 34, 95, 113,
  130, 134, 136, 141, 169, 177,
  180, 215–218, 234, 251, 254,
  264, 291, 292
Dulia 65
Duration of stay 297

E

Ecosystems 234, 235
Empathy 44, 110, 115, 118, 119
Employees 7, 9, 13, 71, 85, 89, 111,
  113, 115, 118, 119, 126, 132,
  133, 136–139, 152, 157, 176,
  212, 213, 221, 223, 241, 250,
  253–255, 258, 259, 261, 262,
  270–272, 275, 281, 289, 290,
  292–296, 300–303
Environment 2, 3, 7–11, 42, 67,
  69–71, 73, 119, 127, 129,
  134, 148, 149, 152, 156, 160,
  168, 171, 173, 176, 180, 213,
  217, 221, 230–242, 256, 258,
  259, 261, 264, 265, 275,
  288–291, 293–295, 303
Environmental impact 233–235,
  237, 295
Ethical responsibility 255, 256
Evaluation 62, 116, 117, 192, 280
Excursionist 232
External customer 4, 7, 8, 126,
  138–140, 294, 295, 302

F

Facebook 87
Fear 96, 178, 212, 221, 274, 275,
  278
Flourishing 7, 60, 62, 69, 71, 72,
  74, 107, 108, 136–138, 212,
  302

Freedom 25, 32, 44, 65, 95, 193, 196, 218, 220, 264, 273

G

Generosity 24, 27, 31, 65, 72, 108
Gift-giving 30, 110, 112, 119, 296
Give 5, 6, 30, 42, 43, 46, 52, 61, 62, 65, 66, 68, 71–73, 81, 89–91, 107–111, 113, 118, 133, 154, 155, 169, 173, 174, 176, 179, 181, 191, 212, 214, 215, 218, 220–222, 237, 254, 260, 262, 263, 281, 292, 298
Global Reporting Initiative (GRI) 293
Guest(s) 2, 3, 6, 7, 9, 10, 13, 23, 25–33, 35, 36, 43, 44, 47, 50, 51, 53, 54, 61, 67–69, 73, 82–85, 90, 91, 106, 108–112, 115, 116, 118, 119, 128, 148–151, 186–190, 192, 197, 198, 200, 212–214, 218, 222, 231, 232, 236, 237, 240–242, 251, 253, 255, 275, 277, 278, 297–299

H

Hausa culture 53
Hilton Hotels & Resorts 260, 261
Homer 20, 23, 26, 27, 29, 34–36, 296
Hospitality 2–13, 20, 23–36, 42–47, 50–52, 54, 55, 60–63, 65, 67–74, 80–91, 93–96, 106–112, 114–116, 119, 126–128, 137, 138, 140, 141, 148, 150–153, 155–161, 171,

186–188, 190, 212–214, 216–219, 221–224, 230–234, 236–242, 248–251, 258, 261, 264, 265, 271, 272, 274, 275, 277–279, 288–290, 293, 296–300, 302
Hospitality management 8, 231
Hospitality profession 4, 6, 7, 31, 32, 110, 111, 113–116, 120, 148–150, 152–154, 157–161, 233, 234, 241, 242, 296, 302
Hospitality school 155, 157, 161
Host 2, 6, 9, 24, 25, 27, 29–33, 35, 36, 43, 50, 53, 54, 67–70, 106, 109, 111, 114, 119, 148, 231, 232, 236, 240–242, 278, 296, 297, 299
Human dignity 4, 134, 135, 223, 256, 270, 273
Human flourishing 3, 4, 7, 10, 11, 22, 71, 73, 107, 136, 140, 151, 242, 263, 291, 294, 295
Humanism 2, 4, 108, 169, 186, 187, 198, 200, 298, 299, 302
Humanistic CSR 251, 257, 263, 264
Humanistic management 4, 7, 130, 140, 263, 300
Humanistic organisations 295
Humanistic view 136
Humanistic workplace 7, 136, 137, 294, 295
Human touch 91, 92, 115, 280
Human work 270, 273

I

Igbo culture 49, 50
Indigenous cultures 46, 299

Index

Induction 116, 117
Information sharing 139, 191, 199
Internal customer 7, 8, 69, 126–128,
130, 134, 138–141, 302
International Organisation for
Standardization (ISO) 293
Intimacy 218–220
ISO 26000 293

Job security 69, 138, 140
Justice 21, 81, 94, 95, 222, 249,
264, 294

Kenya 270–273, 275–281, 300

Lantana 155–157
Leadership 6, 34, 114, 116, 120,
140, 152, 274, 281, 302
Legal responsibility 254, 260
Leisure 12, 69, 214, 236–238, 251,
258
Loyalty 10, 70, 139–141, 186–191,
198, 199, 242, 261, 296, 300
Luxury hotels 186, 187, 192, 193,
197, 199, 200, 297

Materialism 216, 217
Meaningful relationships 274
Mobile technologies 85, 86
Moral virtue 20–23, 26, 30, 31, 33,
34, 81

Nourishment 29, 33, 297, 299
Nursing home 168, 170–172, 174,
178–180, 299

Observantia 65
Odyssey 20, 23–30, 34–36, 296
Openness 33, 34, 47, 67, 74, 127,
140, 212
Organization's framework 141
Organizational culture 69, 126, 127,
140, 221
Organizational structure 127, 129

Pandemic 11–13, 61, 66, 93, 115,
260, 270–275, 277–279, 281,
282, 299, 300
Person 2–7, 13, 21, 22, 24–26,
28–31, 34, 42, 43, 48, 61, 62,
68, 69, 72–74, 81, 89, 92, 95,
96, 106, 108–113, 115, 116,
119, 130, 132–137, 150, 155,
156, 168–173, 175–178, 180,
192, 212–221, 223, 224, 232,
259, 270, 273, 289, 295, 298,
301
Personal attributes 154, 159
Personalized education 156
Personal value 136, 149–151, 153,
160, 161
Person-centred care 174, 176, 288,
289, 299, 300
Personhood 65, 72
Philanthropic responsibility 256
Philanthropy 256, 260, 261, 264

Philosophy of hospitality 27
Physical abuse 221
Physical safety 212, 221
Physiological 232
Privacy 11, 90–92, 219, 299
Professional dignity 134
Professionals in hospitality 231
Protective structure 222
Psychological 61, 66, 68, 71, 73, 107, 221, 232, 273, 280
Psychological abuse 213
Psychological safety 212, 221

R
RATER 6, 118, 120
Receiving 20, 25, 26, 30, 53, 68, 106–108, 110, 112, 113, 128, 133, 150, 174, 180, 212, 220
Recreation 68, 233, 235, 237, 248
Reducing status 139
Reliability 118, 193, 195, 196
Resident 168, 172–180, 232, 299
Responsiveness 116, 118, 119, 189
Retention 6, 7, 10, 188–190, 198, 199, 295, 302
Revenue 5, 11, 87, 140, 232
Rewards 70, 139, 156, 198, 222, 295
Robots 11, 80, 85, 88, 91–93

S
Safety 13, 43, 68, 128, 129, 178, 212, 214, 218, 221, 238, 254, 277, 280, 291, 293, 295
Safety net 225
Service 3–8, 10, 11, 20, 29, 32, 33, 44, 54, 62, 63, 67–71, 73, 74,
80, 83, 85–88, 90, 92, 93, 106–116, 118–120, 126, 129, 132, 133, 138–141, 148, 152, 154–159, 168, 171–180, 186, 188–192, 194, 195, 197–199, 212–214, 216–219, 221, 231, 232, 234, 235, 240–242, 248, 250, 251, 261, 271, 272, 277–279, 294, 297, 299–302
Service Coordinator 168
Service delivery system 187, 190, 191, 194, 196, 197, 199, 200
Skills 7, 47, 63, 84, 107, 111, 114–118, 120, 127, 130, 138, 148, 149, 151–153, 155–160, 174, 180
Smart objectives 72
Smart rooms 90
Sociability 63, 222
Social media 87, 135, 279
Soft skills 7, 111, 114, 120
Space 2, 26, 28–30, 32–34, 64, 68, 72, 83, 112, 132, 135, 159, 168, 174, 178, 186, 255, 258, 260, 261, 274, 278, 293, 297, 298
Stakeholder 2, 3, 10, 12, 55, 127, 131, 132, 136, 137, 139, 141, 190, 240, 242, 248, 250, 261, 263, 265, 288–291, 293, 294, 296, 301, 302
Standard operating procedure 220
Stranger(s) 2, 3, 20, 23–26, 28, 30, 36, 42–44, 46–50, 52, 53, 64, 67, 68, 106, 108, 109, 150, 231, 274, 292, 299
Subordinates 7, 130, 133–135, 141, 172, 300

Sustainability 4, 8, 9, 160, 230–236, 238–243, 259, 261, 293, 295
Sustainable Development Goal (SDGs) 273
Sustainable Reporting 293

T

Tangibles 5, 110, 118, 119, 171, 232
Technology 10, 11, 45, 67, 80–82, 84, 85, 89, 91–93, 95, 96, 153, 186, 189, 190, 199, 218, 254, 299
Telos 221, 222, 224
Temperance 21, 81, 96
Throw away culture 213, 217
Tianjin 187, 188, 192, 197, 199–201, 297, 298, 302
Tourism 2–4, 6, 8, 9, 11–13, 20, 31, 34, 42, 44, 45, 47, 62, 68, 93, 112, 115, 116, 126–128, 137, 138, 140, 141, 186, 187, 189, 193, 212–214, 217, 218, 221–224, 230–242, 270, 271, 274, 279, 288–290, 294, 296, 298, 299, 302
Tradition 5, 20, 24–26, 28, 34, 42, 44, 47, 53, 60, 66, 71, 74, 151, 155, 299

Trainings 13, 130, 133, 138, 149, 151–155, 157–161, 177, 178, 180, 187, 200, 213, 222, 223, 281, 291–293, 295, 301, 302

U

Utilitarianism 81, 217

V

Vulnerability 13, 29, 34, 169, 172, 212–214, 217, 222, 224, 230, 255, 281, 295

W

Women training 161
Word-of-mouth (WOM) 187, 190, 196–200
Workforce CSR 291, 293, 295, 300
Work life balance 221, 222, 300
Work life integration 222

Y

Yoruba culture 47, 48

CPSIA information can be obtained
at www.ICGtesting.com
Printed in the USA
LVHW081054190522
719180LV00004B/158